By Your Side

My Life Loving Barbara Windsor

Scott Mitchell

SEVEN DIALS

First published in Great Britain in 2022 by Seven Dials,
this paperback edition published in 2023 by Seven Dials,
an imprint of The Orion Publishing Group Ltd
Carmelite House, 50 Victoria Embankment
London EC4Y 0DZ

An Hachette UK Company

1 3 5 7 9 10 8 6 4 2

A CIP catalogue record for this book is
available from the British Library.

ISBN (Mass Market Paperback) 978 1 3996 0284 6
ISBN (eBook) 978 1 3996 0285 3
ISBN (Audio) 978 1 3996 0286 0

Typeset by Born Group
Printed and bound in Great Britain by Clays Ltd, Elcograf S.p.A.

MIX
Paper from
responsible sources
FSC® C104740

www.orionbooks.co.uk

To my Barbara

A love like no other
Always in my heart
Always missed
Forever loved

Your Scott x

Contents

Prologue

'One day, Scott darlin', when I'm no longer around, they will ask you to write a book about us.'

Barbara and I were in our little mews house, she was sitting in her cream armchair surrounded by the awards and memorabilia marking a sixty-year showbiz career that she would soon start to forget. I was in my usual place, by her side, on the couch. I shifted uncomfortably. Barbara and I talked about everything; but I didn't want to talk about this.

'That's not going to happen, love,' I said.

She was too smart to be brushed aside. She reached for my hand and fixed me with her piercing green eyes. 'It will, Scott. And if you do, and I think you should, make sure you tell the true story of how things really were for us, what went on between us and who we were together. Will you do that, love?'

I found myself shaking my head. Barbara was nearly thirty years older than me, we'd been together for a quarter of a century at the time and were trying to come to terms with a cruel diagnosis. Over the years I had seen this bright, bubbly little lady dust herself off so many times, perhaps I had convinced myself she was invincible. But she knew otherwise.

'Promise me, Scott,' she continued, 'be honest. Otherwise there is no point.'

Honesty was vitally important to Barbara and had been since we'd first met. I had asked her many times why she had always been so candid in her books and interviews. I knew what she would say before she said it.

'It's who I am, Scott,' she would say. 'I am the one who has to look in the mirror and own who I am. There will be people who like me and people who don't, but at least I know I've been true to myself.'

I did not think I had her strength but over the next few years I discovered that if you love someone deeply, unflinchingly and unconditionally, that love gives you the strength to discover what you are really made of and withstand unimaginably difficult times.

'If you tell them about how we really were together, Scott,' she said, 'you'll be able to walk down the street with your head held high knowing exactly who you are, who we were and who you will go on to be.'

I gripped her hand and made her a promise, having no idea how insightful those words would turn out to be.

I can feel Barbara now, tapping her nails, fixing her hair, standing in a cloud of Shalimar and waiting for me to carry out her instructions and carry on her legacy. She was an outstanding human being and all I wish is to do her proud. So with the help of diaries that I started in 1987, digging into the raw emotional pain of losing her and reliving a million memories, I hope to share with you the true story of our life together. There have been extraordinary highs and challenging lows and all the living, laughing and loving that has gone on in between. I hope you will get to see who this special lady was to me, and to the others lucky enough to count her as a friend off-stage, behind the scenes and away from the screen.

In the early days of our relationship Barbara was kipping on the floor of a grotty dressing room in Clacton-on-Sea between performances of her one-woman show. The once loved *Carry On* films had faded from fashion, a saucy British seaside postcard from another era, and she was yet to take on the matriarchal role of Peggy Mitchell that would propel her back to the top of the British entertainment industry. Whatever she was to the many fans she entertained along the way, she remained, in her soul, little Barbara Ann Deeks. A four-foot-ten-inch kid from the streets of Stoke Newington who fell in love with the adoration of an audience at the age of thirteen and determinedly clawed her way out of emotional poverty to become our very own 'Babs'. To me, as you will see, this complex, talented, sincere, joyful, vulnerable, hard-working, professional, playful, generous, courageous woman with a wicked sense of humour and a heart of gold was quite simply 'Bar', the love of my life and the woman who taught me how to live.

Those lessons have never been more vital to me than in the devastating months since Bar passed away in the midst of a global pandemic. In the last few years of her illness Barbara somehow managed to remain true to herself. It was a privilege to be by her side and she gave me the strength and drive to carry on. But in the final days of her life, I started to fall to pieces. I was consumed by fear and devastating sadness. There had barely been a day spent apart and never a day that we didn't speak. How could I be me without her? How could there be a world without her in it?

As I sat inconsolably weeping by her bed one night, a palliative care nurse put her hand on my shoulder. 'Remember, Scott, her hearing will be the last thing to go,' she said, ever so quietly. 'Just talk to her, she can hear you.'

So I wiped away my tears and, sitting by her side, I took her tiny, bird-like hand in mine and started recounting the story of our life together.

I

Say No More

Sunday, 10 January 1993 was the innocuous day that would change my life. 'My old friend Barbara Windsor is down here doing panto,' Mum said. 'She's coming to dinner tomorrow evening.'

'What, *the* Barbara Windsor, from those brilliant *Carry On* films?' I asked.

'Exactly,' said Dad. 'I remember you and your sister laughing hysterically at those films. She was always so good in them. You know we used to hang out outside the E&A salt beef bar in Stamford Hill back in the day.'

'She's an old friend,' said my mother. 'We performed in Madame Behenna's Juvenile Jollities in Stoke Newington town hall back in 1946.'

'I'm sure she's great. But I'm not being funny,' I said, rolling my eyes, 'I'm twenty-nine. Do you really think I want to have dinner with Barbara Windsor and you lot?' I had driven to Sussex to see my parents in Hove for lunch. I had plans that night. Mum was a bit surprised by my impolite response.

'She's here doing panto. You're trying to establish yourself as an actor and she's got forty-five years of experience in the business.'

That was true. I'd left drama school eighteen months earlier and apart from getting the odd fringe job and revue show I wasn't working that much, but still, in my head, I was an understated, less-is-more, theatre actor with nothing in common with the bums, boobs and bodily fluids British comedy that was the *Carry On* franchise.

'You might learn something,' said Dad.

'All right, all right,' I said, still a bit bolshy. 'I'll stay.'

'Good, because I said you'd go and pick her up tomorrow. She's staying at Victor Spinetti's house in Kemptown.'

'Who?'

'Victor Spinetti, *Hard Day's Night*, *Taming of the Shrew*, a staggeringly talented actor . . .'

I didn't know who he was. They were my parents' generation. In other words . . . old. So reluctantly I drove to Kemptown for 7pm. I knocked on the door and this incredibly attractive lady opened it. She fixed me with these bright piercing eyes and smiled. This was not what I was expecting.

'Hi, I'm Rita's son. Scott.'

'I'm not quite ready,' she said, opening the door a bit wider. 'You'll have to come in.'

I noticed a couple of things immediately. One, she looked much younger than I expected. And two, she also looked ready. So ready, in fact, that I suspected she'd been waiting by the door to go. Bag, gloves, coat, the whole thing beautifully presented in this little ball of prettiness. She later told me that she only asked me in to get a better look.

'Welcome to my lounge,' she said. It's a line from *Entertaining Mr Sloane*, the Joe Orton play about an older woman seducing a younger man. It went over my head but I recall feeling pleased I had dressed smartly.

On the drive she asked me what I did.

'I'm an actor,' I told her.

'You don't look like an actor,' she said.

'What does an actor look like?' I shot back. She giggled.

The banter between us started on that first car journey and continued all the way through dinner. Contrary to my low expectations it was a wonderful evening. Brian Hall, the chef from *Fawlty Towers*, joined us. He was a cockney actor and had become my acting mentor, as well as being a London cabbie on the side. The wine flowed and we giggled the whole night at stupid, silly jokes. Mum asked about how I could best get work.

'Read *The Stage*,' said Brian.

'*The Stage* is about as useful as a nun's fanny . . .' Barbara leant in and whispered in my ear. Wow, I thought, this lady is quite something. She's not only really funny, she's young at heart.

To my embarrassment my dad decided to put on the VHS of my bar mitzvah. Barbara was on the floor, kicking her legs in the air, howling with laughter. In the video I started to say my prayers, then collapsed in tears. I remembered with mortification being overwhelmed with the pressure of the moment, I couldn't do my speech. How utterly surreal to be watching myself as a weeping teen with the former star of the *Carry On* films. Mum and I dropped Barbara back because I had drunk way too much to drive. I saw her to the door and, while it had been a crazily fun evening, I thought that was that.

But a few days later I took myself off to the Brighton Theatre Royal to watch *Cinderella*; Barbara was playing the Fairy Godmother. From the moment she stepped onstage she was undeniably eye-catching, and it wasn't just the cinched-in waist, sequins and crown. She oozed panto. It wasn't hard to imagine she could make anyone's wishes come true. I couldn't take my eyes off her. Being backstage afterwards didn't break the magic of the show; it cast a spell. The flurry of activity, the post-show buzz, the smell of make-up and rails and rails of bigger and brighter costumes, was intoxicating. And in the middle of it all, this tiny lady, radiating an enormous glow.

'Give me your number, darlin',' Barbara said. 'I've got a good friend who's a casting director. He might be able to help you.'

And so I found myself exchanging numbers with Barbara Windsor.

She called me one Saturday morning in February. I was in bed, hungover, feeling really sick. I had to pull myself together quickly when I realised who it was. She asked me if I wanted to go to Brick Lane to see her in her music hall show, so we made a plan, then fell into easy conversation. I enjoyed chatting to her, but apart from thinking how pretty and feminine she was, I didn't think she was making a move. Barbara told me later that she never considered herself a screen siren. She saw herself as the bubbly blonde sexy girl next door. 'They either dig me or don't give me a second look,' she would always say. I guess

I couldn't help myself. I was very happy to give her a second look. Make that a third in under a month.

Barbara asked me if I would be happy to take her agent Barry Burnett with me to Brick Lane. Barry was an old-school agent who had an encyclopaedic knowledge of show business. He sat in the back of my car, very polite, very proper. She told me his father was Al Burnett, the owner of the Stork Room, a club in the West End. Bar filled in the backstory that they both knew so well.

'It was 1960, I was twenty-three years old and had just got a job performing in the revue. Four nights in the manager comes backstage and suggests I have a "drink" with a punter. Well, that wasn't my bag. I politely declined. In my former job at Winston's that sort of thing never happened. Not unless you wanted it to!' She'd cackle at that part.

'In barges Al and tells me I have to get out there, have that drink and earn myself a "oner". Well, I was having none of it and threw the ice bucket we kept in the dressing room to cool ourselves down over his head and promptly walked out.'

I loved that story. That night was the first time I'd heard it but over the years I would hear it again and again. The thing about Barbara, as I came to understand, was that she wouldn't, couldn't, be made to do anything she didn't want to do.

'Please welcome the mesmerising, charismatic, mischievous, spellbinding queen of the cockney community . . . Miss Barbara Windsor!!!'

With a flurry of arm-waving to match the words, Vincent Hayes, the master of ceremonies who owned and ran the magical Brick Lane Music Hall, would command the small orchestra to strike up the first chords of Marie Lloyd's 'Don't Dilly Dally on the Way.' There was a slight commotion at the back of the hall, everyone turned, in came Barbara in her pearly queen finery holding a small birdcage prop. She weaved her way through the tables, smiling.

'Good evenin'!'

''Ello darlin's!'

Barbara had played Marie Lloyd, the famous music hall star, in *Sing a Rude Song*. Marie Lloyd had led a similarly hectic life both on- and off-stage and the two were often compared. I watched the audience beam back at her. There was a real sense that this cracker of a performer was one of their own. The excitement was palpable. Barbara paused at our table, put her hands on my shoulder and gave a little squeeze. I turned round to look up at this beaming, warm, open smile and my heart raced. I felt a rush of excitement and connection then watched her make her way to the stage to perform the number in full. Barbara was one of those performers who had the unique quality to extend their aura and presence over the footlights and make everyone feel special. But I felt especially special that night and I liked it.

After that I decided to do some homework. I realised my knowledge of Barbara was based on a couple of *Carry On* films that I'd watched at Christmas, so I was amazed to read in her first autobiography that she had received a Tony nomination for her role in *Oh, What a Lovely War!* on Broadway and also had a BAFTA nomination for the film *Sparrows Can't Sing*. I started to realise she was a very accomplished and versatile actress and I had done her a disservice by dismissing her as a one-trick pony, like a lot of people. She was so much more than the infectious, fun *Carry On* bird.

We started chatting on the phone and then we arranged to have dinner. She was married and twenty-six years my senior, so although I felt it was a bit flirty, mostly I thought it was just friendly fun. She was easy to have a laugh with and I told myself not to read too much into it.

'I'm reading your book,' I told her.

'That's sweet of you. Are you enjoying it?'

'Actually, Barbara, I found quite a lot of it a bit sad. I'm really sorry about what happened with your parents. That must have been tough.'

There was a pause and I thought maybe I had overstepped the mark. Barbara was asked to give evidence in the family court at her parents' divorce hearing. She was fifteen, but tiny even then, and looked about ten. All she was told was to tell the truth, which she did. Had her father ever hit her mother? Yes, she replied. She was then asked to write down the swear words he used during their lengthy, angry arguments, which she did. All I knew from the book was that her father's face got redder and redder and then he stormed past her when the court awarded her mother full custody and five shillings a week. He did not speak to or even acknowledge his daughter again for twenty long years. I suspected then, and now absolutely believe, that Barbara's father broke her heart when she was fifteen years old, and she spent the rest of her life trying to please the men in her life to make sure they didn't leave her like he had. It was a wound she never fully recovered from.

'Sorry, Barbara, I didn't mean to upset you.'

'That's okay. It's just, you know, my dad was my hero. I absolutely worshipped the ground he walked on. I was so like him. I think that's what made my mother cross. I had his thin blonde hair. "Two hairs and a nit", she'd say. I think she wished I had her thick auburn hair. I think she wished I was more like her, but I was just like him.

'He taught me my first audition song, you know, he was always singing it, "Sunny Side of the Street". I believed in that. I believed we'd always live on the sunny side of the street. But we didn't. My mother wanted out of the East End. She wanted to move up in the world and was always telling me off about my cockney accent, my clothes, my weight, my hair. It was never good enough. She was a very good dressmaker. Did you know that? Very stylish . . .'

And so our long chats began, and I have to say, regardless of whatever happened between us, from that day they never stopped. We never stopped talking.

On the morning of my thirtieth birthday, I woke up and cried. What was wrong with me? I'd been out with a group of old friends in Brighton but it felt like I was missing something. What did I have to show for thirty years on this earth? What would another thirty bring? What was the point? Then the phone rang.

'Hello, Scott. It's Babs.'

Maybe it wasn't something I was missing, but someone. We'd been to see *Sherlock* onstage in Wimbledon and, because I was with Barbara, I got to go backstage again. I was meeting people I'd only seen on TV or onstage before.

'Scott, this is Robert Powell.'

'Hi, Scott, I'm Roy Barraclough. Can I get you a drink?'

Barbara matched me drink for drink that night and we ended up locked in conversation, howling with laughter. I was having more fun with a woman twice my age than with my own friends.

Who could I tell that I was beginning to look forward to Barbara's calls? Who could I tell that I was waiting for those calls? Who could I tell about the swarm of butterflies in my stomach when I heard her voice?

'I've got a part in a stage production of Joe Orton's comedy *Entertaining Mr Sloane*.'

It's a sinister but sexy comedy about an older woman seducing a much younger man, her lodger.

'Do you fancy helping me learn my lines?'

'I'd love to,' I replied. She gave me the address of the casting director's office and we met there to record the lines on tape. This particular casting director specialised in TV commercials; he was witty, flamboyant and fun, and of course knew everyone in the business. It was very intimidating, and I suspected he knew that. Barbara, however, seemed genuinely delighted I was there, and, anyway, I had some news of my own.

'I auditioned for a play at the Man in the Moon theatre. You won't believe it, it's a Joe Orton double bill and guess what?'

'You got the part?'

I nodded happily. 'I'm playing Joe. Isn't that a coincidence?'

'It's worth celebrating,' said Barbara, a wide grin on her face, cracking open a bottle of champagne.

'I knew Joe,' Barbara told me over a drink. 'He always said I would play Kath in my forties.' Barbara was now in her mid-fifties but, honestly, she could easily pass for a forty-year-old. I was bowled over by her youthful looks and vitality.

'He also told me the most important aspect of this play is that you believe Mr Sloane wants to fuck the landlady.'

'Is that right?'

'Uh-huh . . .'

In the original film the landlady was played by Beryl Reid. She was fifty-one at the time and Mr Sloane was . . . yes, you guessed it, thirty. Maybe turning thirty wasn't going to be that bad after all.

I don't remember if I asked Barbara about her husband, Stephen. I knew she was married, but somehow he never came up in conversation. All she said, if she said anything at all, was that he was very busy with the pub he ran, The Plough near Amersham. It was a very successful establishment, she told me. He must have been run off his feet, because I never saw him, let alone met him.

We did discover, however, that learning lines was greatly assisted by a bottle of Sancerre. Or two. When the work was done, we went out to meet her friends and later, on this beautiful balmy June night, she grabbed my hand, and we ran down the road back to her little mews house. That was the night it all changed.

At 6am I remember opening my eyes, looking around a bit wearily and a bit hungover, with a million things racing through my mind. I was thrilled, I was shocked, and also a little scared. What if her husband decided that today was the day to come to London and see his wife? Barbara opened her eyes.

'You all right, love?' And then before I'd had time to answer, she said, 'My cleaner's coming, you've got to go.'

Blimey, I thought, your cleaner comes early.

She pulled a £20 note from the drawer and waved it at me. I must have looked a bit indignant.

'I don't want your money, Barbara.'

'I didn't mean it like that. Just for a cab.'

'Thank you, but I can make my own way home.'

I left, got on the tube and sat all the way to East Finchley wondering what the hell had just happened. At the same time, I had a real feeling of warmth. I was clearly attracted to her, but, more than that, I really liked her. Even in the short time I had known her, she felt perfect, not for me, but to me. Although I could see she was far from it. I told no one. When I got home, I went to bed to sleep off the hangover and, at 1pm, I called her.

'Hello, love, you okay? You all right? Everything okay?'

'Everything is fine, Barbara; I just want you to know I really respect you.'

I don't know how she took it, but I didn't want her to think she was merely a conquest. I didn't hear from her again for a long, agonising week. I went to stay in Gloucestershire. I was there to learn lines and was determinedly not thinking about her, even though I was palpably aware that she hadn't called me. I could hardly call her again; she was Barbara Windsor after all.

Monday, 7 June 1993: Barbara called. Thank God for that.

Wednesday, 9 June 1993: Barbara called me. Twice.

The following day I got a message: she'd like help with her lines. So off I went and over another bottle of wine . . . Well, let's just say the script was put to one side for a while.

Friday, 11 June 1993 [there was a coded note in the diary]*: Done the lines, went out, later wine, back to the mews, drinking wine, smoking cigarettes . . . SNM.* [It stood for 'say no more'.]

Monday, 14 June 1993: Barbara called to say she missed me. Could be in trouble here.

I knew I was feeling the same way. I missed her when I wasn't with her, I thought about her nonstop and I just wanted to see her again. I realised things would get complicated from this moment on. Not only was there the age difference, she was, unfortunately, undeniably married. To be fair to me, it was hard to think of her as married. I had not seen any trace of the mysterious Stephen. To be honest, I was more worried about her attitude to extramarital sex. It was abundantly clear from reading her book that Barbara did not conflate love with sex. It was written in black and white, in her own words. Back before I was born, when she was offered a role in *Oh, What a Lovely War!* on Broadway by Joan Littlewood, she jumped at the chance, even though it meant leaving her newly wedded husband, Ronnie Knight.

'I don't mind if you want a bit of the other,' she said before leaving for the States. He was furious and hurt and wondered who he had married. Barbara on the other hand fell into the arms of the musical director Shepard Coleman, the first of many affairs. It was all in the book! Trouble was, I didn't want to be a bit of the other, which led me to the only conclusion I could make. She was Barbara Windsor and I was going to get hurt. If I could have stopped seeing her, I would have, but I didn't want to. The thought of not seeing Barbara was fast becoming unbearable.

She appeared to feel the same way and we went out a lot. She didn't seem to mind if we were seen together, although we weren't obvious about it. It was exciting, the little secret between the two of us. Sometimes she would pass me off as a driver, other times she said she was just giving me a helping hand. We were careful to show no sign that we were more than friends, but I was around quite a lot. We went to the theatre, we popped in to see her friends. One Sunday she came over for roast chicken at my flat. We had such a lovely afternoon, a couple of bottles of wine, but when it came to leaving she couldn't find her keys. She turned on me, irritable. 'This is all your fault!'

'My fault?'

'Yes! Because I don't know what I'm doing here. This is all your fault.'

'I don't understand. What do you mean?'

'I'm all over the place, because of you!'

I dared to hope that this was a sign that I was more than just a bit of fun. Was it possible that she was stressed because she liked me? Was she scared like I was? What was clear was that we were no longer meeting to read lines and I was falling, hard and fast.

I'd seen her ecstatic, I'd seen her anxious and I'd seen her irritable. Then one day on the phone, I discovered another side to her personality. She was so down that I drove into London. She opened the door and was surprised to see me. 'What are you doing here? You silly sod.'

'I thought you might need cheering up. Put the kettle on, why don't you tell me what's on your mind.'

I was beginning to learn that Barbara was not used to having a person to talk to, I mean really talk to. All her worries, she carried alone. 'I don't have any work after the play ends, it always worries me that.'

'Maybe a break would be good?'

'A break is never good in this business.' Barbara was totally committed to her career in show business, it ran through her veins. I could see that right from the start. Barbara wasn't *in* show business. She *was* show business.

'What about Stephen?' I asked tentatively. 'What does he say?' What I meant was, if the pub is so successful, why are you worried?

'He's a lovely man, Scott, he really is, but the love of his life is that pub, not me. I don't want to be a burden,' she added. 'He's got enough on his plate running that place. It means the world to him.'

If I was Stephen, I thought, I would make sure you knew you meant the world to me. I didn't stay over but after talking the afternoon away I left her in a better place.

'When will I see you again?'

'We'll figure it out,' I reassured her. I wasn't sure how, but from the beginning we were good at talking about the hurdles we faced. The biggest problem would be not seeing each other. This was the start of her and me against the world.

After another drinking session at the casting director's flat we meandered drunkenly back to her mews house. In front of a stranger, she pulled me to her.

'I love you, Scott,' she said.

A jolt of fear went through me. What if that person heard? What if that person told the papers? She wasn't the huge TV star that she became, but she was recognisable. I put it down to the booze and tried to take it with a pinch of salt, but then again maybe she did mean it. There was space in her life for a new love. Stephen wasn't physically, romantically or emotionally connected to his wife. Bar could separate sex and love, but what if this was sex *and* love? It was all a bit of a crazy whirlwind. We were happily sloshed most of the time and if I was absolutely honest, I wasn't entirely sure which way I wanted it to go. Barbara Windsor came with a lifestyle that I wasn't used to, which was both exciting and terrifying, but no doubt could swallow me whole. What if it spat me out too?

I was at a private birthday party at the House of Commons, standing on the terrace, overlooking the Thames, glistening in the late

evening summer sunshine, and pinched myself. Bar on my arm, me
kitted out in a shirt and tie; next to me was Elaine Paige, Shirley
Bassey was behind me and Donald Sinden across the way. How have
I, a kid from Sussex, ended up here? How? I knew how . . . and her
name was Barbara. We left the Houses of Parliament and diverted to
Joe Allen's, after that to any late-night bar that would have us. We
were both irrepressible, irresponsible children in sort of grown-up
bodies; one more drink, one more bar, one more minute together
. . . It was too much fun to think about putting the brakes on. Every
night with her was a heady night.

The night before Barbara's fifty-sixth birthday a coach collected a
gang of us: Nick Berry, Anna Karen – a lifelong friend of Barbara's
who'd played Olive in *On the Buses* – and Paul Bennett, the picture
editor at the *Sunday Mirror* and another of Barbara's most trusted and
loyal friends. Paul knew about us, but never sold her out. Years later
he'd know about the dementia too and, again, never breathed a word.
That night, we were driven to Hornchurch, Essex, where Barbara was
performing in *Mr Sloane*. I was nervous because I knew Stephen and
his family were going to be there. From a distance I watched the tension between Barbara and Stephen build and was upset for her when I
saw them bickering at the front of the bus. This was a big moment for
Barbara, and he didn't seem to be supporting her. I was also strangely reassured to see the state of their relationship for myself. I think it
allowed me to stop feeling guilty and simply fall in love with a great
lady who was all I'd ever dreamed of in a woman. If I thought I'd
been in love before, I was wrong; previous relationships had been dress
rehearsals compared to this. She showed me what true love felt like.

Barbara frequently augmented her work with personal appearances, and the first one I went along to with her was in Nottingham. Can
you imagine watching a white stretch limo pull up knowing it was for
you? Well, only for me because I was with her. We got in and started
drinking champagne, and carried on all the way to Nottingham. I
watched her do her stuff. Just like at the music hall in Brick Lane,
Barbara would work the room, spread her own brand of fairy dust,
and give everyone what they wanted; and then we got back in the
limo and headed south to London. It was a magical evening, and we

canoodled all the way home. We were beyond hiding it now; we just didn't care. It was as if there was nothing else in the world.

'I know Barbara Windsor is here. I'm her godson, I wanted to surprise her. I'll prove it to you, let me call her.' I was in the lobby of a hotel in Gloucester at nine o'clock at night having missed her so much I'd jumped on a train, then into a taxi, to go to where she'd been doing a personal appearance. The hotel staff put her on the phone and we had a chat as if I were back in London. Believing me, they let me up. In the lift I had a sudden panic. What if she has someone here? What if it's the Babs who still has multiple men on the go? I felt ill, but then she opened the door and her eyes filled with tears. She was delighted that I had done something so romantic. I stayed. God knows what the hotel staff thought.

I was a bit scared of the strength of my feelings towards her, but she had admitted she was frightened too; we were in this together and together we were getting in deeper. The feelings were so intense, so passionate, that sometimes they got a bit explosive. We'd be running late. We'd misplace the keys. We'd get lost on our way to an appearance. Boom, the volcano erupted.

'We can't be late. I need that £300.'

'I don't understand where all your money goes.' I felt she left too much of her business to other people. She had told me she co-owned The Plough with Stephen, but as far as I could tell, her earnings were going to a business I was being told was a successful pub restaurant. It just didn't add up.

'Don't start.'

She didn't like being challenged on things that I could see negatively affected her life but that she wouldn't contest. I couldn't understand it and she would fight back.

'It's not your business.'

But she was my business. I was completely involved with her and her life.

'Let's not let this spoil what we have,' I would say, moments later. 'It's only because I worry about you and how hard you work.'

'But I love what I do.'

'I know, Bar, I love that about you, you know that, right?'

'And I love you . . .'

Deep down I think we both feared what we had, what we felt, what we might lose and what we had to face if we really wanted to be together. Those furious flare-ups were quickly followed by passionate declarations of love. We wanted to be together. Completely. And that meant Barbara had to leave Stephen. I didn't think it would be too much of an ordeal; they lived entirely separately, and it seemed to me the only thing he cared about was his precious pub. But I think there was a part of me that thought she would never do it.

She'd been at The Plough all day, leaving me to wait by the phone. 'I've done it,' she said down the phone. 'I've told him it's over.' But it didn't quite turn out like that.

She called me again the next day. 'He won't accept our marriage is over.'

'What?'

'He's slept on it, and he says he just wants to go on as before. Sorry, Scott. He won't discuss it.'

Perhaps we should have stopped there, but we didn't, or couldn't, and instead our affair intensified. I realised it was blissfully dysfunctional. We were happy, yes, but I also didn't want to go on running around in the shadows, creeping through the alleyways, being the dresser or the driver or the kid who helped her learn her lines, forever. Frankly, none of that was especially good for my confidence and wellbeing, and it made it easy for some of her friends to belittle me and talk over me or just ignore the fact that I was there. It was high-octane, yes, but I was often out of my depth. To be honest, the whole situation was somewhat out of control. And so, I drank and drank and drank. And Barbara matched me for every single drink. Sometimes those nights were the best of fun, sometimes the mood darkened.

She had to tell Stephen. She couldn't tell Stephen. Fierce arguments led to just as fierce declarations of love. It was crazy.

We were now so often out on the town together it was stupid or dangerous. Or both. At a party at Planet Hollywood we were photographed with David Hasselhoff. Man, did we look like a pair of munchkins in that one, and Bar also introduced me to Gloria Hunniford for the first time. It was fairly evident that I wasn't the driver, the dresser or the kid helping her learn her lines.

My favourite times were when it was just the two of us. We'd go out for dinner, then back to her mews house, crank up the music and dance and sing until 2am. Sometimes we put on shows, farcical, fast, funny ones, taking it in turn to do a performance for an audience of one. For me, the only one who mattered. It was a good way of letting off steam and reminding ourselves what we had when we were alone and could both just be ourselves.

Then finally, on 11 November, Barbara went to The Plough and told Stephen again that it was over and this time she told him about me. It was awful, they had an almighty row and then he kicked her out. Any illusion it might end amicably disappeared there and then. Stephen started drinking, then started calling. The calls got worse and worse. He wanted to know my name; he wanted to know how old I was; he was horrified to hear I was younger than him. He didn't want it to be over. I couldn't understand it, according to Barbara they'd not had a physical relationship for five years, so why was he so upset?

'His mistress is The Plough,' said Barbara. She said he was happy to be married to her and have his mistress, that suited him, but it didn't suit her. Especially since, as far as I could tell, she was paying for that mistress!

It was the beginning of three very turbulent days. He would call, she would get upset, we would clash then make up, and then it would all start again. At first it was about their relationship, but it soon became clear that this was about something else. Money.

'The pub is swallowing up all the money I earn.'

I didn't understand. 'I thought it was a successful pub, with a successful restaurant?'

'He's told me the pub isn't doing so well as I thought.'

'What do you mean?'

'What I earn goes to the pub.'

'I thought what you earned went to Stephen.'

'I thought he was taking care of things.'

'Why do your earnings pay for his business?'

'It's our business.'

'But—'

'Don't start!'

She told me she'd learnt young to fend for herself and I knew she was very strong, but I was beginning to see that in other ways she wasn't. The calls between them kept going backwards and forwards. I expected him to come round at some point and beat me up. He did phone one time and threaten to rip my head off my shoulders. Bar stuck up for me vehemently, told him that this was about them, not me, but it didn't matter, he blamed me.

'I'll never take the blame for him!' I exploded that evening.

He came round one Sunday morning to discuss finances. I was up and ready to fight him. He phoned, a car drew up fast, but I wasn't quick enough. I flew out after Barbara but she was already in the car and they were off. He looked in the rear-view mirror and saw me jumping up and down like a leprechaun, he later told a newspaper (which actually appealed to my sense of humour as it's something I might have said about myself). I could not bear to think he would charm her back because I was adamant now that I could not live without her.

For an anxious human being like me, running would have been easier, but it never occurred to me to do so. While I understood his pain and upset, I honestly felt their marriage was well over before I turned up. I did tell Stephen eventually that I would own my part, but I wouldn't be blamed for the collapse of his marriage and certainly not his pub.

In November, Barbara's great friend of old, Danny La Rue, opened a bar opposite his flat on Charing Cross Road. We were invited to his flat first. Danny was renowned for talking about himself. It was endearing but people made fun of it. He was lording it up, regaling us with tales about other people telling him how wonderful he was. He trapped about ten of us in his lounge, drinking champagne.

'Darlings, when I did *La Cage aux Folles*, Shirley Bassey said that up till then "I Am What I Am" was her song, but then she saw me and said, "Danny, that's your song now."'

'So you keep telling us,' said a quiet high-pitched voice from the back. John Inman's – the legendary Mr Humphries in *Are You Being Served?* – timing, as ever, perfect. It set me off into one of my nervous laughing fits. Since I was sixteen I'd suffered from horrible fits of giggles when in a stressful situation. Well, the past three days had been nothing but stressful, which is perhaps why, when we hit Danny's bar, we had a mega blow-out and got utterly smashed.

I was beginning to get into the habit of taking sleeping pills and Valium after nights out drinking, and coke had started to creep in more. I told myself I was having a brilliant time partying, but was I really having a good time? I had always been a fearful person and the drink took that anxiety away. While on drink and drugs I was on the same level as everyone else. I had always drunk abnormally. The first time I drank I was eighteen, a New Romantic, and a mad, super, unashamed Spandau Ballet fan. They were playing a club in Bournemouth one bank holiday weekend. It was so small and so packed they had to climb in from the outside. I had my first can of lager that night. After about three I felt a bit sick, went to the loo and threw up. I didn't like being sick but I did like the buzz the alcohol gave me. From that moment on I would throw up two or three times a night, then carry on drinking. That went on for years. I was prepared with mouthwash, chewing gum; no one knew what I was doing. In time, I wasn't even making myself sick, it was just happening.

Our six-month anniversary was spent in Darlington. Bar had an appearance at the music hall. At this stage she was taking any work she could get. We woke up a bit hungover from celebrating the night before; Bar had slept badly. She was really stressed about work, about money, about her precious, beautiful mews house that she had worked so long and so hard for. I told her she could come and live with me in my flat in East Finchley if the worst came to the worst (of course, this was at a time when the general assumption was that I was a gold-digger. How ironic!). It was also all wrapped up in guilt about Stephen. He accused her of ruining his life and it was plaguing her. I was at a loss as to what to say. None of it made sense to me. Not his declarations of love, nor his declarations of poverty.

Meanwhile, I was terrified because I'd got a part in *The Bill*. Actors, we are a nightmare!

When Barbara started moving her stuff to the theatre in Stevenage for her panto run, I decided to move some of my clothes to the mews. Now that Stephen knew, it seemed an okay thing to do. Five days later the panto opened. Officially I was still Bar's dresser and driver. We thought that was the best way to start with.

Then, on Christmas Eve, Dad collected us from the theatre and drove us to Hove for a family Christmas with somebody else's wife. We were adjusting. So much had happened since I'd turned thirty. Now I was spending Christmas with my family and my new girlfriend, Barbara Windsor, the woman who forty years ago had done dance classes with my mother Rita.

'The *Sunday Mirror* are hanging around The Plough,' said a journalist from the *News of the World*. It was always the same with the tabloids, but that first time was alien to me. 'We know something is up, Barbara. Isn't it better coming from you?' They wanted the first picture of Barbara and her 'new love'. I felt sick at the thought of it. I knew she was a well-known lady, walking down the street with her I noticed people looking at her. Not everyone, of course, she was almost on the cusp of being someone who used to be famous, but why would they want a scoop about us?

'Listen, Scott,' she said, 'it's give an' take with the press. They do their job so I can do mine. Sometimes it's good, sometimes it's not, but, darlin', you have to learn to take the rough with the smooth. Life is all about the ups and downs.'

I cannot fully describe the oddity of sitting with a stranger, a journalist, and being asked to talk about things I wouldn't easily talk about to my sister or best friend. In the back of my mind, I knew I was going to be judged. I looked stupidly young, I was an out-of-work actor and I was involved with a famous performer, and I was allegedly the cause of her marriage break-up. I tried to say as little as possible and follow Bar's professional lead. It was excruciating. I was so petrified I was physically sick. But I had to hold myself together for her because she was the one going onstage as Aladdin.

She knew she was going to get some stick for dating someone younger than her young husband, but we kept telling ourselves we had each other and that was all that mattered. I felt bad that all this would mean Stephen would be dragged through it, but mostly I thought how weird it was that the British public were interested in who Barbara was seeing. Almost worse than the questions was posing for the photo. I hated the whole thing. It felt creepy and corny.

On 31 December, after Barbara had done two panto shows, we went home to get ready to celebrate New Year's Eve. We realised there were journalists outside the house, so we had no option but to stay in and celebrate with an M&S ready meal and a bottle of champagne. Why did we draw the curtains and hide ourselves away? Because the *News of the World* had paid for an exclusive, so an exclusive they had to get.

'Happy New Year,' I said, refilling the champagne flutes.

'Bloody better be,' said Bar, as she started to giggle.

2

The Glass Slipper

On 1 January 1994, Yvonne, Barbara's long-standing friend and personal assistant, came to the mews house along with Sharon Ring of the *News of the World* to ask some follow-up questions. I did my best to keep out of the way and let Barbara do what she did best. Answer in witty soundbites, print-ready, perfect. The journalists had left the mews but my nerves were still jangling. Later that day I thought I was being followed by a van with blacked-out windows, so I drove a mad circuitous route back to the mews and managed to lose them, but then there was another journalist and photographer outside the front door. I did a U-turn and we shot off to my flat in East Finchley. Unfortunately, Barbara didn't have her sleeping pills. She'd taken Zimovane for years and she was worried about doing two shows on no sleep. I rang Harold and Miriam Winehouse, old family friends of mine who also happened to be Amy's aunt and uncle; they lived nearby and I thought they might have some.

We were later than expected to the Winehouses' and it set off another silly argument. I knew why we were jumping down each other's throats. We were both frightened. Our secret whirlwind love affair was going to be blown open for all to see. By 11.30 that night Barbara decided she wanted to sleep in her own bed so we drove back to the mews safe in the knowledge that after midnight it wouldn't make any difference if another paper got a photo because the *News of the World* would have dropped by then. This was my world now and frankly it was crazy. Thankfully the paps had gone. Our nerves were shot and we collapsed into bed. Chatting in the dark, we both admitted that we were dreading the morning.

'I'm worried about what this will do to you,' she said. 'Taking me on is such a burden.' There was that word again.

'Where does all this burden nonsense come from, Bar? You could never be a burden.' I was wrapped up in the headiness of it all. I'd never expected to feel like this about anyone, I didn't think it was even possible, but she was more insecure than I realised.

Over the years we unpicked this more, but that night we talked about what 'winning' little Barbara Ann Deeks had meant to her mother at the time. 'My mother got custody of me and then spent all her time criticising me,' Bar said. 'My voice, my hair, my style, my songs. You know, every time I pick out an outfit, I can hear her voice in my head, "Not that Barbara", "That doesn't suit you", "Those colours don't work".

'She never told me I was pretty, not once. Or that she was proud of me. Not once.' She looked sad.

'She hated the *Carry On* films. Said they reminded her of my father, that I was just like him. Well, she hated him, so . . .

'In fact, my mother never told me she loved me. She never said those words. What is a kid supposed to think? I think parents should be really careful about what they say to their children.' She tapped her head. 'It's in there for life.'

Bar told me she hadn't realised how much her mother loved her until after she died and left a box full of mementoes: flyers, programmes and reviews. Only then did friends and neighbours get in touch to tell her how much her mother talked about her and how proud she was.

'How sad is that?' she said. 'What a waste.'

I held her close to me in the dark, I knew she needed reassuring. 'You could never be a burden to me, Bar. I love you,' I told her and I meant it.

'Me too,' she said. And boy did we love one another. It was a powerful, all-consuming love and every minute I wasn't with her, I was thinking about her. I could see her face in my mind all the time, her wonderful smile. I still can. I can conjure the aroma of

Shalimar, Barbara's favourite perfume, even now, and we talked about everything.

Perhaps not everything. We didn't talk about how I was feeling about myself. That was my secret to hold. But what she said got me thinking. For me it always went back to when I was eight years old and my dad took me to a karate and judo class. He was one of the instructors there and he was a big guy, a man who could handle himself. When it was my turn to go on the mat the teacher picked me up and threw me over his shoulder, and I burst into tears. Dad didn't say anything. He just looked at me with disappointment. That feeling of not being good enough landed in the pit of my stomach, and stayed there. I understood why Barbara felt the way she did, because I felt it too.

In my teens that fear took on another layer because it was evident that I wasn't going to be as tall as the other guys. It bothered me. Today I feel like a giant in my own skin but back then I felt insignificant and small. When I started going out it seemed to me that at one-thirty in the morning all the guys on the dance floor were tall. I would wait for the five-to-two-ams – the drunk girls who hadn't been asked to dance who would make do with the short bloke. I made fun of myself. I would send myself up, referring to myself as the little geezer before anyone else had a chance. I learnt to make people laugh as a way of getting people to like me. I was a classic people pleaser. But inside it was stripping off another layer of my self-confidence and I would rip myself to pieces. It is staggering how critical we can be of ourselves. Almost cruel.

Fashion helped disguise my nerves. New Romantics led to a rockabilly look, then drama school. It all helped me build height on to my personality. Booze helped too. When I drank I was the same size as everyone else. People liked having me around even if I doubted myself, and I did doubt myself. I think I was born a worrier. My mother's side of the family carries the hunted souls of the persecuted. Dad's side was tough. Mum's side was scared. I took after Mum. For as long as I could remember, I worried whether the sun would come up in the morning. And now, lying next to Barbara Windsor as the sleeping pill took hold of her, I worried, when the story dropped, if the sun would indeed rise and what the world would look like when it did. Of course, I told her I was fine. I wasn't.

Early the next morning an edition dropped through the letterbox. We went downstairs together and there, staring at me from the doormat, was a picture of Barbara and me. I still hated the photo. We knew it was going to be front page, but knowing it and seeing it are two different things. Reading the article was worse. I was being spoken about as though I wasn't a real person. Outside the house were about fifteen journos and paps.

'What are we going to do?' I asked in a panic.

'Put on a smile, straight back, head up. You'll be fine.' I remember the noise of the camera shutters.

'Morning, Scott.'

'How you feeling, Scott?'

'This way, Scott.'

Hearing my name called out completely freaked me out – the only time that happened was in the waiting room at the doctor's. How mad was that? I tried to copy Barbara, I tried to smile, but I couldn't raise my head. I felt like every movement was under the microscope, it was all exaggerated. Perhaps we all have a secret fantasy about being the centre of attention, certainly actors do, but it was awful. I didn't know what to do. If I looked at them and smiled it would have appeared as if I was enjoying it, but I wasn't. Thankfully no one followed us. We got to the Gordon Craig theatre in Stevenage and there was some excitement among the cast and crew because they thought I was an out-of-work actor helping Barbara out. A very camp panto actor came in with the paper in his hand and flung it on the floor in mock horror.

'Darling,' he purred, 'I thought you were the dresser.'

When we went out for dinner that night it felt different. It was worth it because now we could relax, be ourselves, be a couple. Now that the secret was out, everyone would get bored, move on and we could get on with our lives, I thought, just me and Bar. Naive doesn't come close.

On 3 January we went out to buy the papers. There was a picture of us leaving the house on the front of most of them. For the twenty-seven years I knew Barbara she would read five papers a day: the *Sun*, *Mirror*, *Daily Star*, *Daily Mail* and *Daily Express*. Bar was a consumer of tabloid news. She loved the papers. She understood their mischievous world. In its own way it's a showbiz industry too. Big characters inhabited Fleet Street back then and it definitely had moments of high drama. That day, however, the drama was us. Most regurgitated the *News of the World* piece, but the *Sun* excelled itself: 'BABS: CAN'T STOP, I'VE GOT A-LAD-IN TONIGHT!' The smile on her face was put down to me being a 'Genie-us in bed'. Clever if not surreal.

It wasn't all laughs, of course. Rough with the smooth, right, Bar had warned me. The rough bits were the dissection of Barbara's relationships with men. I was the last in a very long list. The thing is, I never minded her past. Far from it; I admired her for it, was even a bit envious of the things she'd done. The list was long, but it was an exciting one. George Best, Maurice Gibb, a couple of Krays, though she told me only Charlie had been someone she'd wanted, whereas Reggie was someone you couldn't say no to. The article said she always looked for love in the wrong places, that the men in her life didn't deserve her. I was being labelled as another misfit she could lay her head on. Until the next one came along.

What's Barbara Windsor doing with a man who has bumfluff where a beard should be? That stung. I was being portrayed like a plaything, but in fact I was thirty years old. Hardly a boy.

Mum and Dad were fantastic. 'Are you happy, son?' they asked.

'I've never felt so happy,' I told them.

'That's good enough for us.' They both really liked Barbara and in time came to love her.

'It's not going to be easy,' said my dad. 'You're going to have to have broad shoulders.'

I had no idea how broad. The next day a journo got hold of my parents' ex-directory number and called them. That gave me the first tremor of paranoia. Who would have given that to them? It felt awful. They went chasing my old drama school friends, anything in my past, it was like I was being hunted. There were endless follow-up stories as more and more details about our relationship and her marriage came to light. Barbara admitted she'd had four other affairs during her marriage, just to take the heat off me. It made us fiercely protective of each other and what we had.

'It'll die down,' I said, holding her in bed, cocooned and feeling safe. Bar knew better. From the moment Ronnie Knight went to prison she had become tabloid fodder. Before then it was about her career and trying to get coverage. But the gangster–showgirl mix was explosive and the press couldn't get enough. Ronnie had hated it and she was worried press attention would turn me against her as it had him. That's why she told me so many times about how to handle it, how to not take the personal personally, and how to survive the intrusion.

'I use them to promote my professional life, they use my private life to promote their paper. It's give an' take,' she said. 'They've shat on me a lot of times. I get knocked down, get back up, and dust myself off.'

I was in awe. No matter what had been written, when she saw the journalist who had penned it, she'd smile and say hello. I had no idea how to compartmentalise like that but, as far as she was concerned, it was part of the industry she was in and loved, so she would take it. Her life wasn't private. Her personal life was of interest and there was no putting it back in the bottle. She didn't always enjoy it and she was deeply anxious about the impact on me, but she knew how to work it and she did her best to impart that hard-won knowledge to me. Over the years I learnt how to handle the press, but in those early days I was a deer in headlights.

'You all right?' she would ask. 'You okay?'

I kept telling her I was fine. I didn't want her to worry about me too.

Then a week into the intense press interest, Barbara got a bad chest infection. She had to do a photoshoot for the authorised follow-up story and as she drew away in the car she looked like a frightened little lamb, tapping her nails on the glass, looking back at me until the car turned the corner. She was holding it together for me, I knew that, but I realised it was taking its toll. It was the business with Stephen and the pub that was the worst. He was getting angrier and loading all the guilt on her. I thought that was unfair; he was being dishonest about the state their marriage had been in. It was beginning to dawn on me that, while she'd been worried about me, she was the one who needed looking after. It was a lot of pressure and, though I rarely thought about Barbara's age, it was being driven home by the headlines. She wasn't twenty-one any more, she was fifty-six.

The more all this happened, the more strength I knew I needed to have in order to protect Bar. Her wellbeing and happiness were all that mattered.

'So, what's Scott's financial situation?' Stephen asked. I thought that was a bit rich coming from a man who was relying on his wife's earnings. It was my turn to get angry. With him. But Bar was having none of it. She put the phone down.

'You've got to move on,' said Bar, firmly putting me in my place. 'I loved him once. There is no point turning it into hatred. We are happy, so what have we got to be cross about?'

That was the thing about Bar, she never looked back.

After the last performance of *Aladdin*, there was a party, complete with mock awards. I got Best Off-Stage Performance as a Dresser. Bar received a special award for getting the Gordon Craig Theatre in Stevenage on the front page of the *News of the World* – surely a first in history.

Shortly after finishing work Barbara had a flare-up of diverticulitis and was in crippling pain. She would lock herself in the bathroom and I would hear her crying out in agony. There was nothing I could do to help the wrenching, griping pain in her lower abdomen. It was horrible, particles would get stuck in pockets in the lining of her lower intestine. But that wasn't the only health scare we were dealing with.

On 7 February 1994 Bar went into the Wellington Hospital, in St John's Wood, for a hysterectomy. She'd been putting up with heavy bleeding and mood swings for a while. The doctor said the procedure would end all that discomfort. Barbara was very worried about how it would affect us afterwards; she was concerned about how her body would cope and whether it would take away her sex drive.

When I returned to the hospital after the operation she had tubes in her nose and was very drowsy. Later she rallied and we held hands. I was making her giggle but it hurt her to laugh . . .

'Careful,' I said. 'Your catheter will fall out.'

'Oi,' she replied, 'I'd like you to know I am one of this country's biggest sex symbols!'

We both laughed again and it felt good. We thought we'd be home the next day, happy, together and, finally, ready to get on with our life as a couple.

Stephen called her in the hospital to say, firstly, he loved her and, secondly, that the cheques were bouncing. She'd always said he had no understanding of women, but, really, she was in recovery, she didn't need that extra pressure and she was stressed. She had pains in her chest, so they decided to do a comprehensive check-up which revealed discrepancies in her ECG. More tests showed she had furring of the arteries not only in her heart, but also behind her eyes. When I visited the next time, Bar was scared and teary. 'It's not fair to you, Scott. You're a young man, I'm always a nuisance to the men in my life.'

There it is again, this sense of being a burden, just like she felt when she was a child . . . I thought about that journalist writing about how she picked hopeless men and, though I agreed, what I was coming to understand was that she picked them because she didn't think she deserved any better. She thought she wasn't good enough for them. How wrong she was. I was determined to make her see it differently.

'You'll never be a burden or a nuisance to me, Bar,' I told her again. 'Whatever happens, I'll be here with you, by your side, as long as you want me to be.'

Brave words and true, but actually I too was scared. I'd waited all this time to meet the woman of my dreams and now it seemed like she was very ill, or, worse, might die.

I left her at 10pm but by 11.45pm she called, crying. 'The right side of my face is numb.' I drove back to the Wellington and stayed with her until she fell asleep at two in the morning.

The numbness was caused by three small brain seizures, which had been caused by high blood pressure, which had been caused by the shrinking of the arteries, so now she needed medication, statins, to bring the blood pressure down, and regular monitoring. It was beginning to feel like my life was one long Blackpool roller-coaster, the rush of highs and lows coming thick and fast, my stomach lurching, holding on, loving and hating every second. On Valentine's Day I arrived at the hospital with a huge bunch of white roses and a single red one in the middle. Our romantic dinner for two was in her hospital room.

'All that matters is that you get better and that we love each other.'

Bar didn't come home until 22 February, two weeks after she'd gone in for her operation. She rested and, thankfully, by early March she was feeling more herself. We went out for dinner at The Ivy with John Reid, Elton John's first manager, and Christopher Biggins. It was lovely to see Bar laugh again, and it seemed less painful when it was those two. Bar and Biggins made quite a twosome; they were very funny together and would frequently send each other up, and they also both loved all the showbiz gossip.

'Do you remember when . . .'

Bar would stop the conversation. 'You won't remember, Scott, but he played— in—' She would always fill in the gaps for me. I enjoyed the campness, and it felt good to be back out with friends. I enjoyed their world.

A woman approached the table and introduced herself as Jane Deitch, the casting director of *EastEnders*. 'So what are you up to now?' she asked Bar.

'Recovering,' Barbara said. 'It would be nice to play a woman of my own age for once!'

A few weeks later we went to see Barbara's friend and comedian Jim Davidson in his alternative adult panto, *Sinderella*, and then we headed to Joe Allen's for dinner. This time Dawn French was in there and I was a bit starstruck. I kept looking over and Bar noticed. She showed a tiny bit of jealousy that night, which I quite liked. There was healthy jealousy on both sides. Our relationship wasn't volatile, but it was passionate.

In April we booked to go away to Spain to stay with an old friend of Barbara's. It was the first time I realised she had a fear of packing; it really sent her into a tailspin. I often wondered if it had something to do with being evacuated from London as a child. At first her mother hadn't wanted her to go, but then her school friend was killed sitting on the wall while waiting for her, so Bar was sent to Blackpool and fell immediately into the unsavoury hands of a brother and sister pretending to be married. She barricaded herself into her room to keep the man from coming in and thankfully her cries were heard by the girl next door and that family offered to take her in. Unsure what to do with this energetic little tearaway, the woman sent her to dance class. The rest, as they say, is history.

But I think it was probably more about what happened when she got home that created the sense of loss and panic. Her dad was one of the last soldiers to make it home and her parents' marriage never really recovered, which led to the fighting, and then to the divorce and that awful day in court. She was a daddy's little girl, without a daddy.

As we were packing for our trip to Spain, she became flustered, grasping her face with her hands and staring at the wardrobe through her fingers. 'I don't know what to take.'

'Take whatever you want, it doesn't matter.'

'It does matter.'

Sometimes I would storm out of the room. We were like two petulant children trying to get one suitcase packed. It went on for years, we knew it was going to happen, but it still carried on. I had to talk her down as I was putting different things in the case. 'See, there's the swimwear, there's the toiletries.' In many ways it was one of her most endearing qualities, though it annoyed the shit out of me.

We'd been in Spain a few days when Ronnie Knight called the villa. Turned out he was nearby. Barbara's mood changed instantly. It was said he was the biggest love of her life but by now I had read enough about him to make up my own mind. Bar and Ronnie were on the phone for over an hour that day; he knew she'd left her husband, he claimed his marriage was over and they were meant to be.

I heard all his declarations of love but, in the end, she didn't see him. I am sure she felt like the last thing we needed was Ronnie Knight popping up. I certainly did. And she also knew that I would have been upset if she had gone to see him, though I would never have told her she couldn't go. As I've said before, there was no telling Barbara anything. What was different was that she and I spent a lot of time talking and I got the sense she'd never had that before. She didn't want to hurt me and she knew that this would have. Later that afternoon Ronnie called again, but Barbara told her friend to say we were out.

She always used to say that what Ronnie did changed the way people thought of her. 'They didn't see me as an actress any more, they saw me as the moll.' But despite the impact his actions had on her, she was never nasty about him. She always said he was a very nice man from a long line of charming East End hoodlums; cocky, confident, flash, and someone who could always tell a tall tale. A bit like her dad.

Back from Spain and away from Ronnie, I finally got to meet Barbara's family at a wedding. The Ellises were lovely people. Afterwards we went to Stringfellows and saw Jim Davidson, then dropped in at Morton's. When we went out on the town we never wanted the night to end. As usual I would have to deal with the smirks and unpleasant comments. Sometimes we would get sniggers from across the room. I had to double-check it wasn't my imagination. People would look around, a bit of a whisper, a bit of a laugh, but what they were thinking would show on their faces. It would never be from the pros, never from Peter Stringfellow, he couldn't pass judgement about age gaps! From the word go Jim Davidson treated me nicely. He'd call me Scottie. People might try to call him to heel but there isn't any point because he is a fabulous rascal. But despite the mutterings, it was good to be back out in London, having fun, boozy dinners surrounded by friends.

Then, on 29 April, Barbara got a call from the *Daily Mail* to say that Ronnie Knight was on his way home. We were in shock. 'Why would he come back?' Bar kept asking. Later there was gossip that he'd run out of luck in the Costa del Sol. Perhaps prison was a better prospect.

Around this time, we met Jane Deitch again. She reintroduced herself to Bar at a party at comedian and actor Mike Reid's house. After everyone else left we sat up until the early hours listening to some of Bar's stories. It wasn't unusual for industry people to get straight to it. They all had questions about Joan Littlewood and the *Carry On* films.

'So, tell me, what was Kenneth Williams like?' Jane asked.

'Well,' said Bar, 'he was always terrible to the new ones. My first scene in *Carry On Spying* was with Kenneth. Bernard Cribbins had warned me he would try and unnerve me, so of course I messed up my first line. It was awful. Bernard had also told me that Kenneth had a hatred for Fenella Fielding. "Do get on with it," he said, in his famous withering voice.' Barbara could impersonate him perfectly.

'He was wearing this awful fake beard. "Don't you yell at me with Fenella Fielding's minge hair stuck around yer face! I won't bloody stand for it!" There was stunned silence,' Bar said. 'Then Kenneth clapped. Thank God. "Ooooh, isn't she marrrrvellousss!" he oozed.

'From then on, we were the best of friends. He even came on my honeymoon.' Pause. 'With his mother!'

The same old stories would come out, almost word for word, yet each time I would listen intently as if for the first time. I enjoyed these stories every time – who wouldn't love the chance to hear about these acting legends? Later, when she was ill and would tell me something for the umpteenth time, I would still lean forward and look as if I hadn't heard it before. Honestly, I never got tired of hearing them, although Barry and I would wince a bit when that Fenella story was recounted in various interviews.

The next day we got a call from Sue Crawford at the *Sun*. She told us they were bringing Ronnie back on a private plane. He was due to be arrested on landing and they wanted to know if Bar would give her reaction. Sue also suggested we leave London. The *Sun* then promptly whisked us away to a hotel in Sussex. We unpacked and then had sandwiches and tea on the terrace as we watched people playing croquet on the lawn. Could life get any crazier?

Sue came over for dinner that night with the following day's front page of Ronnie looking pleased to be back on UK soil. Bar looked at the photo and I could see she was a bit torn about the whole thing. It was another drama to deal with. As far as she was concerned, she'd stood by him through thick and thin. She told Sue it was Ronnie's affair with Sue Haylock that eventually ended the marriage. The next day another headline: 'WAR OF THE WIVES'.

After that we had lunch with royal photographer Arthur Edwards, and Paul Hooper, both from the *Sun*, and Barbara gave them her version, officially. However, it turned out they had been followed by a *Daily Star* journalist who listened to the whole thing through the open window. She must have got her copy in quick, because somehow the *Star* got the story out first. Canny!

A few days later Barbara returned from lunch to find the police at the mews waiting to question her. Three hours of intense questioning dragged her back to a life she'd long left behind. She always told me she knew nothing about his business and, even if she did, there was no way they would ever have got anything substantial out of her. Bar was many things, but she was no grass. She was from the East End, she knew the rules and she stuck to them. Maybe that was why the East End called her back and also why it then came calling.

Bar was performing her music hall routine on Brick Lane when Jane Deitch came in to see the show. 'I had no idea you did all that singing and dancing as well as chatting to the audience,' Jane said. 'It was terrific.'

When she left I leant towards Bar. 'Do you think she might want you for *EastEnders*?'

'Oh no,' said Bar, 'panto and theatre is fine, but TV doesn't like me. Trust me, I've tried.'

'But what about *One Foot in the Grave*?'

'A one-off,' she said. It was true, it was the biggest bit of TV she had done in a very, very long time.

'But you were so good.'

'You're biased.'

That was true as well, of course, but she *was* good. She was better than good and definitely better than she thought she was.

We went to another party at the House of Commons, and as ever we carried on into the night at Stringfellows. At formal, invited events, I was beginning to feel more accepted; people generally shook my hand and said hello, even if they then made a beeline for Bar. But out and about at bars and clubs like Stringfellows and Morton's, it was a bit more of a bunfight. 'So how many *Carry On* films did you do?' shouted a very pissed lawyer, over me, at Bar.

The music was so loud she didn't hear. 'Nine,' I told him. 'Nine out of thirty-one.'

'Shut up! I'm not talking to you,' he said, literally pushing me out of the way.

'That's rude,' I said and headed to the bar. Barbara tried to follow me but there was another fan waiting for their few minutes with the star. I turned my back to the room and had another drink. The more I drank, the less I noticed people talking over me, or pretending I wasn't there. None of it mattered; I had Bar. I thought I had Bar. I was almost one hundred per cent certain I had Bar.

'I don't want to cause any trouble,' muttered Thomas Powell, slurring his words. 'I just need to see Babs.'

This time I was standing face to face with Bar's past. We were in Brighton and Thomas Powell, one of her old flames, had come to the theatre. He looked like a tramp. He had been madly in love with Barbara since their affair in 1972. Back then he was a musician who took a job as an extra on Ken Russell's film of the musical *The Boy Friend*, which Bar had been in with Twiggy. Barbara sang and tap-danced her way through a difficult time, she and Ronnie were in shreds, and filming was made harder by Ken's constant rewrites. Thomas was already a recovering heroin addict. Beautiful, vulnerable, talented and young, their affair deepened so much Bar nearly left Ronnie a couple of times, but he always managed to charm his way back in. In Brighton that night, Thomas was no longer young or beautiful, he'd been ravaged by drink and drugs, but even though he was in a terrible state, there was something remarkably gentle about him. It really struck a chord.

'Sorry, mate, not tonight.'

'Maybe I can go backstage for a few minutes, just a minute.'

'Best to leave it, Thomas, she's got to work so it's not good for her.'

He took it all meekly, hugged me and I saw up close the aching misery etched on his face. I really felt for him. It made me feel a bit sad and maybe a touch vulnerable. I wrote in my diary:

Saturday, 15 July 1994: I hope I don't end up like Thomas Powell. Poor creature.

*

'When I met you, my luck changed,' said Bar. 'Look, I've been offered a gig as a roving reporter on *The Big Breakfast*.' Gaby Roslin and Chris Evans's show was HUGE at the time.

'It's because we've been in the papers, Scott. It's because of you. See, ups and downs. We can take the up. I'm doing it.'

'Good for you, and, for the record, you were the fabulous, brilliant, talented Barbara Windsor long before you met me,' I told her.

'Less of the *long*,' she retorted. 'Let's go out and celebrate.' So we did, two happy night owls, egging each other on. She always looked good, and we were photographed whenever we went out – though I was usually cut out of the photo.

On 5 August I agreed to surprise Bar with a birthday cake on camera. It was not my idea. I felt a bit cringey inside; I still wanted to be at the RSC at the time and here I was holding a birthday cake on breakfast telly, but I agreed to do it for Bar. She was touched because she knew it wasn't easy for me and, as ever, that made it worth it.

Then on the August bank holiday, slightly out of the blue, Bar was asked to read for a part in *EastEnders* with Ross Kemp and Steve McFadden. They were considering recasting the role of their estranged mum, Peggy. Bar was never usually nervous, but she was about this one. We went over the script repeatedly, but she couldn't get it. It bugged her.

'I don't think TV is my thing. I'm just too much for it. I can do tits and arse, and jazz hands. But I can't do TV drama, not like this.'

'Remember what Joan Littlewood said,' I told her. 'You are better than you think. You've typecast yourself. You're an actress, a really good one. You can do this.'

The trouble was she'd been in the wilderness for quite a long time and her confidence had been knocked. On the way to the studio, she asked me to stop the car. She got out and was sick, right outside where she used to live with Ronnie. This life was mad. All those years of experience and she was still in pieces.

When we arrived, I was shown around the lot (the outside set of Albert Square), while Bar was taken off for what she soon realised was more than a reading; it was an audition, complete with a bad outfit and a cast-off wig. I went back to my flat to wait.

'I did my best,' she said when I picked her up. 'But I have no idea how it went. We did a scene in the pub under the arches, using mugs for glasses and the boys just read off their pages, so it was a bit unnerving, but afterwards Ross came over and showed me around the square.'

'That was nice of him.'

Bar agreed. 'He said he thought this would become my home.' She was really touched by that.

The next day her agent Barry called to say she was being offered the job. It was seeing her vulnerability that had done it. 'We didn't expect that,' said Jane. That was the thing with Barbara, no one ever does.

EastEnders was huge news. Primetime. BBC. I was thrilled for her and she truly deserved it. Bar played it down. 'It's a small part, a side character, a short contract. She's only back because Phil's in hospital. Nothing permanent, they probably won't even renew it . . .'

'We'll see,' I said. Grant (Ross) and Phil (Steve) were at each other's throats because of Sharon; those boys were always getting into scrapes, so it wasn't impossible to imagine they might need their mum about for a bit. Little did I know what they had in store for Peggy.

'It will be good to have some steady income for a change,' said Bar, 'while we sort out the pub.' The pub. Turned out one pub sorted out the other, in the end.

'Talking of that, I've arranged for the two of you to meet my family's accountant, Mark Gold. He can work out why the pub is losing money and where your earnings are going before you give him any more.'

We'd been together for over a year and I was with Barbara all the time, so at the end of September I moved out of my flat in East Finchley and into the mews. It made sense, we were always together, but it also meant I no longer had a safety net to fall back on. Equally, Bar was becoming part of my family. They all adored her, obviously, so I wasn't surprised when Bar said she would like my brother-in-law, Laurence Alexander, to be involved in addressing her business affairs. I think she felt safer having him and our family accountant to help unravel the situation which was getting more confusing by the day.

It appeared that on initial investigation the pub debts were looking considerably larger than Mark had first thought. Bar's money had been going into a loss-making venture: £128,000 in the previous financial year alone, which was still not enough to plug the gap. More worryingly, the paper trail revealed that she, not Stephen, was financially responsible for the debt. Though they co-owned the pub, she alone was the underwriter. She had to sell the pub, unless he agreed to take on all the financial liabilities himself, which strangely he was not inclined to do. But he didn't want to sell his beloved pub either. Bar felt bad. I was irritated.

I felt like a parent sending a child off to school when Barbara went to the *EastEnders* lot for the first time. She was so early, and it turned out they didn't have a dressing room for her, and the one they did have was locked. Once again Ross Kemp came to her side. 'Come on, I'll show you the rest of the lot.'

He knew exactly how nervous she was and very politely turned away when she was sick again, this time behind Meals on Wheels. Bar rang me to tell me she'd been told to bring her acting right down. Sounds like it will be very good then, I thought to myself.

'It felt like I was doing nothing,' she said, downloading it all that night. 'All I had to do was say Grant's name but it came out as "Here comes the baron", all loud and shouty, every time! So much for one-take Windsor. It took five. Oh, Scott, it was awful. Ross was so kind. I'm glad I did my first scene with him.'

Bar was very aware that the show was taking a chance on her. Would the sexy, dumb blonde be able to pull it off as an East End matriarch? When she went back on the lot the next day, she was still nervous. I waited for her to get home. I could tell from the moment she walked through the door that things had not improved.

'I think I redeemed myself a bit,' she said. 'When I walked up to Phil's bed in the hospital he said, "Mum, what are you doing here?", and I was supposed to say, "What am I *doing* here?", but I didn't think Peggy would say it like that, so I offered up an alternative. "What do you think I'm doing here? Waiting for a number thirteen bus?"'

'And?'

'They liked it. It's in. I felt a bit better after that, but then things went downhill. It's so different to what I'm used to, I don't think I can do it.'

I opened a bottle of wine and we cuddled on the sofa. 'Maybe it's playing your own age.'

'It's not that, Scott. It's just I don't know anything. I'm the novice, I feel like a spare part.'

'What are you going to do?'

She fixed me with that steely look. 'I'm going to work bloody hard and hope I can keep up.'

She was beset with worry. She managed to convince herself they wouldn't renew her contract, that it would be over before it had even really started. On the evening of Peggy's return, we sat at home watching on the sofa together. Watching us watching was a photographer from the *Evening Standard*. And so our life in *EastEnders* began. Talk about the twilight zone, it was hard to take in her performance with all the clicking and clacking going on, but still I could tell she was good. Bar was harder to convince. Despite reasonable reviews, she didn't think it would last.

A few weeks later we went to the opening night of the new production of *Oliver!* with Mum and Dad. Lionel Bart had lost all his money so Cameron Mackintosh bought the rights and gave him a share to get him back on his feet. After, we took Dad to Stringfellows. Jim Davidson was there and we sat with Cynthia Payne, who gave us special cards that said 'Thank you for all the custom over the years'. Dad loved it. Bar knew a lot of Dad's old friends and they loved recalling the old stories. Dad was really deaf by then; he would mishear things and repeat it back all wrong, and Bar would take the piss, but they loved each other. Bar always said that Dad was one of the nicest men in the world. Everyone loved Ronnie Mitchell.

After that I got a job in the Basingstoke panto as Dandini. When we got the script Bar made me stand up and do the lines. Because I had been to a drama school I was doing the underplayed Marlon Brando.

'You ain't going to do it like that!' she said, giggling. 'Theatre is bigger than film and panto is twice as big again . . .'

I felt very self-conscious. I thought the only reason I was in the show was because I was Barbara's boyfriend, which probably wasn't far from the truth. If you wanted Barbara Windsor, you got Scott Harvey. I was part of the package. I won't blame it all on that, though. I was self-conscious enough all by myself. Why I had chosen a career in acting, I don't know. It's almost masochistic. I would stand in the wings shitting myself then come off and berate myself. It fed into my already insecure soul and was not good for my health.

As the year came to an end, after years of heartburn, Bar made me go and have things checked out. I was diagnosed with a hiatus hernia. I'd never told Barbara about my tactical vomiting, but ever since that night when Spandau Ballet had climbed through the club window when I was eighteen, I was sick whenever I drank, and I drank all the time. Sometimes we might both be sick from booze, and I would tell her then, normalising it to her and myself, but she had no idea how often it happened. The long-term effect was that the section of stomach that stops the stomach acid from coming up into the oesophagus had been torn. And the result was constant heartburn.

Looking back now, I liken it to a form of liquid bulimia. I was not a normal drinker. But my normal was my normal and so at that time I simply didn't stop to think about it. If I had, perhaps I would have admitted that adding to my lack of self-worth a precarious career, and moving in with a famous and more successful woman than me who had a list of lovers longer than the years that I had lived, might be cause for concern and maybe I should watch my drinking. But I wasn't thinking. I was madly in love with a wonderful woman who was madly in love with me. We only wanted to celebrate.

Then came the best news of all. Peggy was a hit. Bar's contract would be renewed and, better still, they were making her landlady of the Queen Vic. Cheers to that! Drink anyone?

3

A Varied Life

'We loved your episode of *One Foot in the Grave*,' said the binmen collecting the rubbish from the mews.

'Thanks, you keep me in work, you do.' She always said that.

'Don't worry about that other story. We're on your side.'

He was referring to a story that blamed Bar for Ronnie's decision to return to the UK after ten years on the run and his subsequent arrest. It was accompanied by a picture of her in a witch's hat. I think it had more to do with the unsavoury bunch he'd got involved with, but what do I know. Still, it upset her and, when she was signed off work for a couple of nights, I thought the stress of that and the pub was adding up.

It probably didn't help her stomach issues that we would go out for blow-outs to let off steam. One night we went out for a Chinese meal and I woke up on our bathroom floor. I did ask myself whether this was normal, but I didn't stop long enough to get an answer.

Babs was settling into *EastEnders* and her confidence was really growing. Meanwhile, mine was dipping. On one night out we went to the Dorchester Hotel in Mayfair for champagne cocktails, and then on to a club where we met up with Steve McFadden and a young Jake Wood, who I'd met a couple of times previously. All night long people came up to Bar and, although she tried valiantly to include me in those conversations, it was clear they had no interest in talking to me. Instead, I busied myself watching Rick, the boyfriend of *East-Enders* producer Jane Fallon. He was watching everyone so closely I thought he might be a journalist. In fact, it was Ricky Gervais and his observations became comedy gold.

At the end of April I turned thirty-two. Coincidentally, there was a party on the *EastEnders* lot, so we started off there and then went into town with a few of the cast. Bar wanted to leave early, but because it was my birthday I decided to stay out without her and ended up in a new place called Soho House, where I saw the singer Steve Strange. I thought it must be a place to be if he was there.

I don't know if I was becoming more aware of being overlooked or ridiculed, or it was getting worse as Bar's profile rose, but on another night at The Ivy I got really wound up by a couple sniggering about us. They were in my eyeline and, although it had happened before, for some reason they were really bugging me. It was stopping me from enjoying the evening, which was irritating me further. Then the paranoia started to fester.

I should go over and say something . . . How can I? . . . They won't admit it . . . I'll embarrass Bar.

Over the following months the sniggering and sideways glances started to wear me down. I could never completely shrug them off. It would stay with me all night and often over the next few days as well. It became part of my unease and anxiety, so much so that I would often scan the room, looking for culprits. Finding oblivion helped. Alcohol made it all hazy and coke meant I stopped noticing anything other than the fascinating conversation I was having, probably about myself. In the early hours of the morning, I was king. During the day I felt sheepish and small.

I got an audition for a part in the musical *Joseph* that would be put on in a small theatre in Middlesbrough. It was through a friend of Barbara's and I was worried from the off. 'I can't sing and I can't dance,' I told him in no uncertain terms.

'Don't worry, we're looking for a character actor,' he reassured me.

I sang 'You Made Me love You' – a song Bar always did in her one-woman shows.

'You've got a voice in there,' the producer said. 'The others will be doing the heavy lifting in the dance routines. You'll only be in the chorus.'

And just like that I was offered the role and, against my better judgement, took the part. The only thing worse than being pushed aside was being asked the question that every out-of-work actor dreads. 'So, what are you doing now?'

Now at least I could tell the few people who asked that I had a job. My digs were with a local vicar, although he wasn't practising at that time as he'd just had a nervous breakdown. Not an auspicious start. On the first day of rehearsal, we sat in a circle, the musical director went around to each of us and made us go through the scales. I was shitting myself because they were all brilliant and, as it got closer to my turn, I grew more and more nervous. When I did it, I sounded like a strangled cat. Everyone looked at the floor. 'I did tell you I couldn't sing . . .'

Then it got worse. We all stood up and went into a street dance routine. I couldn't do any of it. It was the most painful week of my life. I used to go home and get drunk with the vicar and tell him how terrible I was. We'd end up laughing about it, but it wiped me out. I was rubbish and after a week I realised I had to leave. I don't think I ever recovered.

Now I was an out-of-work actor who couldn't act (not strictly true, but I couldn't sing or dance), going out with a famous performer experiencing a brilliant second act. Peggy had made herself acting landlady of the Queen Vic, and Bar said that as soon as she stepped behind that famous mahogany bar, she felt like Peggy. She was immersed in Peggy's world and it was an explosive, all-consuming one. Peggy blamed Sharon for having an affair with Phil behind Grant's back. It was great telly, and the ratings were rising.

'I don't know if I can cope with this,' she would say sometimes, coming home with fat scripts she needed to learn for the following day's shoot.

''Course you can,' I said. 'You are the best thing to happen to that show. Chris Evans was right.'

Just before her role had been announced, Chris had said that if he were the producer, he'd make Barbara landlady of the Queen Vic. Bar had been terrified at the time. She thought she'd lose the job if they thought she'd leaked the story, but she hadn't – it was just Chris being his usual brilliant self.

Instead of actively looking for acting jobs, I hid behind the role of driver. I'd done it on and off, but now I was getting paid for it. It made sense to us for privacy reasons, but it was a double-edged sword. Part of me knew it was helping both of us, but another part knew I was getting further and further away from being a person in my own right. It was a recipe for disaster. Talking like an actor, living like a driver and getting paid by my partner, through my family accountant, which made it almost feel like pocket money. Probably made worse by the age gap. It was another thing for me to defend and the snide comments were never far away.

'It's pathetic, isn't it,' I heard a group of Bar's friends say at dinner one night. 'The way he's sitting there . . .' I saw them look over and laugh. 'Poor lamb needs a job.'

Titter titter . . . I knew there was nothing I could do about it because they were in a more prominent position than me and were also supposed to be our friends. I didn't tell Bar because she was feisty and would have called it out there and then. And I never wanted to create a scene. But I also didn't have the guts or gravitas to challenge them myself. I'd been bullied before as a child. I remember being kicked in the stomach until I fell to the floor and having my food and pocket money taken. Back then, I was small and sensitive, and an easy target. I wasn't big enough to look after myself. And now, sitting at that table, in that smart London restaurant, I was an easy target once again. When I heard those words, it felt like a blow to the belly, just the same. Bullying had been replaced by bitchiness; different playground, same tactics.

Most often I would find myself with people talking across my face. It was as if I was invisible. That in itself didn't bother me. I always accepted that Bar was the star, the famous one, and I was always happy to walk one step behind her. She was absolutely the main attraction, I knew that. I was proud of that fact and proud to be with her. What I didn't expect was to be treated badly and belittled by so many people, especially those who were supposed to be friends. People would say I was after her money or trying to make a name for myself by riding on her coat-tails, which wasn't true in any way – yes, I didn't have a fortune but I had my own savings and a stake in our family jewellery business. I didn't tell Bar because I didn't want her to feel guilty. I never wanted her to feel bad about being who she was. She was who she was, and I knew that. Thankfully, we were never in competition with one another. But I was in competition with the world, my self-image, myself.

Maybe I thought I had to establish myself as a man about town to level out the scales a bit. The first night I stayed out later than Bar, I noticed people were talking to me, not across me. It was not an unpleasant sensation.

But along with the hard times and the digs, and the constant whispers, there were great times as well. On 27 July we were invited to a garden party at Buckingham Palace. As the Queen entered the garden, the band played the national anthem and we all stood up a little straighter. At one point Her Majesty passed about ten feet away from us. Back straight. Head held high. The Queen . . . We both felt very emotional. And then, in the blink of an eye, we were back at Brick Lane Music Hall for an opening night with Mad Frankie Fraser. One minute Frankie was talking about cutting someone's ear off, the next he was apologising to the ladies in the audience for his bad language. Thanks to Bar, I had a ringside seat at the best show in town. Life in technicolour, Babs style. We appreciated what we'd brought to one another's lives, despite how unlikely our match was.

'If I hadn't met you, Scott, I wouldn't have been back in the press,' Bar said. '*EastEnders* wouldn't have come calling and I'd still be doing that one-woman show.'

'And I would still love you,' I said.

From garden parties to music halls, private dining clubs to boxing rings, we had a varied life and I loved that about us. But, honestly, some of my most cherished memories are of heading to a local greasy spoon on a Saturday morning. Wherever we may have woken up and in whatever state, we would treat ourselves to mugs of coffee, the full English and five newspapers. The soundtrack to my life was Bar's heels clicking and her tongue chatting. It was nonstop and it was wonderful.

In October we went to Mauritius on holiday. I was the last passenger awake on the long, eleven-hour flight, champagne in hand, talking the hind legs off the crew, and inviting all of them for dinner at the hotel when we arrived. I meant well. I loved everyone when I was pissed and probably thought everyone loved me; only in the morning did the dread creep in. Best to have another drink.

At reception they asked if we'd like to have our bags unpacked. 'Oh no,' said Bar. 'I don't like the idea of anyone rifling through my underwear.'

'Why? It's never stopped you in the past!' I must have still been pissed, but Bar just burst into her infectious giggle. The thing is, that laugh was actually her laugh, it wasn't put on. She could summon it for effect, of course, but when she found something genuinely funny, it just erupted out of her. All the British tourists recognised it immediately and would look round in amazement. The receptionist looked a bit perplexed, though.

Dartford panto followed and another stint in *Cinderella*, with me as Dandini and Bar as the Fairy Godmother. I hoped it would be less dramatic than the previous year when we'd had two ugly sisters competing for the top spot. Gordon Kaye – who played René in *'Allo 'Allo!* – was one and the other was Roger Kitter, also famous in his own right and very good at impressions. Two nights into the run Gordon had refused to go on to do the slipper scene because Roger had made an impromptu gag, thereby stealing the show. Bar was top of the bill and stormed into Gordon's dressing room.

'How sad,' she said, getting teary. 'You left a stage full of actors roasting. You made us all look bad and it wasn't fair on the audience.'

She actually cried. Gordon apologised. I thought, what the hell? Show business can be ludicrous. But Bar knew panto was serious business and dedicated much of her career to making sure the audience had a cracking time.

One year on and things didn't start well. First our dressing room was broken into, then our car, and then the badge on the front of my Mercedes was broken off. But I enjoyed it once we got going and loved the part of Dandini, probably because I got a good reception. Dandini was a little Artful Dodger character and I played it well.

I never drank before or during the show, but after was a different matter. There was always someone to have a drink with. But first we had to get out of the theatre. Never in all my years with Barbara was there a time when we walked out of a stage door into a quiet, deserted street. Not once. The panto crowd and fans of *Carry On* overlapped. They were very much Bar's people and there would always be a group of her loyal fans waiting at the stage door after the show. Regardless of time or weather, Bar would make a point of signing every autograph and taking every picture.

'Do you have to talk to every one?' I once asked.

'They've waited in the cold for me,' she said, 'it is the very least I can do.'

I would watch with growing admiration as she chatted to them all. There was one woman who got very emotional. Bar gave her a long hug. It was real, this connection with people, she was never putting on an act.

'You all right?' I asked her when she finally waved the last fan off.

'She was missing her dad,' Bar said. 'They watched all those *Carry On* films together and he died recently. They were happy tears, though, the best kind.'

If I found this odd to begin with, I soon got accustomed to seeing people get really emotional when they chatted to Bar. So I would learn to wait patiently and watch the woman I loved spread some of that precious fairy dust as my feet slowly froze. No one wanted to talk to me but at least they weren't rude or pushing me aside. And then when we got back to the hotel, Bar was always up for a drink, and everyone always wanted to have a drink with Bar. People would feed her famous lines from the films. It's amazing how many people have an encylopaedic knowledge of those films.

'Have you got a large one?' people would shout while ordering a drink.

'I've had no complaints.' Followed by a 'yuck-yuck-yuck' Sid James cartoon chuckle.

At breakfast, someone would invariably pick up a pear. Bar would smile knowing what was expected of her. 'Lovely pear,' she'd say.

'You took the words right out of my mouth.' Yuck-yuck-yuck Sid James chuckle.

Eventually I taught myself how to do it and it came in very useful over the years. Whether we were surrounded by people, or it was just the two of us, there was always so much to laugh about. When we were alone she just had to screw her face up, put her hands up in little fists and go all James Cagney on me. 'You dirty rat . . .' she would say, flailing her arms, and we'd once again fall about laughing. If there was bad press, or someone being rude, we'd joke our way through it. 'Infamy, infamy, they've all got it in-for-me.'

4

Poor Me, Poor Me, Pour Me
Another Drink

Our life together continued with highs and lows. On 9 February 1996 we were heading over to Canary Wharf to have dinner with actor Michael Cashman, now Lord Cashman, the former MEP who was a big character in the Stonewall community, when we heard the news that a bomb had gone off. In Canary Wharf. We turned back. Then on the 18th another IRA bomb went off on the Aldwych, injuring eight people and killing the bomber. I'd been terrified of IRA bombs since one went off at the Grand Hotel in Brighton in 1984. I went down and looked at the hole in the shattered building. The IRA ceasefire was over, filling me with dread.

Better have another drink.

A lunch at the Grosvenor House Hotel with Gillian Taylforth and Mike Reid, both *EastEnders* legends, carried on late into the night when we were joined by Paul O'Grady and Mark Little. Bar could generally match me drink for drink, but she was even littler than me and at some point her eyes would start to roll into the back of her head. That was the moment to call it a night. I took her home, poured myself another drink, then after a while decided it would be more fun to go back out and score some coke. Bar was out cold, so why shouldn't I? It was just a bit of fun. A one-off. Quite quickly this one-off became something that happened every couple of weeks.

It tended to start off the same way. Champagne at home, putting on the gladrags, a car arrived and then we were whisked away to the ball, be it the BAFTAs, an opening night, a book launch, a performance . . . Bar would trot down the red carpet, a wave of noise would follow her as fans spotted her blonde hair and big giggle, and I would follow. The goggle-eyed lenses would follow her every move.

'Barbara and Scott!'

'This way!'

'Over here please!'

'Guys, into the lens . . .'

Bar would be whispering, 'Eyes left' – click – 'right' – click, click, click – 'middle' – another barrage of camera clicks, a blinding popping of bulbs. It was exciting and terrifying in equal measure, a snowstorm of white lights in my vision, but despite feeling a bit disorientated I was beginning to enjoy myself.

Then, 'Can we have Barbara by herself?' a loud voice boomed across the press pack. The clicking stopped. I stepped away and then the sound of picture-taking escalated. Being asked to move away was worse than the walk of shame and I learnt never again to outstay my welcome. The photos the next morning were always Barbara. On her own. The money shot. I was just in the way. But thankfully there was a tray of drinks at the other end of the long red carpet and I was usually on my second before Bar had finished the interviews, desperately trying to hang on to the buzz.

'Go back out. Enjoy yourself.'

'Really?'

'I'm nearly sixty. I've got work in the morning and I've had a hell of a past, so go, have fun.'

'Are you sure?'

''Course I'm sure!'

Bar walked through the front door, and I asked the cabbie to turn around and head back to the West End. It wasn't to hook up with women, though we both had a similar attitude towards sex. Ours was not an open relationship, but it wasn't a closed book either. Bar had talked to me in detail about her many, many conquests on our second date. She said it was always good to brush the cobwebs away . . . sex was not a big thing to her and, to be honest, going back out wasn't about sex for me anyway. It was about keeping the party going. But it didn't feel like a great achievement the morning after. Bar was laid-back, but she wasn't slapping me on the back either.

'I'm cool, Scott, but don't take the piss,' she said, when I stayed out until dawn.

Bar didn't want to stop me living my life to the full, as she had, but it did start to get a bit mixed up. She had always said sex was sex and love was love, and she wasn't one for double standards, so she kept her reservations to herself and never asked me directly. We both had a very similar outlook. We knew what we had and we knew how big it was.

There were other dark sides to those nights I headed back out to the West End, alone and drunk.

'Want to score some gear?' There were two strangers on the street ahead of me.

'Yeah,' I replied, thinking I was Tony Montana from *Scarface*. Earlier in the evening I'd been at a press party with Richard Branson tapping fags off me, making Piers Morgan laugh. I was invincible. I followed the strangers down a street, money in my hand like a fool. Suddenly, the money was gone, I was pushed to the ground and they were going through my pockets. I was so shocked I barely fought back. They tore my trousers, flipped me over, grabbed my watch and were off. I walked home very shaken up.

It wasn't the last time I was mugged in the West End. I don't remember the club, but there was another night when I got some coke off someone in the toilets, and then at the end of the night the resident drug dealer pulled a knife on me.

'This is my patch . . .' I had been warned.

What was I doing? I had waited all this time for this wonderful woman to come into my life, why was I fucking it up? What if I got caught? I would berate myself, beat myself up, then go back out on another self-destructive mission.

I know how perverse that sounds, but Bar said to tell the truth, so I am doing my best to honour those instructions.

Despite Bar's divorce, the money issues and the unkind spotlight on an insecure young man, between the two of us everything was fantastic. We were both being judged for our relationship, which mostly brought us closer together, but in me it also created a huge building tension. What if I'm not good enough? What if they are all laughing at me? What if she moves on . . . leaving me to become the next Thomas Powell? How do you adjust to life after Barbara Windsor? The seeds of doubt being sown in my mind were enough to reap a forest of insecurities.

The thing is, by then, I had become the master of masking my insecurity. I was the charmer, the geezer, the self-deprecating party boy, the entertainer, the schmoozer, the man who was always up for taking the party on. In a nutshell, by now I was an insecure man about town, both invisible and known, drinking and taking drugs, and crazily in love with a woman I had to share with the world, who was beginning to slightly tire of my antics.

When we were in synch, it was great. When she was worried about an early call and needed to get home, it could lead to some heated arguments.

'Take it easy, love,' she said, when I went to the bar and ordered another drink.

'Stop watching me!' I'd snap. 'I'm finally enjoying myself.' With all the booze and coke and late nights and social slights, my moods were a bit up and down.

I popped the cork from a bottle of champagne and filled two flutes to the top. We clinked glasses. It was 8 May and Bar's divorce had finally come through.

'To being a free woman!'

'To being a poor woman you mean!' Stephen had got a settlement in the divorce, on top of leaving her with a £1 million debt hanging over her head. But at least the lawyers had ring-fenced Bar's future earnings, meaning Stephen couldn't come after her for more money.

'It doesn't matter. We have each other and that's all that matters,' I said.

'I'm sorry that you get such a hard time from people.' I did. We both did.

'You're worth it,' I told Bar.

By the time we'd finished our first 'toast', I had refilled my glass several times. I opened another bottle, cranked up the music and we danced around the living room, until we fell on the sofa laughing. We chatted late into the night about the mad miracle of us.

Marvellous miracles continued to happen. At 10.30am on 30 June I felt the brute force of Concorde leave the runway at Heathrow and, like a couple of children at Christmas, we held hands and watched the speedometer race up and reach Mach 2 as we broke the sound barrier and everyone cheered. We were flying to New York on Concorde! Bar had mentioned to John Reid that we were planning to go to New York and he had sent over a car with two tickets to join him on the famous flight. We landed in New York before we'd taken off in London and were taken to John's impressive fiftieth-floor apartment. Our eyes were on stalks, the views were astounding, as were the racks of suits and drawers of watches that went on for miles. I'd never seen wealth like it. That's what you get for 'discovering' Elton John. We freshened up and by 3pm Bar and I were sitting in a matinee performance of *Rent*. Not bad for a Sunday. We hit the theatres and bars of Broadway and lived it up in the city that never sleeps. Perfect for us.

Unfortunately there was bad news from home, so we felt very glum leaving our Big Apple bubble. After twenty years of working hard repairing jewellery for H. Samuel, my mum and dad heard they were going to take their business elsewhere. They had to make twenty-two people redundant and fold the business Dad had built from three to a hundred shops. He was in his sixties but was ever the fighter and, after a week or so, he was back driving a London cab and putting food on the table. Gone were the Range Rovers and luxury holidays but his self-esteem was intact. He was a man who'd always held himself well. In Steven Berkoff's autobiography, *Free Association: An Autobiography*, he tells the story of my dad walking back into the Royal Tottenham dancehall like a ship swaying on the ocean to find two guys sitting where he'd been sat.

'That's my seat,' he said.

'What are you going to do about it?'

He was going to fight them, of course. Unfortunately, the two men were the Kray twins, who were quickly joined by two more burly men. I met a woman years later who told me she couldn't believe how he kept getting back up to fight them, even when they were four against one.

'How did it end?' I asked.

'I don't know,' she said. 'When your dad's eye popped out of its socket, I fainted.'

'Scott? What are you doing?'

I woke up and got dressed. I felt terrible. My head was pounding and I was on the sofa.

'You never made it to bed.'

I was trying to get my bearings.

'Have you been here all night?'

I shook my head, it hurt like hell.

'Did you go out after I'd gone to bed? Again? Where were you, Scott?'

That was the thing. I didn't know. 'I can remember leaving here . . .' My voice trailed off. Nothing. No recollection, not even a hint of one.

'That's a bit convenient,' she said as she walked into the kitchen, leaving me feeling sick and afraid.

She was right, but I honestly couldn't remember a thing. Had I been functioning? Walking and talking? Or face down in a gutter? I could have been attacked, abused or died. Or maybe I had amused a room of strangers in the wee hours of the morning with my staggering wit and humour. I hunted for some clue. I had my phone. No cash. A bruised elbow. Where the fuck had I been? This was my first black-out and it was terrifying. Not quite terrifying enough to stop me, though.

A month later, on 11 October, I woke up having a panic attack. Bar was leaning over me as I tried to catch my breath. 'What is it? What's wrong?' She looked scared.

I couldn't speak.

'What's happened? What've you done?'

We had a very open channel of communication and could tell each other anything. We didn't always agree but we always chatted. There were no 'conditions' attached to our relationship, so no reason to lie. That was the true meaning of love in our eyes.

'I don't know, Bar. I don't know.' It was petrifying.

Worried, Bar rang my brother-in-law, Laurence. 'I can't leave him,' she said, 'but I've got to go to work.'

She was in the middle of Mark Fowler's HIV-positive story, a plot-line she really had to dig deep for, because prejudice was not her style, so she needed full concentration. Now I really was getting in the way. Drink, it's guaranteed to make all your worst fears come true.

'He's in a total state,' she said. I could only hear her side of the conversation.

'Well, it's hard, isn't it? Peggy is everywhere. I've been really busy and you know how people can be around him.' She was blaming herself.

Laurence came and took me back to Hove so I could clear my head. It was embarrassing for me and hard for my family. They couldn't understand why their decent, kind son, and loving brother, was hitting the self-destruct button with such a vengeance.

'What's going on, son?'

I honestly didn't know.

'Is it getting too much being with Barbara?'

Wouldn't that be easy, just to blame it all on her.

But it wouldn't end there. The next time it happened, the note said it all. 'Ring me. Haven't slept. Gone to do a PA in Trafalgar Sq.' It was 11am and I had been out all night. On my phone there was a list of missed calls that had started at 1am and gone on until 9am, when she must have given me up for dead. I didn't dare listen to the messages. I had been supposed to drive her to that personal appearance. It was my one job. To drive her. I dialled her number, shaking.

'Scott! Oh my God, where are you?'

'Home.'

'What? Where have you been? I've been sick with worry, are you okay . . .?' There was a mixture of terror and fury in her voice.

'I'm sorry, I lost track—'

'You're not hurt?'

'No, I'm fine, got a bit of a headache.'

'I've got to work.' I didn't blame her for being furious.

'Bar, I'm really sor—'

She put down the phone. Maybe she really couldn't talk, though I suspected she didn't want to. It was one thing to stay out to the early hours. It was another thing to stay out all night, not pick up the phone, fail to get Bar to work and put her through a night of intense worry. I had hit a dead end. There was nowhere for me to go.

Laurence drove to London again, and again I broke down as soon as I saw him. I slept a bit then broke down again when Bar came home.

'You've got to sort yourself out, love,' said Bar. 'You're going to get hurt.'

She was being kind, but I knew she was cross. Work was full-on; she was about to go into her first cancer diagnosis story, the HIV story was still running and then there was the question over the paternity of Tiffany's baby. Peggy was everywhere and Bar needed space. 'Scott, I think it would be best if Laurence took you back to Hove.'

All I could do was cry. I broke down again when I saw Mum and Dad. I tried to eat but couldn't get anything down – God knows what had happened the night before. I will never know. I had been playing Russian roulette with my life, but the people I hurt were the people I loved most in the world.

The next day John Reid called me. He wanted me to see Beechy Colclough, the addiction specialist. Beechy phoned me but I was in a foul mood. He had a kind voice, a soft Irish accent, and said he would call me again in the morning, which he did. He had a free appointment the next day, so Laurence took me back to London. I walked to Harley Street, sat in the comfy leather chair and thought, *Now what?* Part of me didn't want the help, the other part was desperate to tell someone what had been happening.

During that first session we barely covered the basics, except that I couldn't control what happened when I drank. Honestly, I barely scratched the surface, but still he seemed to think I had a problem.

That his words came as a surprise is staggering to me now, but, truthfully, I didn't believe him. I was angry with myself, but mostly because it meant the party was over, and I didn't want it to be. *You've really gone and blown it now*, I thought.

'What is wrong with you?' I said, as I stood in front of the mirror and hit myself.

Deep down I knew the black-out drunk wasn't me and yet I was looking at a black-out drunk. There must have been mornings when I drove Bar, the love of my life, to work, drunk, maybe stoned, definitely sleep-deprived. The shame burned.

'I don't even know you,' I would say to my beleaguered reflection.

Then I would be angry again because we'd been on this fabulous ride, and I had ruined it, I had spoilt all the fun. We were always invited to opening nights, glittering parties, and now I was going to have to do this sober. This was incomprehensible to me.

Despite Beechy's soothing, non-judgemental voice, I was very jumpy and angry after the first session. I was reeling from how out of control my life had become. I had these enormous feelings of self-loathing and self-doubt but no medication to soothe the pain.

'Scott, we've all done it,' said Bar. 'I've got myself into loads of messy situations over the years, honestly. You're going to be fine. It's not the real you. You've just got to cut down a bit.'

I so wanted to believe her. She wanted the real Scott back, so did I, but it was much easier said than done. I had covered up my fear of not being strong enough, or brave enough, or big enough, since I was eight. And then at eighteen I had discovered a way of making myself feel strong and brave and big. What was I going to do now?

I went to see Beechy again. I got profoundly upset about the near misses, the way I had put Bar in harm's way. 'I promise you, Scott, if you don't have another drink then you will never feel this bad again,' he said.

For a while it looked like I was getting on top of things, but I knew it was an illusion. I was existing. I was getting through the day. I could be relied on to drive Bar safely back and forth to the studio, but then I was treading water in between. My diary entries don't reveal a man scraping his soul, tackling his demons or particularly enjoying his new-found sobriety. Mostly I was bored and angry. I was thinking about everything I had messed up, not because of my drinking, but because of what I would now miss out on. I still wanted to be able to drink. I couldn't imagine life without it.

'Mine's a Coke.' I learnt to say this very important line every time I went out with my fellow cast members from Jim Davidson's panto. It was good to be doing something other than driving Bar and the cast were great. I was shitting myself, obviously, but I was in good hands with people like Victor Spinetti – whose house Bar had been staying in the evening I laid eyes on her the first time – Roger Kitter, our long-time friend who'd played Bar's ugly sister in Basingstoke, and John Bardon, who went on to play Jim Branning in *EastEnders* a few years later. Dinners were muted. I was withdrawn and sometimes could be quite sullen. Without my crutch and the platform of booze, I was no longer the giant, no longer the life and soul of the party. But I stuck to it, and I was at least able to be proud of that.

I came home for Christmas and we collapsed in a heap, just the two of us. And with tea and cake, we curled up together to watch the *EastEnders* Christmas special.

Peggy knocked on Pauline Fowler's door. Reluctantly she let Peggy in to talk to Mark, in private. Peggy wanted to apologise for all the horrible things she'd said about him being HIV positive.

'How do you cope? Aren't you scared?'
  'I go to a counsellor and talk to them about this and that.
You can't just bottle it up. I tried to at first, everybody does, it's only natural, but you waste so much time that way and time's so precious. You've got to learn to enjoy now and make the best of what you've got . . .'

At which point, Barbara and I held each other tightly on the sofa. It was an incredibly poignant scene and groundbreaking at the time.

After Christmas Bar came to Bristol to see the panto and, contrary to my fear, we had real fun. Victor called our room at one-fifteen in the morning. 'Come over,' he said. 'I've got hot chocolate!' Boy, how things had changed, but we did go, in our dressing gowns, and sat gossiping and laughing with him till the wee hours. It must have been a funny sight for the night waiter. A very wholesome showbiz afterparty.

On New Year's Eve I drove home after the second show. We got a late Chinese takeaway. 'Can I get you a drink?' I asked Bar.

'No, no, I'm fine.'

'It's okay, you know. I don't want to stop you from having a drink.'

'I don't need one,' she said. 'It's been a tough year, Scott. My divorce, your dad's business going under, owing so much money. No wonder it all got out of hand. You're going to be just fine, Scott, I promise. All right?'

I nodded, wanting to believe her.

'That's life, darlin'. Full of ups and down.'

'Joan Littlewood is in the theatre looking for you,' Victor said, as soon as I took the call.

'*The* Joan Littlewood?' I asked incredulously.

'Yes, Scott, *the* Joan Littlewood. Barbara's Joan Littlewood.'

Joan was a RADA-trained maverick director, ahead of her time, who turned the middle-class male-dominated world of theatre on its head after the war. It would have been a welcome boost to meet her and hear what 'The Mother of Modern Theatre' had to say, but I was already in the car heading back down the M4 on my way home after the show.

'She's here, she wants to talk to you. I'm putting her on.'

'Hi, Scott, it's Joan. I just wanted to say I really liked your performance. You move well onstage.'

'Thank you.' I gripped the steering wheel, bowled over.

'You are very good; thought you should know.'

Her words could not have come at a better time. It is said that the good news about being sober is that you get your feelings back, but the bad news is that you get your feelings back. My belief in myself was at an all-time low and I was seriously considering giving up acting altogether. I got home and as soon as I walked through the door I called out, 'Hey, Bar, you'll never guess . . .'

We always swapped notes about our days. I don't know who was prouder. Bar had known Joan, well, since she'd mistaken her for a cleaning lady when she first went to audition for *Fings Ain't Wot They Used T'Be* in 1959. Joan saw something in Bar and made her raise her game back then, on the cusp of the Swinging Sixties. She was a tiny, very bright, cockney girl who spoke her mind, loved her community and gave back to it with 'joie de vivre'. No wonder the two women connected. As a director, she was a straight talker who changed the theatrical landscape with *Oh, What a Lovely War!*

'She was the person who told me that if I ended up playing the ditzy blondes my whole life it would be my fault,' Bar said.

'Bet she's proud of you now. There is nothing ditzy about Peggy!'

'If she told you you were good, you should believe it, Scott. Compliments don't come often from Joan and she knows what she's talking about!' It was gold dust to Bar.

'Praise from Joan. I can retire,' I said.

'Rubbish, it means you should go on.'

Both Bar and Joan made a good point and I wish I had listened, but I found life hard to deal with and praise hard to take. An addict's lament. Poor me, poor me, pour me another drink . . .

5

The Invisible Man

'Sobriety is impossible on your own,' said Nick Love, a filmmaker friend of mine who was married to the actress Patsy Palmer at the time. 'Please come to my AA meeting. It's in The Boltons in Chelsea.'

'Scott doesn't need that,' said Bar.

'Barbara, I assure you, you can have a glittering career, a life of luxury and still have addiction problems,' said Nick. 'Addiction is a great leveller.'

And so I found myself at my first AA meeting. I sat at the back and listened. When I first heard someone laugh, I was stunned. How incredible would that be, I thought, to reach a point where I could laugh about this situation.

My fellow attendees had been in similar scrapes to me. They weren't laughing because it was okay; they were laughing because it was not. I could see it was obviously very bonding for the people in the group to be surrounded by others who were non-judgemental, but I held back. Whatever the story, there was one similarity: we'd all become powerless, and that was why we'd ended up at AA. To get some of that power back.

Trouble was, I wasn't ready to enter the circle of trust. I had doubts. I was looking for the differences, as opposed to the similarities. I was scared to be honest about how frightened I was, how 'less than' I felt. Those were words I could not say out loud, so for eighteen months I had one foot in and one foot out. I was going through the motions because it looked good, but I never really grasped the true redeeming spirit of it. The long and short of it, I wasn't ready to accept I had a drinking problem. Instead, I listened, and cherry-picked the bits that I was prepared to accept. I was ticking the sobriety box, but I wasn't fixing anything inside.

Around this time there was an unfortunate incident with a friend of Barbara's who also worked in the industry. She got off the phone in tears one day after they spoke to her very curtly. It was all quite petty, but Bar was distraught and for some reason I'd had enough. The red mist descended. Maybe it was months of pent-up fury at being pushed aside, talked over, dismissed and generally belittled by various people. I had taken all of this because it had been directed at me. But this was a direct attack on Bar and I wasn't going to stand for it. Maybe I was beginning to feel braver in myself. I just didn't recognise it, so alien was the feeling without a drink in my hand. I was prepared to be intimidated but it was quite another thing being rude to the lady I loved. I called this person and told them I was not happy about it.

'Be very careful how you talk to me, Scott. I could make your life very difficult!'

'I don't give a fuck,' I replied. 'Don't ever speak to Bar like that again.'

Bar and I were fierce in our willingness to defend others. She told me stories of how she'd picked fights with the bullies at her school when the playground thugs went for the Jewish kids during the war. I can just see it, her tiny fists bunched furiously, a pocket battleship. 'Lemme at them . . .'

She was right, too. When you stand up to the bullies, they back down. We never spoke to this friend again. Their loss, I believe.

We were invited, through John Reid, to Elton John's fiftieth birthday party at the Hammersmith Palais. I was nervous about it. I'd been plodding along with AA and with Beechy but deep down I wanted a drink. How the hell was I going to cope at Elton's fancy dress party without one? Just the thought of it made me feel awkward. However, as we started to plan our outfits, it was impossible not to get excited. We opted for Pearly King and Queen costumes, black velvet suits with wide floppy hats on to which hundreds of drop pearls were sewn. The classic East London look evolved from the 'costermongers' – barrow boys working the dockside markets. When they did well they would attach pearl buttons to their jackets. The better they did, the more buttons were sewn on.

Our many pearls were matched only by the many flashes of the packed-in press photographers as we walked the short distance between the car and the front entrance of the Hammersmith Palais. Celebrities spilled out of cars and each time the crowd went mad.

'Over here please!'

'Look this way!'

'One more, both of you.' We were wearing matching outfits so perhaps this time I wouldn't be cropped out of the photo.

As soon as we entered the foyer we were in an Elton-inspired wonderland. That man really knows how to throw a party. Floor-to-ceiling flowers, lights and colour, it was full of the biggest show-offs in the business all trying to outdo one another with flamboyant costumes. John Reid came as a male swan from Matthew Bourne's *Swan Lake*, Jean Paul Gaultier was a French maid, Janet Street-Porter was Wonder Woman, with mile-long legs, but nothing could top Elton's enormous wig and white marabou cloak.

'What, this old thing?'

Even the staff looked immaculate and were floating around making sure everyone's drinks were full. Inevitably, Bar got quite tipsy and I remember wishing that I could too. Elton and his partner David Furnish sat in their eighteenth-century finery looking across a room effervescing with joy, quaffing fine wine and vintage champagne. It was like being at Versailles. But all I could think was, what a great party to be drunk at. I was on edge all night, surrounded by mega celebrities who were having the time of their lives. John later told us that someone who'd been sober for seven years had relapsed at that party. I could relate.

The following day there were many press photos in the papers. As usual I had been cut out of all of them. It was around then that I started to call myself 'the shoulder'. It made me both smile and feel insignificant. I was Barbara's partner, not a spare part, but no matter how hard she tried to pull me into the circle or include me in a conversation, it never seemed to work.

'Scott's very much like that, aren't you, love?' she would say.

'Scott's good at that, you should ask him . . .'

Or, one of her favourites, 'I was saying to Scott earlier . . .'

If the people we were with didn't make room for me we would give each other that knowing look and, as soon as she was able, move on together and have a laugh about it.

'You all right?' she'd check.

'As long as I'm with you,' I always replied.

That was our way of dealing with the slights and put-downs. As long as we were okay with each other, it was okay. Though I realised it wasn't really. The humiliations started to add up and in turn my anxiety began to build. My scalp was flaking so badly, I looked like Liam Gallagher had sneezed on me.

There were certain friends it was different with, though. I'll never forget the brilliant night out we had at *EastEnders* actor Paul Bradley's party in Stoke Newington. Bar spent most of the time telling stories about being brought up there after the war. At the end of the night we, together with Ross and his partner Rebekah Wade, decided to go into town for a drink. We got into a cab and headed towards Joe Allen's. As soon as we pulled into Trafalgar Square, Bar piped up. 'Thank fuck we're back in the West End.'

She loved being an East Ender, but she was very much a West End girl now. I've heard Ross tell that story a few times; I think it's one of his favourites.

'I OWE £1 MILLION POUNDS', the *Sun* headline read.

Barbara needed the money, that was why she did the story. The Plough owed just shy of £1 million, which meant Bar owed just shy of £1 million.

'I can give you £150,000,' said Dale Winton, calling her up as soon as the story came out. She thanked him and turned down his kind offer. She said she would pay back every penny. And she did. I have huge respect for her for that. Unfortunately, the story reignited the antipathy from Stephen and in early August we got a tip-off that the

People were printing a tell-all story by him. I went out and got the early edition from King's Cross station at 10pm.

'You don't need to read this,' I said.

'Hand it over!'

It was a deeply unpleasant article, which focused mostly on her appearance in bed. Stephen described in detail why he hadn't been sexually attracted to her once the wigs and make-up were off. We could only assume it was in retaliation for the debt story, but it went far beyond that. It was cruel and Bar sobbed and sobbed as she read it.

'I'm not going to the party tonight,' she declared. 'I can't.'

'Bar, it's your party,' I said. 'It's to celebrate your sixtieth birthday and all your friends will be there, everyone who loves you.' I didn't add that it had also all been paid for by the *Mirror*.

So Bar did what she always did. She dusted herself off, put on her war paint and faced the world like the trouper and survivor she was. She truly was an astounding woman.

I'll never forget the moment I looked around the Belvedere that evening as it started to fill up with her guests. It was very Barbara, a mix of showbiz and the underworld: many of the *EastEnders* cast, Danny La Rue, Dale Winton, Gaby Roslin, John Reid, Freddie and Janice Foreman, Tony and Wendy Lambrianou, Mad Frankie Fraser and his partner Marilyn . . . the list went on and on. There was an undeniable feeling of warmth and positivity in the room that night. It was as if each and every one of our friends was embracing Barbara with love, holding her tightly and saying, 'We've got your back.'

It was a wonderful night full of laughter and dancing, and smiling faces, and one I still remember clearly (not least because Bar and I wore these strange matching lime-green jackets that evening). Whatever were we thinking? There was a brilliant moment when Joan Collins's daughter, Tara Newley, said to me, 'I'm having a great time talking to bank robbers and serial killers.' There weren't any serial killers there, but it sure sounded funny in her terribly 'English' voice. By the end of the evening the horrendous article had been forgotten, or so I thought. But the words lingered and, unbeknownst to me, a self-doubt was starting to take hold deep inside Barbara.

*

On 30 August 1997 we went to dinner at Joe Allen's with Dale Winton and Steve Allen, the LBC presenter. Little did we know, while we sat drinking and chatting, that Princess Diana had been killed that night in a car crash in Paris. Like the rest of the nation, we felt numb and so sad for her and for her boys when we heard the news. We bought some flowers and joined the many thousands of people at Kensington Palace to pay our respects. Bar wore a hat so as not to draw attention to herself, but lots of people still recognised her, now she was being beamed into millions of living rooms three nights a week. We joined the queue at Harrods to sign the book of condolence; it was important to Bar that we did the whole thing properly. A real royalist, my Bar. She really was the best of British.

The country was in mourning but we all had to dust ourselves off and get back to life, unsure why we felt so bereft without a woman that most of us had never met. In Albert Square Peggy was dealing with Phil's drinking issues, which meant Barbara was busier than ever and in practically every pub scene. I had stopped drinking, but my life was still spiralling. Nothing was happening in my career. I was getting rejections from agents the whole time and my self-doubt was growing. Then I was hit with another blow. On 17 September Brian Hall died from cancer. To the nation, Brian is probably best known for playing Terry, the chef in *Fawlty Towers*; to me he was a beloved family friend and mentor. He was there the night Bar and I first met and I loved him dearly and felt his loss profoundly. He had tried to make it easy on us all, saying he wasn't afraid of cancer or death. And, as for everlasting life, he had his own take, saying, 'I'm getting ready for a nice long kip.'

I slipped from being subdued to sad. I was not enjoying my life and no longer had the crutch of the booze to push me through the days. My unhappiness was making Bar unhappy. She blamed herself, but of course it wasn't her fault. She'd been Barbara Windsor the showbiz queen for years and I had known that from the beginning. The fault was all mine, but this was the tipping point. I was making the love of my life miserable because I was a miserable dry drunk. I may not have had alcohol in my system but all the reasons for wanting a drink were still very much there, and being constantly under a spotlight just made it feel worse.

'It's all my fault,' said Bar. 'My life ruins people.'

'No, Bar, it's my fault. I'm holding you back. You're doing so well. You are brilliant as Peggy and I'm . . .' I was nothing. 'Well, I'm holding you back.'

'Don't say that, Scott, please.' We'd hug.

'It'll be all right,' I replied. But deep down I didn't think it would be.

The downward spiral was shockingly fast. A fog rolled in. Everything became overwhelming. I couldn't feel joy. I couldn't see the good. I couldn't see I was in a wonderful situation with this wonderful lady who was still with me even though I had messed up. I couldn't see the positives. Everything was negative. It was like walking through quicksand. Everything was dull and heavy and constantly within me. It was like being awake in a bad dream. I couldn't move my legs, I couldn't escape. I was stuck but I wasn't asleep.

I called Beechy and made an appointment to see him that afternoon. As soon as I walked in the room I broke down. I had to tell him what I felt. My relationship was killing me. I believed my misery was circumstantial, basically being with Barbara, so I decided the only option was to change the circumstance and not be with Barbara.

'You have to tell her,' he advised. I walked home ever so slowly.

'Hi, darlin', how was it?' she asked.

I closed the door slowly behind me. 'Bar, we need to talk . . .' I couldn't believe I was going to do this. 'Will you sit down?'

'You okay, love? You look terrible.' I could see in her face she was worried about me.

'Bar, I know I've looked as if I'm coping but . . . it's too much. I don't think I can live like this any more.'

She gripped my hands, her eyes widening.

'I'm sorry, Bar, I've got to leave.'

She cried out like a wounded animal, leapt off the sofa and ran out of the house. The door had slammed before I was even off the sofa. I was bereft. I knew telling her was going to be awful, but this was worse than I'd thought. I went out into the rain to look for her, up and down the streets, but couldn't find her anywhere. What had I done? What if she did something stupid? I was terrified. Basically, I was terrified all the time.

When I got back home, she was there, soaked through and weeping. We immediately started arguing about who was feeling worse. There was pain on both sides. One person in the limelight seeing for the first time how dark it was for the person standing just outside the glare. And the other, the invisible man, believing he had to escape the glare to become visible again. I wasn't asking her to step out of the light. I knew that would have meant us both being plunged into darkness and it wouldn't have worked. I wouldn't have asked and she wouldn't have agreed. I believed we were in an impossible situation with no other way out.

She felt very let down. I had told her I loved her the way she was. I had told her she could rely on me. And now I was going back on all my promises. I was so torn inside. I had never felt so bad in my life.

The next day Bar was angry at me. 'Where will you go?'

I had no idea.

'Where will you live?'

Again, I had no idea.

'We've been through so much. I don't understand.'

She'd never trusted anyone to be there for her before. Not only was I her emotional support, but I also took care of all the practical stuff. I ran everything at home so that all she had to do was learn her lines and go to work. For the first time in her life she was being properly looked after and looked out for and protected, and now I wanted to take all that away. She was devastated.

The thing was, so was I. But in my mind I thought I needed to go away. That only by distancing myself from Barbara could I carve out a life of my own. It was the constantly being recognised, constantly having people coming up to her, having to stop what we were doing because I was with her . . . I thought a new life without her would mean I was free. I was running to an imaginary world where everything would be better. But that was terrifying too, because Bar wouldn't be in my life and I never stopped being in love with her. Sometimes I feared what she might think of me if she knew what a wreck I was on the inside, but she always knew I loved her completely.

After a tearful start to the day, I took her to work. We were both in a bad way, especially Bar. I spoke to Beechy and Nick Love to double-check myself. We had more rows at dinner that night. I was unreasonable and angry with myself because I was feeling scared and alone. I was all over the place.

'We can sort this out, Scott,' Bar said. 'I love you.'

'I love you too, so much. I don't know what I'm doing.'

I wept at my AA meeting. A couple of people came up to me afterwards; I recognised one as an actor who kindly gave me his number. I think he could see what a mess I was in. I went home and slept for an hour, then woke up having a panic attack so cancelled going to the theatre that night.

'Go to Henlow Grange health farm,' Bar said. 'You need a rest.'

So I did. Alone. But rather than take care of myself I went up to the smoking room and hung out with some nice mothers from Hornchurch. I was racked with nightmares and thought the treatments helped, but as soon as I picked Bar up from Elstree Studios I felt low again.

'You okay to come to the party with me tonight?' she asked.

The last thing I wanted to do was go to the *EastEnders* party. 'Sure,' I said, but in truth I hated the whole night. Nobody there was doing anything wrong. The actors, producers and crew were people I had got to know well. I hung out with many of them socially, but I felt like a beggar at the feast and it was about to get worse.

'Scott, come on up to the stage! Come on up!'

I shook my head.

'Oh come on, Scott!'

It was late October and we were sitting at a large round table in the Grosvenor House Hotel at the glittering Lady Ratlings Ball, surrounded by clinking glasses, bottles of wine and everyone in their finery. I did not want to be there. I now felt like I was walking a tightrope at each of these star-filled events. I definitely didn't want to get up onstage and do a turn with Ann Emery – Dick Emery's sister.

Christ, an unrehearsed song and dance? No way. I shook my hands. 'Not tonight,' I shouted back. 'Please, ask someone else . . .'

She thought it was false modesty. I was supposed to be an actor, remember. 'I am not taking no for an answer.'

I stood on that stage feeling like an imbecile. All the faces smiled back at me, waiting. I just stood there. *What's wrong with him? Why can't he do it?* It was a sign to me. The final humiliation. I knew I was letting Bar down and I felt awful for that, but there was nothing I could do. In that moment my world crashed in, and everyone was watching as it happened. What could I say? That to be inside my head and body at that moment was the worst place in the world? Who would understand? Who would believe me?

If my plan to escape Bar's life was about being able to drink without the world watching, I did not admit that. I was learning about the link between feelings and drink, but I wasn't prepared to accept it, so instead I manoeuvred the pieces so I could escape. What I wanted was respite from my own sober pain. And I had a perfect get-out for explaining why I was feeling the way I was feeling. Even though we didn't want to let each other go, I felt I needed to escape everything that was Barbara Windsor.

Sorry, Bar. It was never you.

6

Three Pink Cups

I sat down opposite Hilary Gagan, my very underused agent, in a small café in Soho. 'I have moved out of the mews house and have a new address,' I said, building up to say out loud what I had actually come to say. 'I am ending my relationship with Barbara, it's over, thought you should know because you might get some press questions.'

'I'm so sorry,' she said. Clearly it wasn't going to affect her revenue stream a great deal but she was sweet about it. We chatted a bit more, then a woman walked in and sat down at a table in the corner. Joan Littlewood. In a better frame of mind maybe I would have read that as a sign that she believed I was a good performer, so I should persevere. But I didn't. I took it as a sign I would never escape. Bar's life was always popping up in front of me. And filling the rear-view mirror too. It was not a clean break. The trouble was, we still got on, I was conflicted and it was hard to sever ties when I knew how upset Bar was.

In December the *Sun* ran a story with the headline: 'TV BABS DUMPS TOYBOY'. It wasn't true but I was happy to take the hit for Bar's dignity. Either way, it was over.

Then, early in 1998, a newspaper ran a horrible story about how she had laundered £25,000 of Ronnie Knight's stolen money into her personal bank account in used notes. There wasn't a dishonest bone in that woman's body, she was a grafter not a grifter.

'It's not true, Scott,' she cried. 'It's not, none of it. I can't believe he's stitched me up after everything we've been through. I'll lose *East-Enders*, Scott, and what if I lose the mews?'

She was devastated. I knew it was muddying the waters but I rushed straight over there and ended up staying. In the end she decided to call the police herself. At 5.30 the following morning, having waited on tenterhooks for twenty-four hours, there was a knock on the door.

'It's the police!' she said, now terrified that she would lose everything she'd worked for, plus me, and was alone in the world. Her greatest fears realised.

'It's all right, Bar, you don't know anything, just tell them. I'm here.'

I went to open the door. Bar was ready.

'I'm a friend of Ronnie's,' said the man at the door. What the hell was this guy doing here before dawn? 'Can I come in? It's all a misunderstanding. He's doing a book from inside jail and needed to beef up the story to get more money. He's really sorry.'

It didn't go any further with the police, but what followed was like a storyline from *Carry On Spying*. The friend created a codename so we knew it was him calling – 'three pink cups', because that was what we'd been drinking out of. When he called to update us on Ronnie's moves, he would not acknowledge Bar until she'd uttered the codename.

'Three pink cups . . .'

I cannot express the stress it caused Bar. We wanted to sue the paper for the defamatory and untrue article but was scared off by the lawyer who said it would go on for a long time and take its toll on her health and finances. First Stephen had humiliated her, now Ronnie had betrayed her and besmirched her good name. I took a tray up to her room where she was resting and knocked on the door. I slid the door open, just making visible the tray with the three pink cups. It was good to see her laugh, but then she looked at me.

'Don't go,' she said.

'Sorry, Bar, I've got to get back to house-sit John's place.' (John Addy was a friend of ours.) 'I'm not staying.'

The combination of it all wiped her out. In February Bar started coughing and she was soon so weak the doctor checked her into UCH for observation. Of course I went to see her; the press were already outside by the time I got there. I don't know how they knew so quickly. How do they ever know? It's easier if you don't ask yourself those questions because it can make you quite paranoid.

The next day Bar's picture was on the front pages again. 'TV BABS IN HOSPITAL'. I immediately reverted to the role of carer and shuttled back and forth between the two mews houses and the hospital. Once people read Bar was in hospital, flowers from co-workers, well-wishers and mega-fans started to arrive – ninety-two bouquets in total.

One of the biggest bunches was from Robert Dunn. I saw his name on the card and shuddered. I had never met the man but Bar's friends had told me that when his name came up they'd cross themselves. Anna Karen said it was the only time she and Bar didn't speak in their lifelong friendship because she didn't like who Bar became when she was with him. In fact, Bar told me herself that though she was attracted to him the relationship had been unhealthy at times. I saw the huge bunch of yellow roses and saw red. All this time I had been telling her she'd sold herself short when it came to men, settling for losers because of how her father had treated her, but this guy was the worst of them.

'You cannot see that man!' I told her and threw his card away. I knew it wouldn't be good for her and I cared too much. But it was a mistake telling Bar what not to do. The moment I was gone she got the card out of the bin, phoned her PA Yvonne and asked her to track down the florist, call them and get the man's contact details. She was cross with me – who was I to tell her who she could and could not see? I was the one who was leaving her. I had done what the others had done, despite all my promises. She was feeling vulnerable and alone and in that state she made bad choices.

I got home and turned on the TV. 'Barbara Windsor home from hospital' was being typed out across the screen on Ceefax. I thought it was mad, but it reminded me what I was up against. Her past and present made her news. I had given up my place beside her, yet here I was very much looking after her again. I made sure she ate, tried to take care of her and ran the errands I'd always run. I was quickly sucked back into the Barbara Windsor vortex and I felt trapped.

It was one day when I was staring at Bar's face on the front cover of *Inside Soap* that I decided Lancaster Mews wasn't far away enough. I needed some distance to clear my head without the daily reminders. Perversely, she was the first person I told.

'I'm going to America to stay with family,' I told her. She was upset but what did she do? She bought me the ticket.

'You go, sort your head out and everything will be okay,' she said. I knew she hoped there was still a chance. I don't really know what I was thinking beyond just needing to go. I was in the public glare and yet no one cared about me. Why would they? I was the shoulder, the invisible man, a joke.

'I don't want you to go,' she cried as soon as she woke up the next day. 'I feel so scared. What am I going to do without you?'

I felt awful but she was better, and it was time for me to extricate myself, but then when I started to pack the car, I felt this huge wave of emotion break over me. I sobbed on Bar's shoulder like a child. 'I'm so sorry I'm leaving.'

'Then don't go.'

'I can't stay, Bar. We can't go back.'

But if that was true, why did it hurt so much to leave? I cried all the way to the motorway and was pretty foul to be with when I got home.

'I just want you to get better,' said my dad, weeping as he pulled me into a hug under the Gatwick departures sign. Like Bar, he could see I was not in a good place but he couldn't reach me.

My aunt Bessie, a cockney bombshell, and my cousin Barbara, who swore like a trooper and was always easy to talk to, were waiting at Los Angeles International Airport. They drove me to where they lived in Huntington Beach, Orange County. My eyes were on stalks. Palm trees, blue skies, big cars, the rolling surf of Laguna Beach was exactly what I thought I needed. America looked like a fantasy world, laid-back, col-ourful and easy, and it suited me perfectly. I was ready to start a new life.

What did I do as soon as I'd unpacked? I called Bar. I had put an ocean between us, but she was the first person I thought about when I woke. The first person I thought about when I went to bed. She was the one I wanted to tell everything to. So much for distance.

Three days in, I relapsed. I'm amazed I waited that long. It was 6pm, it had been a beautiful Californian day, perfect temperature, deep blue skies, sun just starting to dip in the sky. My cousin had a double garage attached to the house she shared with her husband. I remember simply walking back towards the fridges stacked with Corona and, without thinking or blinking or hesitating, I opened a bottle, inhaled it, then opened another one and drank that too. Straight down without stopping. They were followed by two margaritas. Then, to prove I didn't have a problem, I made a cup of tea and went to bed.

At three o'clock in the morning I sat bolt upright in a panic. What had I just done?

Within days I was back doing what I'd done before, getting drunk in a club with people I didn't know, fuelled by an alcoholic's foolish sense of security. It had taken four beers and two vodka tonics, and I beat myself up about it as soon as I left the club and was back in bed. I swore to myself I would not do it again. It's the sort of false promise that only a drunk can make. Soon that changed to a very laissez-faire attitude. I decided I would one day give up again but until that time I may as well enjoy it.

If anyone noticed or told my family back at home, I couldn't say, they didn't make much of a fuss about it. I got a job through an Iranian guy who was trading energy futures. It was a small office and he would pay me to answer phones and keep an eye on the markets. I didn't have a sodding clue what I was doing and spent the time surfing the internet all day, partying all night. LA, Vegas, bars, bars, bars . . . my British accent got me a long way. Pretty quickly I was suntanned and looked younger than I was, but I had more confidence now. With a drink back in my hand, I was happy to talk the talk. Now I was really living, right? Not really. There was always something not quite right, something missing.

Bar and I were talking regularly. We wanted to keep the connection because we cared so much for each other. I believed we'd moved to a new stage and were now proper platonic friends, but I was deluding myself.

'I'm staying,' I told her one night.

'What do you mean?'

'I like it here. I think I can make a life for myself.'

Bar was not happy. 'I thought you just needed a bit of time to get this . . .' – she sounded cross – 'break out of your system.'

The thing was, Bar had lived such a wild life and she wanted me to have that, but she wanted me to have it fast and get back home to her. 'I'm sorry, Scott, I'm not sure I can keep talking to you like this.'

'But what about when I eventually come home? Can't we see each other?'

'I can't. It's too difficult. I've got to get over you.'

I tried to understand, but I was shocked at how upset I was by the thought of not seeing her. I squashed the thought with more nights on the town, but it wasn't working. In fact, I could feel the paranoia creeping back in. I could hear Beechy saying, 'You keep doing what you are doing and get what you have got.'

That was me. I'd forgotten how empty one-night stands could be.

I was sitting at my desk when I decided to look up Barbara on the internet. What madness was that? I'd moved to escape the constant news about Barbara and now I was seeking it out. I got a real shock. Robert Dunn was back in her life; there was a photo of the pair of them leaving the mews house, another with Ross Kemp, another at Wayne Sleep's fiftieth birthday, at the Queen Vic! It was like being hit in the stomach. The man she described as looking like Al Pacino, whose card I had thrown in the bin . . . I couldn't understand. I'd heard such negative things about their relationship in the past. How could she? I knew the answer of course. She was hurting, and that was my doing. Barbara was never on her own for long, but Robert Dunn . . . That made me sad. I put the guilt to the back of my mind but I couldn't put the thought of it there too. Her getting back with Dunn really affected me. I called her from LA to talk to her about my concerns, but it led to a row.

'It's none of your business,' she said.

'I still care about you, I'm worried.'

'You don't have the right any more.'

She was right and I hated it. So I went off partying, pulling and working, but was I happy? Not really. A couple of weeks later she called me. 'I've made a mistake,' she said.

Bar was confirming everything I had suspected about their relationship, which was awful for her, but at least it meant we were talking on the phone again. 'It's not good, there are some more stories about to come out . . .' More stories, more men.

'It's your life, Bar.'

I understood it but I didn't like it. I could see what was happening from the other side of the world. Bar's way of dealing with me leaving was to go out drinking and go a bit wild. Not that dissimilar to what I was doing, except I was the one who had walked away. I was supposed to be happy. I thought going to America would stop Bar's life and fame from affecting me. It wasn't working and towards the end of July I decided that staying in the US was futile. I decided I needed to return home, find a new career and make a new life.

I sat at the bar in the departure lounge of Los Angeles International Airport and ordered a double vodka. 'I know you,' said a woman sitting opposite me. Turned out we'd met at a party. We had another drink then boarded the plane. As soon as the seatbelt lights were turned off, I was up, found my new English friend and carried on drinking with her. We were having a grand old party for two on the plane. In my head I was being erudite, charming, telling amusing anecdotes, I used to go out with Barbara Windsor . . . In reality, I'm sure I was being a loud, obnoxious nuisance. I passed out as we came in to land at a grey, wet Heathrow.

I stumbled into arrivals, swaying and talking jibberish. Dad was there to collect me. I thought I was Dudley Moore in *Arthur*, but there was no convincing my dad. He quickly realised I was in a worse state than when I'd left. Some friends of theirs were at the house when we got there and he had the good sense to bundle me off to bed and blame it on jet lag.

I wasn't the only drunken mess. 'I've fucked up,' said the voicemail. I could tell Bar had been drunk and unhappy when she'd called. 'I miss you. Why are you living with your parents? It's not right.'

By the end of the message, she'd turned nasty. I thought it was best for her if she hated me. We were both so unhappy but still I thought it was the circumstances, so I wrote to her saying we shouldn't be in contact. I was still seeking a clean break but was unable to see it through. What a mess.

'No, Scott, I want to be your friend. Please.'

It went on like that, a game of emotional tennis. We'd speak, then not speak, then speak, then argue about speaking. 'Please, Bar, you have to let me go and not be in contact.'

Another agonising week would pass and one of us would fold under one pretext or another. And then the depression that had flirted with me previously came back with a vengeance.

On 24 August 1998 I wrote what I believed would be the last entry in my diary:

> *It's been 11 years of telling myself the same old thing: I am scared, I am hungover, I am confused. My conclusion to the previous 35 years? I had wasted the first half of my life.*

I went to bed in my childhood room in my parents' house in Hove and stayed there. For a month. I couldn't speak. I completely shut down. It was as if I was paralysed. What a waste, that was all I could think. I was a waste of space. I had wasted my life. I was wasting away. Eventually I went to see our family doctor. The words 'I am depressed' will never convey or express or explain the heavy darkness that slips uninvited into the soul and stays there. 'I have nothing to live for,' I told him. 'I've messed my life up.' I'd met an amazing lady who loved me and who I loved and I had managed to mess that up too.

'I am a complete failure.' There, I'd said it. My secret fear.

'Scott, I am going to prescribe Prozac,' he said and, just like that, for the first time in my life, I started on medication.

As autumn became winter, I slowly, so slowly, started to feel a bit of positivity creep into my life. My mother told Bar, who continued to call and check in on how I was. Mum told her what was going on. I lied and pretended I was okay. I didn't want her to think I was weak. She was still with Robert Dunn and it was my fault. Otherwise she was flying, or so I thought. Great storylines in *EastEnders*, a record deal with Telstar, 'You've Got a Friend' and a new play about her life. Written by Terry Johnson, *Cleo, Camping, Emmanuelle and Dick* was based on her affair with Sid James. She also had endless television

appearances . . . you name it, she was everywhere and doing brilliantly. The only thorn in her side was her boyfriend, who had a habit of
selling her out.

'He's not good for you,' I would say when we chatted, which was
getting more frequent.

I couldn't stop thinking about the demise of our relationship, but
then something changed. My wonderful 84-year-old aunt Bessie had
returned from California due to ill health and, while I was visiting
her in hospital, she had a heart attack and suddenly I had something
very real to worry about. I ran for a nurse, but they were horribly
understaffed so the nurse told me what to do and somehow I was
able to assist. I stayed with her, in a state of shock. This was real life.
I had to stop besieging myself with dark thoughts and focus on what
was actually in front of me. When Bessie woke up, she smiled. 'If you
hadn't been here, I'd have been a goner.'

Then she looked deep into my eyes for a long time. She had these
extraordinarily deep blue penetrating eyes. I couldn't look away. 'You
still love her, don't you?'

I knew in that moment, I did. I nodded.

'Be happy, Scott. Sod what others think. Live your life. I know
why Barbara loves you. It's because you make people feel safe, you're
a good man.'

Those words meant the world to me and gave me the impetus to
restart my life. But things had to change and that change started with
me. The Winehouses introduced me to a friend of theirs called Lee
Panayiotou, who had a recruitment agency. I had no qualifications,
but I was determined. She offered to train me up and I was ecstatic.

'I'm going to make you so proud of me,' I said to Bar over dinner.

'Darlin', I've always been proud of you.'

'I'm going to get myself together and really make something of
myself. I want you to see how strong I can be.' Then, feeling braver
than I had for a long time, I said, 'And I'll tell you something else, I'm
going to woo you back, Barbara.'

'Are you going to be my knight in shining armour? Are you going
to come riding through the mist to rescue me?'

'You may laugh, but you watch. I will.'

She didn't talk me out of it, though Robert was still very much on the scene. Luckily, he made it easy for me. On her way to present an Olivier Award to the unsuspecting cast of *Carry On Cleo*, now in Bath, she stopped off at Robert's manager's house. He had wanted her to go to his pub but she didn't have time, she was squeezed as it was. A limo pulled up outside. Nice touch, thought Bar, until she saw the photographer and journalist pull up alongside it.

'Sorry, love, I can't do the photo,' she said. 'BBC rules, no advertising.'

'But it's all organised,' said the limo company owner, pissed off he wasn't going to get the shot. Bar knew what that meant, although Robert denied any part in this. I believe it sealed his fate, though not immediately.

Our Christmas arrangements were far from traditional that year. Initially Bar went to Southampton with Robert and his sons from his second marriage, but she was coming to ours for Christmas itself. There were two elephants in the car with us when I picked her up. The first was that she'd been with Robert, who she knew perfectly well I didn't like. The second elephant was that we weren't behaving as though we were just friends. Nothing happened between us, but we were a bit too excited to see each other, got on a bit too well, laughed too loudly, talked too much, caught each other's eye one time too many. Seeing her back with my family both filled and broke my heart. It was where she belonged, but I had messed it up. When I dropped her back into the arms of Robert I was cross with myself for having left a gap for him to return. I was determined I would do whatever it took to win her back.

7

The Demon Drink

'Bar, how would you feel if I looked for a place near you?' I asked one day. John Addy was selling the Lancaster Gate mews house, I was doing well at work and was feeling more confident in myself. I had picked up the business of recruitment pretty fast and had managed to bring in a big contract via my brother-in-law. I was settled enough and earning enough to get a mortgage. It felt a lot better than waiting for rejections from agents.

'It would be nice to be near you, if you ever needed a hand with anything.' I loved it around Marylebone High Street, I had many happy memories there. Since my declaration that I would woo Bar back, we had continued to meet up, but things had remained strictly platonic. Bar was still seeing Robert and a detective called Nigel, a lovely guy who I got to know quite well.

'Sure,' said Bar. 'I'll help you look. It'll be fun.'

Sometimes she went on her own, sometimes with me. Funnily enough, nothing ever seemed good enough for her. 'You can't live here,' she'd say, 'too dark.'

'Pity it doesn't have any outdoor space,' I'd say.

'You ain't living here . . . Too small.'

'I am small . . .'

We'd giggle stupidly and make another appointment. What we weren't admitting to one another was what we were both thinking. How can we be part of each other's lives without risking walking straight back into the challenges that had brought me so close to the brink the first time round? What we had now was a precious friendship. I wanted to protect that above all things.

After another unsuccessful viewing Bar grabbed my arm. 'I've got a spare room,' she said. 'Why don't you just move in with me?'

'Wow, that's a kind offer,' I replied.

'As friends,' she insisted. That was the tricky bit. While some things had changed, others hadn't. I was still attracted to her and I thought, hoped, that maybe the feeling was mutual. So how would that work as housemates?

'Maybe until I find somewhere.'

'Great, that's settled. You can move in straight away.'

We will keep it casual, I told myself. That way no one gets hurt. Who was I kidding? The first night I went to the spare room it felt wrong. We met in the corridor, instantly fell into each other's arms, and, well, *say no more*. I was deliriously happy and relieved. The last year had seemed like a nightmare, but we were back where we always should have been. Together. I hadn't blown it. I had proved myself worthy after messing up. Age aside, we could meet as equals. We jumped back into our relationship and fell deeper in love than we'd been before. So much for casual.

What we never talked about was the demon drink. As far as Bar was concerned, I'd had a moment and was now back on track. 'He thought he was an alcoholic, but he's better now.' I was willing to go along with Bar's version. *Life is short. I like a drink, so what? I'm going to die someday anyway*. I wasn't fooling myself, though. I knew deep down that I was someone who should not drink, mainly because I liked it too much, but from that first night we were in full celebration mode. We hadn't fucked it up. Our blip was over. Whatever had gone on, we were always meant to be together and that made total sense to us. We weren't a conventional couple, nor did we want to be a conventional couple, and we celebrated our non-convention. Lots of people wouldn't get it, but that no longer mattered to us. We were now fully, head-over-heels in love and we knew we wanted to be together. Not despite our differences but because of them.

By July 1999 I was sure of one thing: I was going to marry Barbara Windsor. My dad came to Hatton Garden with me to help me choose the stone. I had saved a few grand, which was a lot for me, and though I knew I would never be able to buy the sort of rock a star like Bar deserved, it would come with my full and purest love.

We were sitting in bed talking when, as the clock struck midnight, I reached into the drawer and pulled out a birthday card. I walked around to Bar's side of the bed singing 'Happy Birthday'. 'Silly sod, I told you not to get me anything for my birthday.' Bar was turning sixty-two. I put the card to one side, held out the small jewellery box I had been hiding underneath it and dropped to one knee. She clasped her face in her hands.

'Bar, will you marry me?'

Her answer 'Yes!' was lost in squeals of delight. We were both so happy.

'Thank God,' I said, feeling a rush of gratitude.

'Why did we have to go through all that misery?' she said.

'It was worth it to get us here,' I said. We talked long into the night about what had led us to this wonderful moment and fell into a deep sleep. The celebration continued. But I no longer had the urge to get obliterated and, anyway, my wife-to-be had back-to-back filming days, and I was happy to stay by her side rather than run out into the night without her.

Our 'normal' life as a couple was nicely summed up when one day a photographer jumped out at us from behind the crockery in John Lewis. 'You're engaged, Barbara, there's a ring on your finger,' he shouted.

'Actually, yes,' said Bar, with a shrug.

'Well, that's that now,' I said, 'our secret is out.' What did it matter? We were happy and wanted the world to know.

Neither of us thought it would make the front pages, but it did, and the reaction was wonderful. Immediately people wanted to know where and when we would get married and, for a moment, we got sucked into bridal madness, complete with visions of tulle and taffeta as far as the eye could see. Then, the cherry on the multi-tiered wedding cake, Bar received a letter from the Honours Committee asking if she would accept the offer of an MBE. I was over the moon for her; I don't think Bar could believe it. Little Barbara Ann Deeks, MBE!

'What would Mummy have said?' she shrieked. 'Her little girl from the East End.' She looked lost for a moment. 'I wish she was here to see it.'

Barbara always regretted learning too late that her mother had indeed loved and cherished her, even if she wasn't able to show it. I would not make that mistake. I wanted Bar to know I loved her with all my heart.

We were truly flying until Bar got ill again. She'd been bent double in pain on several occasions during the year, she told me, but this was worse. She could barely stand. Immediately we were terrified. She thought of Len, her beloved stepfather, bent double in pain from stomach cancer, and although we didn't say it to one another we feared the worst. Bar went in for a series of invasive tests and we were allowed to feel blessed again when the doctor came back with a diagnosis of diverticulitis. It was nasty, painful and difficult, but at least it wasn't cancer. Her health issues continued and on the biggest New Year celebration of the millennium, when the world partied, we were tucked up in bed by 11pm and I could not have been happier.

Barbara had been asked to be the first actor enlisted in the BBC's *Hall of Fame*, a lavish sixty-minute television special where show-biz friends helped celebrate her achievements. It took a staggering amount of organising and planning. Dale Winton would be the host. They invited Danny La Rue and John Inman. And the list started to grow: Maurice Gibb, Anna Karen, Martine McCutcheon, Ross Kemp and Biggins, of course. Joan Littlewood also made a very rare TV appearance, which really overwhelmed Barbara. She said what an excellent actress Barbara had always been and still referred to her as 'her little bird's egg'.

In the Square, Peggy was soaring high with cracking storylines; she'd married Frank Butcher, Tiffany had died, and a holiday to Spain had revealed Frank and Pat's feelings for one another, leading to one of Peggy's greatest ever scenes: the Dear John letter that she read out before slapping Frank and Pat hard and walking out. Peggy the meddling matriarch ruled Britain's most famous square. She'd high-jinksed her way through a collection of Britain's best-loved films. She absolutely deserved to be the first person inducted into the BBC *Hall of Fame*.

*

At the same time, we were working out how, when and where we could get married. A designer had approached Barbara about the dress, and the magazines *Hello!* and *OK!* had both offered to cover the cost of the wedding. My stomach dropped at the thought of such an enormous event getting out of control. Bar had already been fined by the BBC for accepting a vacation from *OK!* boss Richard Desmond as a gift for our engagement, as the magazine had slipped some product placements in. Richard kindly paid this fine. But imagine what it would be like juggling the constraints of the BBC and a giant star-studded wedding. The money would have been nice, as most of Bar's income was still going towards paying off the debt from The Plough, but I was worried we'd lose all control of our special day. We already couldn't get the month we wanted, as the executive producer of *East-Enders* couldn't guarantee Bar the time off, so we settled on April. The 8th to be precise. It felt alarmingly close to organise something so damn big.

'You awake, Scott?'

'Yeah, I can't sleep.'

Bar turned on the light. Neither of us was sleeping. 'What are you worried about darlin'?'

'The wedding,' I said honestly.

'Me too.'

'I'm worried people are going to laugh at us. You, of all people, in bridal white . . .' I got a cackle for that. 'And me trussed up in tails. They'll think I'm the pageboy.'

Bar was laughing, but we both knew it was true; we'd always been able to be honest with one another about how we appeared to the outside world.

'Let's have a quiet wedding,' Bar said.

'Yes!' I said immediately, flooding with relief. 'A day for us, about us.'

'Our secret,' she said. We both fell asleep, holding hands, me with a smile on my face, determined to plan a wedding to a showbiz legend and keep the whole thing secret. Easy!

We hired a wedding planner, Siobhan Craven-Robins, and she contacted the Dorchester for us, but other than that we told no one. Four days before our tiny 'big day', I told Mum and Dad on the phone. They were pretty shocked, but, along with my sister Marsha, they were the only guests. Laurence stayed at home with the babies.

'We've got something on at the Dorchester,' I told Gary Cockerill, Bar's long-standing make-up artist. 'Could you come and do her make-up?'

'You two tying the knot in secret?!' How on earth had he guessed? 'Scott, I know about every event Barbara's got going on and there's nothing down for the 8th. Don't worry, my lips are sealed.' He didn't let us down.

It was a beautiful, crisp, blue-sky sunny day. I went ahead of Bar, checked the wedding suite and the honeymoon suite and made sure everything looked perfect. I opened a bottle of champagne, looked across to Hyde Park and felt an overwhelming sense of happiness. Mum, Dad and Marsha were taken into the room to wait for us. We were so determined it was going to be our secret, just for us, we didn't even book a photographer. The wedding planner's husband with a little camera would do. Bar and I were led down the hallway to the special room. The closer I got to the door, the more overwhelmed I was becoming. I'd had a couple of glasses of champagne and my emotions were rocketing. I knew I wasn't going to get through the ceremony without breaking down. A couple of times I thought I was going to have one of my laughing fits, I was literally gulping down the emotions to stop myself from erupting.

The registrar started the ceremony. A few times she had to stop to hand me a tissue. I was sobbing with genuine happiness and huge relief that we'd made it to this day. I felt so lucky and every time I thought about how close we'd come to losing one another, how much I loved her, I would convulse with emotion.

'Pack it up, Scott, or I'm going to go . . .'

We were all crying and laughing now, a tidal wave swept through the Dorchester. The vows were over and we sat and signed the register. Then our three precious guests came back to our room for more champagne. It was 1.30pm on 8 April 2000 and we were married. The best way to start a new millennium.

Our first big date. At the Houses of Parliament with the great and the good.
My eyes are on stalks but Shirley Bassey, behind us, has seen it all before.
Maybe not all, maybe not this . . .

Drinking, dancing, having fun.

We never wanted the night to end.

'That's a stretch!' First time in the back of a limo.

Pretending not to be a couple.

Getting less good at pretending.

Joined at the hip. In matching belts.

Taking a bite out of The Big Apple.

What a Liberty! Token tourist picture for the papers.

I was a very young-looking fourteen years old, trying to get myself heard and seen.

Panto eyebrows and Fairy Babs.

Sid Snap. Life as a jobbing actor in a BBC kids' programme.

Early Hamilton? No . . . Dandini.

The real deal.

Father and son at home.
My hero.

The film producer Nick Love
and the great Lionel Bart. A day
out in Whitstable

A wonderful mentor and friend,
Brian Hall.

If you can't stand the heat . . . my
close friend and sponsor, Ian Kay

The Mitchell clan at Brick Lane.

The happiest day of my life. Our wedding, 8 April 2000.

Our small, select, special wedding party. Mum, Dad and my sister, Marsha.

Don't dilly dally on the way . . . to Elton John's fiftieth birthday party.

Around 2.30pm we had a call from reception warning us that the press were downstairs; they'd found out, but it didn't matter, we'd achieved the impossible. We had got married on our own terms and now we would be married on our own terms. It was incredibly important that I was Barbara's husband now. They could laugh all they liked, but we were man and wife, and immediately I felt more secure, more settled. On our way back to the honeymoon suite the cleaners came out to have a peep and wished us well. It was lovely. Our marriage was all over the papers the next day, which was fine. 'BABS MARRIES TOYBOY IN SECRET!' One paper got in a jibe about hoping it wasn't a shotgun wedding, clever little sods.

We were supposed to be going to Gloria Hunniford's sixtieth masked ball the following evening but didn't want to steal any thunder so thought it best not to. Her husband Stephen Way popped over and told us we were absolutely welcome and she wanted us there. So, carried away on our bubble of love, we went to the ball. Gloria even asked us up onstage to toast our wedding. It was special. We were in honeymoon mode even though we weren't actually away on honeymoon. For the first time in my life I felt whole. I don't think I had ever felt naturally happy before. I'm not saying that the old insecurities had been dealt with, they hadn't, but they weren't dictating terms. I was just a happy man, married to an exceptional woman, having a bloody good time and, unlike last time, I liked the party and wanted it to go on forever. Bar was in a great place too. It may have been a risk her being cast in *EastEnders* but she was a hit. Now there was the album, the book deal, lots of PAs, TV jobs and chat shows. We weren't rolling in it, but we were safe.

Thanks to Jack Barclay, on 19 July we were sitting in a pristine, polished Rolls-Royce driving down the Mall. 'Barbara, this is the greatest privilege I have had since Charlie Chaplin entered these gates,' said the policeman, as we arrived at the gates of Buckingham Palace. My wife beamed at him, leant through the window and briefly squeezed his hand. I had seen this so many times; Barbara would reduce barrel-chested men to tears and everyone wanted to hold her hand.

'How can this be happening to me?' Bar asked as we drove through.

'How could it not? If ever anyone deserved it, it's you.'

Barry Burnett, her agent, and I were taken to the big hall and an usher whispered what we'd hoped to hear. 'It is Her Majesty doing the honours today.'

I could not have been happier for my wife. Barry and I were bursting with pride and love when Bar came out in all her finery to curtsy for the Queen. I'm sure in that moment she was thinking, *I wish my mum could see me now*. A real pinch-yourself moment. As we emerged outside, Bar demonstrated her perfect curtsy to the newly anointed Dame Shirley Bassey and someone got the snap. It is a perfect photo.

After that we dashed home to get changed as we were due back on the Mall later that day for the Queen Mother's pageant. Back in the mews, Bar in her underwear, hat and shoes, we scoffed a quick fried egg sandwich and a glass of champagne. I have always loved the extremes of our life – one minute she's chatting to the Queen, the next she's eating an egg sarnie in her pants! Bar was a true royalist and I believe that day was one of the proudest days ever for her. In the evening we went to The Ivy on a massive high and celebrated with friends. It was a wonderful night.

'Welcome to the Colony Club, Ms Windsor,' said the receptionist. 'You're booked into the Windsor Suite.' That was surely a good sign.

'Thank you very much,' said Bar, beaming. Finally, we had rewarded ourselves with a proper holiday, a belated honeymoon in Barbados.

'And would your son like a separate key?'

'Actually, she's my wife,' I said.

'Oh my God, I am so sorry . . .'

'Don't apologise, it happens all the time. She is definitely old enough to be my mother!'

Bar gave me a shove and we left laughing, hoping the hotel receptionist would be put at ease. We never wanted anyone to feel bad about making an honest mistake. I was and would always be twenty-six years younger than her. It was the snide side comments that I didn't like.

But there was none of that on our honeymoon. We had a truly brilliant time. We spent the weeks getting a bit pissed, having a laugh, meeting lots of people. You couldn't go anywhere with Bar without her talking to strangers, everyone wanted to talk to her, but the thing is, she felt just the same and was mostly really happy to stop for a chat. The whole public adored her. I've never seen anything like it. The bond was very special. She made people feel like they were the only person in the room, and it came totally naturally to her.

As the year progressed I was working more and more with Barry Burnett, making sure things ran smoothly for Bar on a professional level. I was lucky to get to work so closely with him and was learning a lot. Barry was charming, he knew showbiz inside out and was highly respected. A long time back Barry had given a young and hungry Cameron Mackintosh desk space in his office. I was now becoming Barry's man on the ground and Bar was increasingly busy, so there was a lot to do. As she got busier, it felt natural for me to stop working for the recruitment consultancy and start working full-time with Barry, for Bar. It felt good to be available for my wife and involved in everything, but there was one downside: less structure meant more time to party and drink.

Around the same time, we started having problems with the house. 'Your house is a sponge,' the builder said, looking at the growing patches of damp seeping up the wall. 'Looks like the membrane has failed. We're going to need to dry it out, retank it and then redecorate.'

Bar and I looked at each other. 'Don't worry, I'll sort it,' I said.

Thankfully, the insurance covered the work and also paid for our accommodation at Clifton Ford Hotel. Imagine a penthouse flat in a busy hotel, with a bar that's open all hours. Bar loved to chat and meet people, I liked to drink. Bar had to go to bed to get up early for work. I did not. For me the combination was terrible.

Barbara had long filming schedules. With Peggy Mitchell leaving the pub under duress, Bar was once again filling the pages of soap magazines: Frank had gone, Grant had gone, Phil had been shot, and Sharon was now the owner of the pub. The scenes were always great when Peggy and Sharon were at each other's throats, and Barbara loved filming days, even if they were tough.

Most evenings I would collect Bar from the studio. We would get back about 7pm, then we'd go to the bar, then we'd order some room service with more drinks, and then I might go back down to the bar after Bar had gone to bed. It was like being on holiday, with friends popping in and out, or calling up from the bar. My wife was happy to turn a blind eye to the more excessive evenings. She wasn't a judgemental person and, anyway, I was better to be around now. Certainly for the first half of the evening. But the mixture of meds and booze was not sustainable.

'Ms Windsor, do you think you could come and get Scott?' the doorman asked. 'He is distracting the staff.'

Bar looked at the clock by her bed. It was 1am. She came downstairs and found me holding court in my dressing gown in the foyer, determined to order more wine. She took me upstairs and put me to bed. She was concerned about where this might be heading. But Bar was very private in many ways. When faced with a problem, she preferred to take herself into a corner and work it out for herself. I woke up the next morning with no memory of the night before, so Bar filled me in. 'You probably need to slow down a bit, darlin'.'

I agreed. And I meant it.

'Wake up! Mr Mitchell!' I opened my eyes, a fireman was standing over us, a loud alarm oscillating around my pounding head. I had passed out, leaving a cigarette under the fire alarm and the London Fire Brigade were filling our room.

I knew it was getting out of hand, but the trouble was, I was happy. So maybe I had no off button, and maybe I had lost the sense of danger that had beset me for so long, but it was bloody good fun. And I wanted more of it.

'It'll calm down when we get home,' said Bar. I agreed again.

But unfortunately, just as we left the hotel, we hit the Christmas party season and, for six weeks, it was go, go, go. Bar's star status meant there was rarely an invite list that we weren't on and I was happy to go to every single champagne-fuelled event. Bar wasn't stupid. She could see by now that I had a drink problem and it wasn't going away, but she wanted me to deal with it.

After one Christmas party, I took Bar home and then went back until someone put me into a cab because I was literally stumbling about trying to buy coke from staff. Bar and I told each other everything, but I think I failed to tell her that. But deep down she knew. People were beginning to mention that, party season aside, I always seemed to push it a bit too far. She knew what they were saying was true, and, worse, that I had started drinking until I blacked out at home too. What she didn't know was how to help. Be kind, get cross, shout, cry, beg, plead . . . Why was I jeopardising everything? Why couldn't I go out, have fun and then go home like everyone else?

It all came to a head on New Year's Eve 2001. The end of my life as I knew it. We went to our friend Greg Foreman's pub in Mayfair (Greg is Freddie Foreman's son and actor Jamie's brother). It was really nice to start with, everyone drinking fine wines and cocktails, then people started getting properly drunk as the night wore on. I got home at 1.30am and continued drinking on my own, which led to taking coke in the kitchen, until I ended up on the floor, unconscious.

When I woke up, I peeled myself off the floor, still drunk, and Bar and I headed out to the high street for the papers and a pint of milk. 'Let's have a quick one in here,' I said.

'Scott, it's barely midday.'

'Come on,' I said, pushing the door of the Marylebone Tup open. 'It's our day off.'

There was not a soul about. The pub was empty. 'Double vodka and tonic please . . .'

Three more followed in under an hour. Bar was chatty enough, but even in my alcoholic haze I could tell she didn't want to be there, so we went home. Two bottles of wine chased the vodka and by the evening I had started back on a bottle of vodka.

I was having a great time, waffling away, talking shit, thinking it was absolutely fine to pour this much booze down my throat. I was now well into a two-day bender. Then a voicemail came through on my phone from Jamie Foreman: 'Scott. Phone me.'

Great, someone to party with, I thought, and immediately called him back. 'Hey—'

'What the fuck do you think you're doing?'

'What?'

'You called my house last night.'

I did? Shit . . . Shock and fear ran through me. What had I done? I couldn't remember, not one thing!

'You left me a totally inappropriate and foulmouthed voicemail. And my partner and kids heard it. Do you understand what I'm saying, Scott? My family. I should come over and clump you.'

I looked wild-eyed at Bar. I had no recollection of any of it, but Jamie was very angry, and he was not a person you wanted to upset. He was more than capable of pulverising me. I was terrified now. He was also a friend who had been nothing but respectful to me. He had only ever shown me kindness and inclusion.

'I'm sorry,' I started to splutter, trying to explain. 'I can't remember, I'm sorry. What did I do? What did I say?'

He told me. And I have never felt so ashamed of anything in my life.

They say you have to hit rock bottom before you can rebuild. I hurtled downwards and smacked into rock bottom with soul-shattering force. I was sobbing now.

'Stop crying,' he said. 'Look, I like you, Scott. I think somewhere in there you're a decent bloke, but you're very unwell. You've got to sort yourself out. I'm not going to be your fucking nursemaid. I'm not going to hold your hand and take you there. You have to do it. Now. Sort it out. You're not well. I will not say this again and if you don't that's on you, but never, ever call my house again talking like that.'

Bar snatched the bottle of vodka out of my hand and poured it down the sink and I went to pieces. 'That's enough, Scott!'

All I could do was sob. But I nodded – it was enough. No sane man would upset Jamie, so I must be insane. 'Help me,' I wept.

I knew I needed it now. I wanted it, too.

Jamie's phone call saved my marriage and my life. Thanks to him, I was able to get sober and stay sober. Thanks to him, I was able to find the strength to be the person Bar needed me to be. Thanks to him, I was able to stay by her side even when she had no idea who I was.

8

Life Begins – One Day at a Time

I stood on shaking legs and looked over a room full of people in Hinde Street. It was 1pm on 2 January 2002, the moment my adult life began. 'Hi, my name is Scott and I am an alcoholic. Please can someone help me because I am killing myself.'

I was thirty-eight years old, my head was like scrambled eggs, but when I sat down I breathed the first easy breath in my living memory. I had finally said what I had been running from for years and perhaps would have continued to run from, until I'd run myself into the ground, if I hadn't made that awful drunken phone call. I had woken still shaking at the thought of it, the panic coursing through my veins. Bar had helped me get dressed and walked me slowly to the park. I was going to pieces. There was nowhere to hide this time. Sitting on a bench, barely able to breathe, I realised there was only one thing for it.

'I'm going back to AA,' I said.

'Whatever you need to do,' Bar said, agreeing instantly. 'I'm here for you.' We both had to look at this full in the face for the first time.

The people in AA did what people in AA do. They caught me, scooped me up, held my pain and helped me through. Bar went to work and I went to AA, every single day. And every day, as I participated in a meeting, I shuffled a little closer to learning to live sober. Make no mistake, getting sober is a really hard thing to do, but it *is* possible and that became key for me.

The beauty of AA is accepting with grace and humility that you are no different from the person sitting next to you, and if the person sitting next to you can do it then you can do it. Equally, if the person sitting next to you can relapse, then so can you. It is that simple. Turn up. Do the work. Day in. Day out. The fact sobriety can happen has to be enough for a while. I was certain of one thing: that whatever life awaited me without alcohol it was going to be better than the one I'd been leading. But let me say this again. It is not easy.

I was walking around in a daze for weeks. Though I was physically present I was emotionally all over the place. I would find myself crying, filled with remorse that I had put Bar through this, followed by remorse that I couldn't drink any more. Ever.

'One day at a time' was the mantra. One day at a time. That made sense to me, because the moment I started thinking that I would never be able to have another drink, it would overwhelm me, and then I feared I might give up.

Just for today, I won't drink, I won't touch drugs. Just for today. That was my mantra.

I was glad Bar was busy with one huge storyline after another – a bust-up with Pauline in the pub, a tussle over baby Louise, reunited with Frank in Marbella, as ever it was all kicking off in the Square – but for a while it skimmed over me. I would bring my body along and sit on the seat and go through the motions, hoping that eventually my head would catch up and, over the years, that is what happened, but there was no quick fix. The quick fix was what had got me into trouble in the first place. Though, like any addict, I was very good at replacing one source of comfort with another. Chocolate for one.

Within a few months I began to feel the pink cloud of sobriety. Colours were brighter, I had a spring in my step, a song in my heart. Alcohol is a depressant, who knew? Better still, I had a new friend. Ian Kay was Jewish, six-foot-three, five years sober and three years older than me. I asked him to be my sponsor and then waited for him to make excuses, but he amazed me by saying it would be his honour. He is still my best friend today.

We talked a lot about the reasons for the insecurity that leads to the need to drink. It didn't take long to unpack mine. I believed I had let my father down. He was a huge man, tough, could look after himself. I was a tiny kid who wasn't up for the fight.

'Have you asked your dad about that?' Ian queried. So one day I did.

'Dad,' I said, feeling a bit embarrassed, 'do you remember that day in the judo class?'

'You didn't do judo?'

'Right, I only went once, I was thrown on the mat and started crying.'

He shook his head, perplexed.

'You don't remember being disappointed?'

'I don't remember it at all, son. But I do know I have never been disappointed by you, ever. You and your sister are my pride and joy, never forget that.'

The years I had wasted carrying a story in my head that I had disappointed my dad by not being a hardman like him, and he couldn't even remember it. And, just like that, the fear that I hadn't been good enough for my dad vanished.

Feeling buoyed by the achievement of not drinking and by some new-found confidence, Bar and I started going out again. I was tentative at first, but I had Bar by my side. We were in this together. 'Everything's going to be all right, sweetheart,' she'd say. 'I'm really proud of you.'

We talked about where the insecurity came from and, in a strange way, we worked out how similar we were, though for very different reasons. 'It takes a lot of courage to face all this,' she said. 'I just keep ploughing on.'

When people asked me what I wanted to drink, I would say, 'No thanks, I'm not drinking.'

'Why not?' often came the reply.

'I've given up alcohol.'

'Really? Forever?' It surprised people. 'You were never that bad.'

Bar and I would share a smile, she would change the subject and launch into some bawdy tale.

'Scott?' It was Nick Love, my friend who had first taken me to AA. 'You're back.'

'I am. I'm really sorry.' Nick and I hugged.

'I'm sorry I couldn't be there for you when you started drinking again,' Nick said. 'I just needed to protect my own wellbeing, above all things.'

'I understand,' I said. 'A friend turned up at mine in a bad way recently, following a marital bust-up. His partner had taken the kids. He'd been out all night and was swigging Bacardi from a bottle. He gagged and coughed the Bacardi all over me. I was frantically wiping it off my face, then had to escape the house while he was being sick in the toilet. It was all too familiar. I was so scared he wouldn't let me leave. I came here the next day and shared with the group that I was afraid I'd relapsed. I didn't taste it, but I could smell it.'

'I don't think that's a relapse, Scott,' Nick said, kindly.

You have to be a very strong swimmer to save a drowning man and, although I'd been sober for three months, I wasn't yet a strong man. I had done eighteen months sober before and then relapsed, so I couldn't take anything for granted.

'Well, it's good to see you giving back,' Nick said. I was there early, making teas. It was a voluntary role and part of my service in giving back to AA. I was always on the lookout for the hapless soul walking in on their first day, taking that brave step. I wanted to be as welcoming as that first cup of coffee had felt for me.

Ninety meetings in eighty-nine days. I was nothing if not committed. The payback was immense. Walking through the rose garden in Regent's Park, I suddenly noticed that everything had gone back into colour. I took Bar's hand. 'It feels good to be alive.'

'I am so proud of you,' she said.

The ground beneath my feet felt solid, I was back in the world. 'Thank you,' I replied.

'For what, you daft sod?'

'Constantly being supportive.'

'I'm just glad it's helping. It's all going to be all right,' she said reassuringly.

I am not sure she totally understood the sacred circle or the twelve steps, firstly because I didn't talk details for confidentiality reasons, but also because it is a hard process to put into words. But she saw the change and that was enough for her.

Bar was working constantly but now I could be relied on to take her there and back and to be good company when she got home. She could trust me and the mews was our safe place. The place she wanted to come back to, to take off the make-up and wig, put on some slippers and relax. We loved the simple act of sitting in the kitchen together while I made dinner and she learnt her lines. Eventually we'd collapse on to the sofa and watch telly. We loved all the soaps and entertainment shows.

Bar loved kicking her shoes off and just being when she was at home, because when she was out and about, she was always recognisable and, though she didn't court attention, attention came her way. She talked to everyone. It would take forty minutes to cross a room.

She often told me stories about being bored at home during the holidays as a kid. 'I would go walkabout and chat to anyone who would talk to me,' she said. 'Sometimes I went back to school to have a natter with the caretaker.' Deep down she was always that East End street kid, making friends wherever she went. Duke or dustman, Bar could make friends with anyone. Wherever we went, she was always at ease. Be it at Gary Farrow and Jane Moore's wedding on a table with Piers Morgan, Richard E. Grant and Nick Faldo, as Elton John sang 'Your Song', or in the private box at a Liza Minnelli concert with Jonathan Ross popping champagne and stars as far as the eye could see. Joanna Lumley, Roger Taylor, Cliff Richard, David Frost, Tony Bennett, Sir John Mills, the big guns were out for this one. Barbara lapped it all up, effortlessly.

'You okay, love?' she asked, as we watched Liza perform.

'I'm good,' I smiled back. I was blown away by Liza's star attraction. Even if she wasn't at her peak, she gave a hell of a performance.

'I'm so glad you can enjoy all this now,' said Bar on the way home. Me too, I thought.

Bar got a phone call from her cousin Kenny to say that his daughter Karen had died. She collapsed to the ground. She was all dressed up, about to leave for the British Soap Awards.

'I'll cancel,' I said. 'Don't worry.'

'No,' she said, as she pushed herself up off the floor and visibly shook off her feelings. She was committed to her job, and nothing would get in the way of her professional duty. Paul O'Grady once said, 'If Barbara Windsor were a stick of rock at the seaside and you snapped her in half, it would say "Showbiz" the whole way through.'

Sometimes I worried she bulldozered on to her detriment, but I understood why. She was driven. Work had given her independence at the age of fifteen and she valued it above all else. In Albert Square, she was behind the bar in the pub, so she was in nearly every scene and was often on set from seven in the morning until seven at night, in back-to-back blocks, often out of sequence and filming at different lots. It was nonstop and our house was piled high with scripts.

'I don't want to let anyone down,' was her constant refrain.

'I worry you might be working too hard, Bar.'

'I don't work that hard,' she snapped back. 'It's not like I'm a doctor or a nurse.'

She would remind me constantly that she loved, loved, loved her job and, turning up to pick her up, I could see why. June Brown was leaning out of her dressing room having a fag and Bar was leaning out the other, having a nonstop natter. I tell you, neither of them drew breath. I wasn't sure where those two got the energy from. Their corridor was called Bishop's Avenue by the cast and crew because it housed the top-notch stars of the show. But in fact there was little hierarchy, the cast and crew were family to Bar. Showbiz had become her home from the first time she'd called out 'Here comes the baron' at the age of thirteen in the Golders Green panto. It wasn't about what that show did for her, it was about what that show meant to her. Family. Peggy must have said that a million times.

For the first time, it felt like I was Bar's equal, but equally I knew my place. One step behind. Knowing this allowed me to make the most of the golden opportunities and events I was privy to. For example, meeting the legendary George Best. George was a shy man. I saw it for myself when we went to his house for a family party. Bar was surrounded by the kids, putting on a show, so we sat and chatted. I feel genuinely lucky to have met the man. He was such a legend; a footballer turned into a rock star. It made me think about drink and how similar alcoholics are.

'Oh look, there's Barbara Windsor!'

How many times had I heard that, or seen someone lean over and say it to the person sitting next to them, but never live on telly. And never when it was the Queen talking to Prince Philip. It is one of my most favourite memories. I was at home watching the Queen's Golden Jubilee. Bar, wearing a fabulous white trouser suit, was on a float full of showbiz people, sipping champagne, and howling with laughter with Sir Cliff and Ronnie Corbett, when the camera cut to Her Majesty. My phone went mad.

But I will not pretend it was all easy. As the months ticked by, I noticed sobriety getting a bit more challenging. I persevered, but the old feelings were bubbling back up to the surface. The fear of rejection, of not being liked, of not being good enough. Without the suppressant, those thoughts were getting louder. But I did not miss a meeting.

By the beginning of July I had been to 139; I was even going to meetings in Spain. When it got hard I would think about that New Year's Day phone call; the beating I could have, should have, received. I was not going back to that. To be honest, that part was easy; what was more awkward was being at a big event without a drink in my hand. The subtle pressure to join in is huge. It was fine when people were on their first or second, but then the witching hour would come, voices would slur, people would get loud and repetitive; then I knew it was time for this pumpkin to get home. Our roles reversed. Now it was me telling Barbara she didn't need another drink. It was me heading for the exit. 'Bar, when are we leaving?' I would ask. Sometimes it was easier if she went out alone.

And then life took another turn. It all happened in slow motion. It was 29 October and we were in a black cab on our way to meet Ross and Rebekah at The Ivy. The driver was so taken by the fact that Babs was in his taxi that he kept looking in his rear-view mirror. Bar was sitting behind him, chatting away and sharing stories about Sid and Kenny, as if she had just left them. I saw the red lights of the white van in front suddenly glow red. The driver wasn't watching, he wasn't watching.

'Stop!' I yelled.

The driver slammed on the brakes. Bar flew forward, her head hit the glass, instantly knocking her out and she crumpled on to the floor.

'Bar!' I screamed. Nothing. I thought she was dead.

'Barbara!' Her eyes flickered open.

'Thank God! Call an ambulance,' I yelled to the distressed driver.

The paramedics took us to UCH and I called Ross and Rebekah to tell them we wouldn't be making it to dinner. 'Keep us informed,' they said.

The medical staff let Bar out at 10.30pm and Rebekah sent her driver to pick us up, which I really appreciated.

'It was nothing,' Barbara said, when anyone asked her about it, but I've always believed that knock on the head marked the beginning of her health issues. One way or another, she was never a hundred per cent after that accident.

9

The Kissing Disease

At the end of my first year sober I knew that those 307 AA meetings had made the difference. I owed them everything. A while back, Beechy had said to me, 'If you stop drinking now, you will never have to feel this bad again.' I wish I could have heard what he'd tried to tell me, but I had to learn the hard way. Whatever I have been through since, losing Bar and Dad, I've never felt as awful as I did after that two-day New Year's bender. Beechy was right all along. Never forget the day, the hour, the minute you got sober. Never forget what led to that day, hour, minute; because if you do, it's too damn easy to think, *Fuck it, just the one . . .*

My sponsor, and dear friend, Ian gave me a silver yo-yo to celebrate one year sober, as a symbol of life in perpetual motion and full of ups and downs. I was mastering the yo-yo. I was starting to believe that I could now manage the ups and downs. I went to two meetings and celebrated with my group. There was a real feeling of gratitude and a deep sense of pride that I had made it. As I walked in, I got a round of applause.

'That's my one round of applause for the year,' I told Bar.

'What about taking Jim's offer to do his pantomime again?'

Jim Davidson had offered roles to both of us, but I was hesitant. I didn't really feel like an actor any more. I liked taking care of my wife and, although I knew Bar wanted me involved in the business, I wasn't sure the combination of my well-documented stage fright and sobriety went well together.

'I'm not sure it's worth the risk,' I said to Bar.

'I'd prefer it if you were there,' she said.

'I will be.' That was the thing now – wherever Bar went, I went. We were a double act. A team.

'Then take the job. You'll get paid and have something to get your teeth into.'

In the end we said yes. I had a year to get my head around it and I was deeply fond of Jim.

Barbara was exhausted. She would never let on to the team, but I saw her crawl out of bed every morning and collapse into bed every night. She would be sixty-six in August. I was not going to be the one telling her to slow down, but I suggested that maybe we could talk to the producers about easing off on her storylines. She'd recently completed her thousandth episode of *EastEnders* and was a victim of her own success. On 1 February we went to meet them and proposed they write her out of the Square for a while, so she could get a proper rest. And it wasn't just tiredness that I'd noticed, it was her mood as well. She seemed to be getting increasingly anxious and she wasn't quite herself. I worried a lot about that bang to Bar's head. Perturbed, I took her for some blood tests.

'BARBARA AND THE KISSING DISEASE' was the headline in the *People*. According to them, she had also signed up for not one but two pantos and a musical. Not sure how they expected her to do that. She was a workhorse, no doubt, but that seemed a bit extreme even for her. But they were right about one thing. The blood tests were showing that Bar had some kind of glandular fever and so she'd been booked in for more tests.

Concerned about her energy levels, she decided to pull out of the panto; even this far ahead she couldn't see herself having the energy to do it. Then we went back to *EastEnders*. This time it wasn't a suggestion. Barbara wasn't well and she needed to take the rest of the year off. They were very understanding about it, of course, and immediately put in motion writing her out of the current storyline. Poor Bar, she was so upset to be leaving. Another headline quickly followed. This time it was the *Sun*: 'TV BABS FORCED BY VIRUS TO TAKE 2003 OFF'.

It was true, she'd been diagnosed with Epstein–Barr, one of nine nasty herpesviruses that is a known precursor to glandular fever. The news breaking didn't help her mood. She considered herself a trouper, not a quitter, so the press coverage made her feel worse, which upset me too because she was always such a fighter.

A couple of weeks later, I was downstairs in the mews house when I heard a thump from the bedroom. 'Are you okay?' I shouted up, but heard nothing.

I rushed upstairs. Bar was on the floor of our bedroom looking dazed. 'Are you okay? Did you hit your head?' I had flashbacks of the accident in the taxi.

'No, my legs just went, Scott,' she said, looking up at me, frightened.

'What do you mean, *went*?'

She was trying to make sense of it. 'I tried to get out of bed and they just gave way under me!'

I got her back into bed and called the doctor. He came round and examined her. 'This is your body giving you a warning shot,' he told Barbara. 'You have to rest.'

Leaving Bar in bed, I explained to him that she was already in her last couple of weeks of filming her storyline. 'Two weeks max,' I told him.

'No, Scott. Sorry. Absolutely not – she is not to go back in at all.'

'Really?'

'Really! This woman needs to rest.'

So that was it. At the end of March, Barry and I told *EastEnders* that she could not come back, and then I went up and told Bar the news.

'Oh God, Scott, I've let everybody down,' she cried. *EastEnders* meant the world to her. Not only had it completely revived her career, it had given her an extended family and she loved the people she worked with, the buzz, the camaraderie.

'No, love, you've done the opposite of that. Now, you need to rest.'

She was devastated. Her age, which she had defied for so long, was catching up with her and it made her fearful for the future. However, I have to admit there was a bit of me that was relieved. I had watched her squeeze every last drop of energy out of herself for the show and it was not sustainable. She couldn't make that decision for herself, but

now medical advice had taken it out of her hands. She would have
to rest.

What happened, though, was something else. It was as if now she
had the permission to stop, her whole being was crumbling. She had a
swollen stomach, pains all over her body, and not an ounce of energy
was left. She started to cry, a lot. All I could do was build a routine
around getting her to rest and eat well. I would get up, make her
breakfast, potter around, make her lunch, go to an AA meeting, run
some errands, and that was about it. I would make her juices and
smoothies, trying to get some goodness back into her body so she
could fight the virus. She didn't have the strength to go out; she
would rarely even get out of bed.

And then her blood pressure started rising. So I took her to see the
heart specialist. As we left the house, there was a pap waiting at the
end of the mews. I don't know if someone had tipped him off, or
he was just waiting there hoping to get a snap on the off-chance she
ventured out. In those days the papers had so much money the paps
were just sent out to sit and wait, even if it took a few days of hanging
around. It was our normal back then, but, looking back, it feels a bit
barbaric, because she really wasn't well and there was no disguising it.

On that day, she was as white as a ghost, she had no make-up on,
and even I could tell she looked frail. I got her into the car as quickly
as I could and hoped that any snaps wouldn't be used, but then got a
tip-off the next day that the *People* were going to run a photo. I faxed
a letter to the paper, asking them not to print it as Bar was not well
and it would not help the way she was feeling. What happened? The
whole front page of that Sunday's edition was a massive unflattering
picture of Barbara looking terrible. The actual article was all flattery
and praise, concern for her health, proud of their Babs, but I knew
better. They used that photo knowing people would look at it, be
shocked and think, *My God, what's happened to this poor woman*,
and buy the paper. She was the bait. The words were irrelevant. The
damage was done by the photograph. I was not pleased about it. It
was a low blow. Regardless of Bar's attitude to the press, I hated seeing
anything upset my special lady and I am sad to say that the photo did
really upset her.

After that she got quieter and quieter, and sadder and sadder. I could see she was sinking into a place I recognised but I couldn't rescue her from. Then one morning it all erupted. A lifetime of pent-up emotions exploded out of her in relentless, endless racking sobs. It was agony to see, but I hoped there would be some release. I was still seeing Beechy and continuing with my daily AA meetings, so I knew that unexpressed emotion caused disease. Maybe she needed to get it out of her in order to get well.

I turned forty that April, 2003, but with Bar so unwell we weren't going to do anything, so I got up, went to the gym with Beechy and then we treated ourselves to a nice breakfast. When I got home, Bar had arranged for a lovely selection of clothes to be delivered for me to choose something from as a present. She felt so bad that I wasn't having a proper birthday celebration. She was always coming up with thoughtful generous gestures like that.

Still obsessed with numbers, I noted that 2 May was my 400th meeting in sixteen months and I was thankful, because it was getting me through this really hard time looking after Barbara. But I was still in early sobriety, so I knew I couldn't relax yet. Knowing my hard-won sobriety was at stake, Laurence suggested I join him and some of his work team for a week away at their villa in Majorca. Mum and Dad offered to look after Bar. She wasn't happy when I took her down there and she cried on the morning I left – I had become her safety net, and she felt that everything was going to be okay if I was there – but she also wanted me to go. And my family were right, I needed to recharge my batteries. I had five glorious sunshine-filled days but, on my return, Bar's health took a darker turn. 'I don't think I want to be here any more,' she said. 'I can't go on like this.'

She was already on pills for depression. I rang the doctor immediately. 'I think she is more petrified of what is happening to her as opposed to being suicidal,' he said. I could only pray that he was right.

'Think about it, Scott, she's been dealt some serious blows in her life: being evacuated, her parents' divorce, her father disowning her, her husband in prison, lying to her, people selling her out, the divorce, the debt . . . and through it all, she's just kept on going. Her body has never let her down, until now. She has worked herself to the point of collapse. She will get better. She just needs a lot of looking after.'

Thankfully, he *was* right and by the end of the month she was out of bed and trying to do a few things for herself. She went to the nail bar around the corner, saw a friend for a quick lunch. Nothing too strenuous. And I was taking her for walks in Regent's Park, which were becoming more regular. It was good to get her out and I thought maybe we were turning a corner, but at the same time I was clearing out Barbara's dressing room at Elstree, which she found hard.

We plodded on. Day by day. It was very up and down. She'd be good for a couple of days and then suddenly she'd be back in bed, exhausted and tearful. That was the thing about the Epstein–Barr virus, some days she couldn't get her head off the pillow, other days she suddenly had a surge of energy. When she did, we would jump on them; walk to the shops, enjoy a coffee in the sunshine and have a proper natter. Those were good days, and I was thankful for them. Two weeks at Henlow Grange also helped.

In August 2003, Barbara turned sixty-six, but she didn't feel like there was a great deal to celebrate. It had been six tricky months, she still wasn't better and there was no work on the horizon. Then we were approached by an agency to film an advert for a retirement villa in Spain with Mike Reid. It was a riff on their *EastEnders* characters, Frank and Peggy, as if they'd gone off and bought a place together. It wasn't too strenuous and was good money, which she was thankful for, but more than that it was good for her mental health to be taking part in life again.

Even in September the virus was showing up in her system and the impact on her mood was instant. 'I've become such a burden to you.'

'Nonsense, I love you.'

'I feel like I'm this old woman you have to drag around on your arm.'

I thought of something that might cheer her up and took myself off to Selfridges. 'Where've you been?' she asked when I got home.

I pulled up my sleeve. I'd had the word 'BABS' tattooed on to the top of my right arm with a star around it. 'Well, I'm really going to have to drag you around on my arm for the rest of my life now.'

She burst into tears. 'No one's ever done anything like that for me.'

'Do you like it?'

'I love it!'

'Right, none of this burden stuff any more then. Promise?'

'Promise.'

I walked into the kitchen with a smile on my face; I was forty and I'd just had my first tattoo. I'd always been too scared to get one, but I wasn't too scared to get one for my wife, especially if it put that famous smile back on her face.

Shortly after that, we went for dinner at The Ivy with our friend, the comedian Roger Kitter, and his wife Karan. Bar wasn't well enough to attend big parties, but it felt good for both of us to get out and small dinners were better for me too.

I was just locking the car when I heard her calling from inside the house. I opened the door and there was Bar at the bottom of the stairs, crying in agony. I knew at once there was something very wrong – her ankle was at ninety degrees to the rest of her leg. My stomach flipped. Bar was delirious with pain.

'I heard the car,' she cried. 'I was in my socks. Oh my God, oh my God—'

I called 999. 'Ambulance?'

I tried to explain what was happening, but I was panicky. Anytime she moved she screamed in agony and at one point she passed out in pain. 'We need help, she's not speaking!'

'Is she conscious? Has she hit her head?'

All these questions. I had no answers.

'I wasn't here. Please, come quickly.'

The person on the phone was trying to reassure me that she'd probably passed out from the pain, but what if she'd hit her head? The crash in the taxi. The fall in her bedroom. I was really scared. Thankfully, the paramedics arrived within fifteen minutes and somehow managed to get her into the hallway.

'What have you done to yourself?' they asked.

Bar had come round. 'I heard the car. I wanted to surprise my husband by coming downstairs to the door. I slipped on the carpet and fell right from the top. I'm so sorry.'

Her ankle had come right out of its socket. There was a young female medic who, after a few minutes, looked at her and said, 'I've just realised who you are.'

Here we go, I thought. *Please, now is not the time for an autograph.*

Then the other paramedic said, 'Barbara, I'm going to have to pop your ankle back in for you.' I started back up the stairs, covering my ears, but it's a small house and of course I heard the pop and yelp. 'There. All done!' They gave her oxygen. I think I could have done with some myself.

'Well, that's the first time I've ever had to do that,' said the young medic on the way to the hospital. 'I'm glad it went well!' Luckily Bar was now too woozy to notice.

The break needed an operation and so, at 10pm, a private ambulance came to take her to the Princess Grace Hospital in Marylebone. By now the drugs were working and she was having a great time. High as a kite, her famous giggle was turning heads as she was wheeled out on the trolley. Talk about *Carry On Matron*. And then a nurse trotted up, followed by a doctor. 'Barbara, would you mind signing my clipboard?' Her reply was always the same, even that night, flying on morphine. '"Course I don't mind, darlin'.'

It was so Barbara to go from the terror of the fall to the ludicrous situation of her signing autographs for people with her leg in a stir-rup. Without the anaesthetising effects of morphine, I did wonder what else could possibly go wrong at this point.

Bar was in the Princess Grace recovering for a week but it was hard to keep the visitors away. First June Brown popped her head round the door. Bar had her leg up. 'How camp is this?' she cried.

'Oooh, Matron! Where's Dr Nookey, Babs?' replied June.

'I'm here!' announced Biggins, joining the party.

They wouldn't stop making her laugh, and the *Carry On* jokes came thick and fast, but in actual fact it wasn't that funny. The fall prolonged her absence from the show and her recovery from the Epstein–Barr virus.

'Two hairs and a nit' was how she, echoing her mother's disapproving words, always described the thin, wispy hair she'd inherited from her dad. She had now finally ditched the wigs and had hair extensions instead, and they needed redoing. So I borrowed a wheelchair from the hospital and drove her to the hair studio in Chiswick. I was just in the process of wheeling her into the salon when I noticed the pap. 'Bollocks!'

'What's he doing here?'

'Waiting for you, I imagine.' I can understand why people get paranoid.

'Who bloody told them?'

Who indeed?

Click, click, click, clickety-click . . .

What could we do? Once we knew we'd been papped, we decided we may as well go with it and ham it up. I look at that photo now and it is one of the few pap shots that I am fond of. It's just the two of us, having a giggle, in a way that was us most of the time. Not the dressed-up, glam, red-carpet shot, with a caked-on smile. We were genuinely having a laugh because that's what we did. We had a bloody good laugh. I guess it was the picture they'd wanted since the day we met.

As our fairly miserable 2003 ended Bar finally had her plaster off, which she was absolutely thrilled about. Then shortly after that she was presented with a Lifetime Achievement Award at the Women in Film and Television Awards. She was still on crutches but, when she heard it was Ross Kemp who was presenting the award to her, she burst into tears. She'd hardly seen anyone over the past year and, though she missed lots of people, Ross was special. She absolutely adored him. They clicked from day one. He was very kind to her right from her first day on *EastEnders* and she hadn't forgotten. It was really good for Barbara's mental state to be given that award. It made her feel a little bit relevant again after spending literally the year in bed. She hated being out of the game.

10

Doll's Feet

'We'd like to make a fitness video with you,' said the producer of a small media company. I thought it better not to look at Bar during the conversation, the woman had literally never done an exercise class in her life.

'Fitness videos are very popular,' they went on. 'Lots of celebrities do them.'

'Are you sure? Do you know what happened the last time I did a keep-fit class?'

Barbara's bra flew off with the help of some strategically placed fishing line in *Carry On Camping*, which launched her into the British showbiz hall of fame.

'Actually, we think it will really sell to our older customers who are trying to get back up on their feet, after an illness, like you.' Odd kind of pitch, but Bar was now feeling a lot better after a quiet end to the year and took it well, signing up to starting a training programme and mapping her progress. Just knowing there was work ahead put a spring in her step.

And then slowly, with a few more visits to Henlow Grange, Bar was ready to don her high heels again. 'Are you sure, Bar? Maybe just add a few more inches to the wig?'

'Cheeky bugger.'

'You're walking a bit like Frankenstein.' Straight legs, small stiff steps.

'Oi, it's not funny. I'm an ageing sex symbol and this is not a good look!'

After walking up and down our hallway many times, she finally got the hang of it again and was back in her heels. What she lacked in stride, she made up for in speed, so anyone walking next to Barbara quickly got used to the clippety-clip sound of her signature tune trotting down the road. I always knew when she was coming home because of that sound. Fast and loud!

I can hear her giggle. 'That's me, fast and loud!'

She had teeny-tiny size 2 doll's feet. She either had to go to special shops that sold small sizes, or for special occasions she might go to Jimmy Choo and have a pair made. After she died, I gave all her shoes away, because every time I looked at them, my heart broke.

Seeing her all dressed up, hair and make-up done, teetering on high heels and back onstage, was a real sight for sore eyes. We were in a huge bingo hall in Bracknell and seven hundred avid bingo players smiled back at her as she started her usual *Carry On* patter.

'I was always the busty blonde tempting the weedy man away from his portly spouse. Innocent titillation, that's all . . .' – she paused, little wiggle – 'with the emphasis on the *tit*!'

The famous giggle would ring out.

'Right, I'm going to come round and see all you darlin's.' And she was off, her tiny feet trotting around the room, working the crowd, telling stories, getting a smile out of everyone, lapping it up. 'I remember one day when Kenny . . .'

'Eyes down!' announced the caller. That was that. The room went silent and not one of those seven hundred cared any more about what Kenny or Sid did. All that mattered was the winning line. Bar came back to sit with me. 'May as well not be here,' she'd quip, but she didn't mind; she loved bingo halls, and music halls, and all things that embodied classic British entertainment and culture. I think it took her back to being a little girl listening to her grandad Ellis's stories of all the East End variety performers. Marie Lloyd was his favourite. He had told her she reminded him of Marie.

Once news got around that she was literally back on her little size 2 feet, nightclubs and bingo halls, from Glasgow to Portsmouth, requested her. Occasionally, she was asked to do smarter corporate after-dinner gigs, which can bring in a lot of money, but she always turned them down. 'I know my audience,' she said, when I asked her why. 'Look, I've never been the greatest singer, dancer or actor, but put it into the melting pot and somehow it works! You see?'

I did see. Cabbies, coppers, workmen and women; wherever she went, she was a hit. It wasn't about the money. It was about connecting with people, but of course there were other upsides. On St Patrick's Day our taxi got stopped at a barrier. Barbara wound down her window and two lovely policemen grinned back at her. 'Oh, it's you, you can go through.' She was one of them.

It was great to see her back in the limelight, doing what she loved best. But I did notice that she wasn't as fast and loud as she used to be. I spotted it on *The John Daly Show* first. Although she was good, it wasn't the old Bar, talking like a machine gun and firing on all cylinders, with her classic clarity and wit. I wasn't sure if it was the after-effects of the Epstein–Barr virus or just that she was a bit rusty. Now I wonder if it wasn't an early hint of things to come.

As we got to March of 2004, I got in touch with Louise Berridge, the *EastEnders* executive producer at the time, to talk about Bar going back in October. We put some story ideas forward where she could be used a lot less but still be in it. Unfortunately, they needed her either in or out, and said if she couldn't manage full-time they would rather wait for when she could. To be honest, the idea of going back to that crazy schedule wasn't what either of us wanted. We were having a good time. It was easy, work wasn't insane and we got to hang out together and just be. It was really nice and I treasure that time now.

But we hit a sudden and unexpected backwards step when I felt the compulsion to drink again. I didn't, but it was frightening to feel that uncomfortable and awkward inside my body again. I tried to find the reason. 'Why now?' I asked my AA group. They explained there was probably no specific reason for the resurgence of those feelings. It was just another phase you have to go through in sobriety. I distinctly remember that a man, fifteen years sober, started talking. 'When I think back to my early days and by that I mean the first ten years . . .'

Oh my God, I thought, am I really going to feel like this for ten years?!

'The more important question to ask, Scott,' they said, 'is why did you drink in the first place?'

That was the big question I wasn't sure I could answer. But I kept talking about it in meetings and slowly the reasons why I had drunk in the first place started to emerge. 'I have always felt scared of life, but it wasn't manly to be afraid, so I hid my fears. Men are supposed to be big, strong and brave. I was none of those things, so I guess I decided I wasn't enough. I was *less than*.'

After I shared my deepest inner fears, people kept coming up to me and saying thank you for being so honest. I was amazed. These big men told me that was exactly how they were feeling most of the time. *I'm not alone.* It gave me the courage to really examine myself and I started to realise how sensitive I was, oversensitive actually. If two friends got together and they didn't ask me along, I took it as a rejection. I knew it was childish, but it was also a real feeling. I started to look at myself. I was really starting to know and face myself and understand who I was. I even started to have a little compassion for myself. This was the moment the real growth started.

When Bar had Epstein–Barr she developed a sudden aversion to drinking. She used to put the drink to her mouth and then almost gag. She said she couldn't bear the smell of alcohol. At first, I thought she was just trying to be supportive to me. 'You know you don't have to do this for me.'

'Scott, I swear to you,' she said. 'You know me, I love a drink. I cannot stand the smell of it at the moment.' She'd try a couple of sips then screw up her face as if she'd sucked on a lemon. In many ways, it was a saving grace for her as well. She was telling the truth about liking a drink, but the world was filling up with mini paps, smartphones with cameras were beginning to appear and a few pictures had started to emerge where Barbara looked quite drunk. It wasn't a good look, so, in a way, it was a win-win for us that we'd both stopped drinking and this was the beginning of Barbara's own sobriety.

In May 2004, Barbara presented an award at the BAFTAs. She was in her element and I was delighted to see her looking so well, but the following day Ally Ross, the TV critic at the *Sun*, reviewed the televised show and wrote, 'What lunatic wolf-whistled at Barbara Windsor?!' She pretended not to be hurt, but I took offence and I emailed him.

'Dear Mr Ross, thank you for your comments regarding my wife. It was a great confidence booster for a 66-year-old lady who has spent the last year being really unwell and feeling low. I hope you were pleased with yourself but for the record I think there were kinder things to say.'

Immediately I worried I had made a bad enemy for Bar, but I also genuinely wanted to stick up for her. The next day I had the most charming email back from Ally Ross. He thanked me for my measured and dignified response and said how sorry he was. Then he sent Barbara a lovely bouquet of flowers. And the really funny thing is, since then we got to know Ally and I still have the odd lunch with him. He's a really lovely guy. The vagaries of showbiz, eh!

The way I looked at it, a critic could comment on a job or a performance, but why get personal? If anyone said anything rude or insulting about my wife, I felt it was my right to stand up for her. Don't forget, Bar was also perfectly capable of looking after herself. Leslie Grantham once took a dig at Barbara in an interview, saying, 'I don't think there should be famous people in *EastEnders*.'

When Bar was asked about this a few weeks later, she retorted, 'Well, I was a bit upset because I never said they shouldn't have murderers . . .' That's my girl!

On 15 May *EastEnders* offered Bar a new short-term contract to return as Peggy in the summer. We were delighted, but our high was short-lived – just four days later we received the sad news that Bar's father had passed away. By the end of the phone call with her stepmother, Bar was in tears and they were rowing. We were supposed to be going away and immediately I thought about cancelling the trip, but Bar was adamant. She did not want to go to the funeral. Her father had turned his back on her years before and she disliked her stepmother. It was clear the feeling between the two women was mutual.

So we went to Spain as planned and, on the day of the funeral, we stayed at the villa and Bar lit a candle. She was quiet and contemplative all day. There was so much loss, regret and hurt. They had been a right little pair, then the war, aspiration and life had got in the way and continued to get in the way. And that was what was so sad; it was such a waste because, underneath all the hurt, there was this abundance of love for her dad. Her stepmother sent back the card that had been attached to the wreath that Bar sent. It arrived in the post on 11 June. Bar was shocked because it felt so bitter and spiteful. Her stepmother must have been hurting too, but she had made it so hard for the two to reunite and it was a loss for them both. And then the stepmother kept the saga going by doing a piece in the *Mirror* in which she called Barbara vile and revolting. It could not have been further from the truth. It was a dark end to a completely unavoidable family breakdown.

With Bar heading back to the Square for a few weeks' filming and me free from life as a carer, I decided it was time to give acting one last crack, just to be sure. But life did not run smoothly for long. Other old feuds were brewing. Two strong females playing two strong females, one square. Kat Moon and Peggy Mitchell, Jessie Wallace and Barbara Windsor.

It was the summer of 2004. I know now that Jessie always admired Barbara and in fact was a fan long before she met her, but at this stage there was a lot of tension between them. Bar couldn't stand people being late and Jessie was often late, or cutting it fine. This particular day she'd kept the actors waiting two hours, swanned in and didn't apologise.

'You're late!' said Bar.

'What? My car ain't a Harrier jump jet!'

Kat Moon was a big name in the show at the time and Peggy had been out for a while. We never missed a show and we both recognised Jessie's exceptional acting skills, but it was her first main role; she wouldn't be the first to let success go to her head. Bar wouldn't stand for the unprofessionalism. I remember the day it kicked off because I was rehearsing for a part in *Androcles and the Lion*, which would be performed in the stone amphitheatre in front of City Hall in London. My final foray into acting wasn't going well and I was hating every second.

'Hello, Barbara,' said Jessie Wallace, all attitude and bravado the first day back after another press story had gone out with Jessie singing Bar's praises. It was the tone. Bar knew when she was being riled rather than respected. Within minutes there was a full-blown slanging match between them. Bar was mortified and ran crying to the producers, ashamed that she had let herself down, ashamed of her own lack of professionalism. She was sixty-seven years old and shouldn't be effing and blinding like an alley cat. She liked setting a high professional standard for the younger actors. The trouble was, they were two formidable ladies and neither would back down, so for a while they just kept out of each other's way. But over time respect grew, then camaraderie, and then finally a deep and lasting friendship. Jessie was a regular visitor when Bar fell ill with dementia. Some of the other key characters we never saw again.

Towards the end of the year Barry and I had a meeting with the new *EastEnders* producer about renewing Barbara's contract and what that would entail with regard to workload. I really didn't want Bar to get ill again. Her name was Kathleen Hutchison and I found her quite reticent. There was a strange feeling the whole way through the meeting, which I couldn't put my finger on. Julia Crampsie, the casting director, was also there. Barry and I had always got on well with Julia, but she stayed pretty quiet that day. After long discussions about possible storylines and roughly when Barbara could go back, we got up to leave. As we stood up, Kathleen Hutchison piped up, 'Well, that's if it happens at all.'

I was taken aback. I did not think this was an 'if', but a 'when'. The show's audience had been steadily falling. I thought they'd be clamouring to have her back. I was expecting to set the terms, not be sent away. It made us worried for Bar and what it might mean for her return.

A few weeks later Barbara met Kathleen at a BBC Christmas drinks party. 'I don't think she likes me,' Bar said when she got home.

It was unusual for Barbara to make a comment like that because most of the time she didn't give a monkey's about who liked her and who didn't, but this was different, Kathleen held Bar's career in her hand. 'How so?' I asked.

'It was weird. She asked me if the necklace I was wearing was real diamonds. That is a strange question, right?'

'What do you think she meant?'

'I don't know, but it was a bit disconcerting.'

'Barry and I felt the same when we met her,' I said.

None of us could work out why the sea change. They'd always been so enthusiastic about Bar's role of Peggy.

II

Turkey Neck

As we ended the year Barbara was busy on the promo trail for her fitness video, *The Windsor Workout*. She'd already done one interview with Jonathan Ross and she was now pre-recording an episode of *Parkinson* with Paul O'Grady and Rod Stewart, which would go out on Christmas Day. I was a bit concerned by her appearance. Again, she wasn't as slick as usual, but when it was edited it was a good interview.

We went straight from the pre-record to the Royal Variety Performance because Barbara was presenting one of the artists. She shared a dressing room with Olivia Newton-John, which was pretty cool, and right opposite was Liza Minnelli's dressing room. It was a hive of activity, with people coming and going through Liza Minnelli's door, which remained open most of the time, so we could clearly see and hear that famous throaty laugh. As call time approached, I went to the green room with talent agent Addison Cresswell, actor Shane Richie and his wife Christie, and the Girls Aloud girls – they were a great bunch. I also saw David Furnish backstage and as he walked past he smiled and said, 'Hi Scott.' I was finally feeling confident that I belonged here just as much as the next person. But watching Bar carefully on the monitor I noticed she didn't appear as confident as she usually did. Her eyes were darting about as if she was chasing the conversation, rather than steering it.

Still on the promo trail, after that we went to Cliveden House, the beautiful country estate where the Profumo scandal took place. Bar was appearing live on *This Morning* with Phillip Schofield. Sir

Cliff Richard was also on the show. It was a great interview and I was happy to see she was back on top form. Then we were taken straight to the airport to fly to Ireland for *The Late Late Show*. She could not have done more to make the fitness video work but, when I popped into an HMV store, it hadn't even made it into the top 20. I had this niggling feeling it was because she wasn't back in *EastEnders* full-time and now it looked possible Peggy Mitchell was not the direction the show was moving in.

Back in London, we went to visit John Inman and Ron Lynch in their mews house in Maida Vale. We had a lovely afternoon with tea and cake, but John was looking very frail, which worried Bar. On the way home it was clear she was feeling glum and a bit vulnerable. I had been told, off the record, that the new *EastEnders* producer Kathleen Hutchison had said to a director that the show didn't have room for Barbara Windsor any more. It might have been true, or it might have been hearsay; either way, it was unnerving. Seeing John and Ron had made us both think. They'd been together for thirty-three years. Time was precious. We both felt it might be time to consider other work avenues and so we rang Barry.

'Funnily enough, a film director has been in touch and was wondering if you'd be interested in having a part in his film.'

'Let's have a look at the script,' we suggested, so Barry gave them our address.

We waited for the script to be delivered, but nothing ever arrived. There was no film. What did happen was a series of 3am prank phone calls. This went on for a couple of weeks and was very unnerving. Back in 2000, Barbara had published her memoir, *All of Me*, and true to form she had been absolutely candid about sex and abortions, and the hoax callers were spewing it all back at her. Fame is an odd existence. Lots of people want it because they only see certain parts: the fabulous nights out, the smiling pictures, the parties surrounded by other celebrities. But when you dig a bit deeper it can be incredibly intrusive. It plays games with your mind, it makes you paranoid, and can really affect you. Bar was constantly recognised in the street. Occasionally that person would think it amusing to follow her home. I can tell you, it is never amusing; nor are phone calls in the middle of the night.

It wasn't just the public who used tricks to get stories. I noticed a blue car around the mews on and off one day. I took a photo of it. Then tapped on the window. 'Look, she's away till the weekend.'

She was away because she was in hospital having a few procedures, this time cosmetic. I guessed that was why the blue car was there, but I was always staggered by how quickly the press picked up these stories. Bar was not feeling at her best. She wasn't an internet person, but she read every paper, and she started to feel slightly under attack. After the release of her memoir in 2000 there had been an article in the *Guardian* in 2002 calling her a gangster's moll and referring to her as careless for having had five abortions. It was vitriolic and kept bubbling up in different versions on the internet and in the press. The critical tone fed her fear that the jobs would dry up. She was beginning to doubt the wisdom of being quite so candid in her memoir, but that was her, she was an open book. Absolutely and completely, even if that meant writing about taboos, like abortions and links to criminal London. Sometimes I think she was her own worst enemy, but she was determinedly honest. The abortions kept coming back at her, comments about her age were hitting harder and finally the threat of never going back to *EastEnders* moved her in favour of having the surgery. She felt washed up and needed the lift.

The blue car pulled away and I waited until the coast was clear. I drove with one eye on the rear-view mirror, often suspecting I was being followed. When the car behind me turned off the road, I would beat myself up for being paranoid.

'Scott, it's Barry. Julia Crampsie just called to ask when Barbara could come back to the Square!'

'What? Really! That's great news. I'll talk to her as soon as she's home.'

A second call followed. The executive producer, John Yorke, wanted Bar to know it would be full-time and long-term, for as long as she was up for it. I went to pick her up from the back entrance of the clinic and told her the good news. Bar was ecstatic. She'd feared she'd be back to the one-woman shows in second-rate venues.

When we got home I washed Bar's hair and could feel the staples around the top of her hairline. The paps were outside all day trying to get a photo of her coming home, but this time we had outfoxed them.

She was already safely back, on the sofa, having a TV dinner with me. But, as ever, that wasn't the end of it. 'Hi, Scott, it's Fiona Cummins at the *Daily Mirror*, could you call me back? It's urgent.'

I could drive myself mad second-guessing what it was, so I ignored it. Within the hour there was a clack of the letterbox, and a note landed on the mat from another paper telling us to call them immediately. My phone rang again. This time it was a journalist we knew, the late Peter Willis. 'The thing is, Scott, they know she's had surgery and they are running the story, so why don't you get your story in first?'

This is how it always works. They hook you in and then you give them the story they were fishing for in the first place. I told them nothing. Medical records are protected, right? Yet somehow we were suddenly prisoners in our own home, hounded for a comment, camera lenses aimed at the door.

Two days later I got up at 6.30am to see Sky News commenting on the *Mirror*'s headline: 'TV BABS' NEW £25K FACE'. Inside, on a double-page spread, was a computer image of what she would look like now, post-surgery. The details were astounding. It was all there: that she'd had her hysterectomy scar neatened up and a melanoma removed from her face. They knew about the lipoma. The only detail missing was the face tucks themselves, despite the headline. The awful thing about these situations is that you then start asking yourself lots of questions. How did those details get out? Who actually knew? It's a horrible place to be and you don't want to go there.

My phone started to ring, but I didn't call anyone back. I just tried to look after Bar. She was really upset, not so much about the invasion of privacy, which made me cross on her behalf, but because she thought it might risk her being rehired by *EastEnders*. That show was her lifeline, as well as her bread and butter, and she knew it.

The next day they called with the official offer for a year to July, plus the option to renew for another year. Bar said yes, instantly. But how come the turnaround, we wondered? 'Keep it quiet,' a friend in the show told us, 'but Kathleen Hutchison has left.'

I have to be honest and say we were both relieved. Our brief experience with Kathleen had left us feeling concerned. Sadly, there was more to come. The next day Bar was back on the front page of the *Mirror*. The *EastEnders* press release about her comeback had hit Fleet Street, but the headline was that Babs wouldn't go back unless the exec producer got the sack. Bar got blamed. I guess there always has to be a fall guy, but it really wasn't her.

Never one to take it lying down, Bar decided to do an article with the *News of the World* about her surgery. Their first suggestion for the headline was 'I've had my turkey neck lifted'. Errr no, guys, I don't think so. The headline was changed and the article was great. Searingly honest as usual, with Bar talking about her Bridget Jones post-surgery pants.

'Anyone seen Bar?' I asked the guests at my nephew Harry's bar mitzvah. Bar had always loved Jewish culture. Indeed, many years ago, after abandoning her desire to be a nun (complete with a tea towel fashionably placed over her wispy blonde hair), she had announced she wanted to marry a Jewish London cabbie. As it happened, she ended up married to the son of one. No wonder she loved Dad so much. In fact, she loved all our big family events. She never hid away, happily working the room as if she were in a bingo hall, safe in the knowledge no one would call, 'Eyes down!' What was really funny was that she wouldn't restrict herself to just our family event. Someone pointed to the large reception room next door. Sure enough, there was Bar having photos taken with the bride and groom. Typical Bar.

In March 2005 we took a trip to Paul O'Grady's farm in Kent. He and Bar had been friends for over thirty years, having met at a murder mystery party in the Lake District with Beryl Reid and Su Pollard. They sat on the sofa all night chatting at that party, and remained firm friends for the rest of her life. Paul was hand-rearing a lamb called Warpy when we visited. He fed it with a baby's bottle and it clipped along behind him as he walked around his kitchen.

'Is that you, Bar?' I called out.

'No,' said Paul. 'It's Warpy.' It was one of the most surreal and campest things we'd ever seen.

'Right, heels off,' Paul declared. 'I need to introduce you to Ronnie and Reggie.'

Bar and I looked at each other nervously.

'A couple of hefty bulls in the farmyard. Boots on, we'll start with the pigs. They've got prizes, you know.' And so we found ourselves knee-deep in mud.

'And lastly,' he said with a flourish, 'the geese-stapo.' A battalion of grey geese marched past. I swear I could hear the click of boots.

It was a truly marvellous, memorable day. Farmer Paul, who'd have thought?

A few weeks later we were back with the family in Henfield, West Sussex, where my parents, sister and brother-in-law now lived. There is always a big Easter procession through the village and I was quite used to crawling along at a snail's pace while Barbara said hello to everyone in the crowd.

'Lovely bonnet!'

'Great eggs, did you paint them yourself?' There was a comment for everyone.

I wandered up the high street to get to the top of the floats where they had stopped to sing a hymn. As usual I had lost my diminutive wife in the crowd. I wasn't worried, she had a habit of turning up. Then I heard a very familiar voice. I looked to the front of the parade and there was Bar right in the middle of the congregation, singing loudly with the good folk of Henfield. The village loved it, but not as much as Bar did.

We'd had a good six months. Life had been a little less crazy. Bar was well again and we'd had a lovely fifth anniversary at Henlow Grange. She was ready to go back to full-time work and we had dinner at The Ivy with Ross, Rebekah and Steve to celebrate Peggy's imminent return to the Queen Vic. After dinner, Rebekah and I came out on to the pavement. All seemed quiet. But when the three Mitchells appeared it went crazy – bulbs flashed, cameras clicked, paps emerged from the shadows and swarmed Bar, Ross and Steve until they got their shot. Here we go again, I thought.

Two days later Bar went back to Albert Square and every tabloid paper carried the 'Mitchell Three' photo. I was apprehensive, but I also had a more secure outlook and felt I was better placed to enjoy it this time round. Peggy was right back in the thick of it, filming the brilliant scene at Den Watts's funeral when she threw his widow, and murderer, Chrissie into his grave. It was a cracking performance and came out on her birthday, which was a double win for Bar. Dissenting voices got noticeably quieter because Bar was simply too good at her job for them not to admire her.

By September our life was moving along nicely. Bar was busy but managing. I was also busy doing AA, work, keeping fit and managing our home life. Halcyon days.

In November I was offered a new job casting for pantomimes for First Family Entertainment, the panto division of Ambassador Theatre Group. That I had the confidence to accept the offer had everything to do with recovery. Once upon a time it would have been a case of fear everything and run; now it was face everything and recover. I hit the ground running and started making calls to agents for the following year. I took to it very quickly; it was the ideal job for me, combining what I'd learnt in recruitment with my up-close-and-personal relationship with showbiz. I was busy visiting theatres, Bar was filming *Children in Need* with Catherine Tate, I was in casting meetings, Bar was collecting more awards, including one for best return. The Mitchells were on a lucky streak. We had lots to feel positive about.

As ever, we'd get home at the end of the day and chat, chat, chat about everything that had happened. In this business, many of the brightest lights go out early and in December we sat on the sofa together and sobbed watching George Best's funeral on telly. He died on 25 November 2005, aged only fifty-nine, three years after a controversial liver transplant, but he had once again relapsed. How does a shy boy thrust into the football equivalent of Beatlemania deal with that sort of attention? He drinks himself to death. On George's request, the papers printed a photo of him looking jaundiced, close to total organ failure, with the strapline 'DON'T DIE LIKE ME', to highlight the dangers of alcoholism. I was devastated by the tragic waste of it and the gnawing truth that death had once awaited me.

For New Year's Eve that year we went to see Danny La Rue in panto in Croydon. I was struck by how frail Danny looked onstage. At one point he sang 'Somewhere Over the Rainbow' and I could hear Bar sniffling beside me. When I looked over I realised she had tears pouring down her face.

'You okay?' I asked as we walked out.

'Scott, don't let me get like that. I never want people saying, "Shame, look at her now."'

I won't, my darling, I thought. I will never let anyone see you like that.

'Promise me, Scott,' she insisted. 'Promise you'll always be honest with me. Don't let me go on too long.'

'I won't.'

'I hated seeing him like that,' she continued. 'He was one of the most flamboyant showbiz stars of his time, and now . . .' Her voice trailed off. 'He looked so shrunken.'

12

Baron Hardup

On 18 February 2006 there was a big party at London Bridge to mark the twenty-first birthday of *EastEnders*. I was looking forward to it, and Bar was always happy to honour the show that had turned her life around. By this time there wasn't a panto I hadn't seen. While some might think this could turn a man to drink, I loved it and busily scanned the room looking for the next Captain Hook or Dandini! Bar could not have been happier that my work placed me firmly back in her world and there is no doubt it made my place there easier. When we attended the civil partnership of Paul Cottingham and Michael Cashman, twenty-five years after they'd been introduced by Bar, there were several well-known faces I would have happily put into panto. It might have been harder to cast the politicians who were there, though I'm sure Neil Kinnock and Gordon Brown would have made excellent ugly sisters. Michael and Paul thanked Bar for introducing them, which brought a tear to her eye.

EastEnders won the BAFTA for Best Continuing Drama that year. Bar was so passionate about it, it was like her favourite football team had been crowned champions of the world. But with her seventieth birthday approaching, I couldn't help but think it would be good for her to take a little time off. She had been good for that show. They were back up to big numbers, regularly pulling in 18–20 million viewers per episode and at the British Soap Awards that year they won seven out of sixteen awards. There was no doubt in my mind that they needed to take care of her too. They agreed to a break, but not for long because immediately after that they asked her to sign another two-year deal. A credit to Bar. Whether pissed in an ice-cream van, hurling a punch or laughing her head off, she could do it all with perfect aplomb. When filming got a bit hectic and there were early calls, Bar would often stay near the studio with June Brown. I would have quite liked to eavesdrop on one of their dinners. Then again, maybe not! June and Bar always watched out for one another, theirs was a sweet and deep friendship.

That summer Bar was asked to film an episode of *Who Do You Think You Are?* She was thrilled and honoured, and it was fascinating discovering the full extent of her East End lineage. A film crew came and filmed us chatting in the kitchen, very true to life, though I felt painfully awkward inside. And then there was a scene in the office with me looking stuff up for Bar. Also absolutely real – Bar never touched a computer in her life!

Delving into the past was a real eye-opener for Bar. She felt quite removed from her family, especially her father's side because they had been estranged for so long. It turned out Barbara's paternal grandfather, Jack Deeks, was a costermonger, a barrow boy street trader selling fruit and vegetables around the docks. He was also one of the original 'Flash Harrys', so named for the pearl buttons the costers wore on their jackets that would glint in the light. In fact, Flash Harrys were the precursors to the Pearly Kings and Queens of old London town, the very costumes Bar and I had worn to Elton's fiftieth birthday celebration. They also invented a secret language so they could talk among themselves and not have the punters work out who was fixing what price. This secret language became known as 'S-lang'. Slang. How much great stuff had come out of the melting pot that was the East End of London.

Her paternal grandmother, Granny Deeks, or Fat Nanny Polly, as she'd been called in her day, had been a hoofer in Hoxton and performed at the Britannia Music Hall. Crazier still, they'd only arrived in the East End because they'd been forced to leave Ireland in 1845–51 during the potato famine that killed a million people and displaced two million more. So actually that side of the family came from Cork, same place as Danny La Rue. Bar loved that. When we went to Cork to visit the mass graves, Barbara personally apologised on behalf of the nation to the gent who took care of the site, so anti-British was he.

Bar's mother had labelled the Deeks 'lowlifes', but they'd actually been up-and-coming tradesmen, and quite remarkably she could be linked through the Suffolk-dwelling Deeks family all the way back to John Constable, the English landscape artist. It was her maternal side, in fact, the Ellises, who'd been dirt poor; some ending up dying in the workhouse, others working as 'in and outers' making matchboxes in the infamous Old Nichol slum. It was a rather overwhelming confluence of history, all flowing down to one little girl with size 2 feet, a brawny voice and a big heart.

We continued to try to balance our busy lives, both independently and together. One minute Bar was living it large with her favourite drag queen Dave Lynn on the Terrence Higgins Trust float for Pride, the next minute she was dragging Dale Winton off a pap who was taking his desire for a close-up with Bar a bit too literally. I was strong enough to become an AA sponsor myself and it felt good to help others. However, as the year went on, I started to feel less buoyant. Thankfully, I quickly recognised the signs of anxiety building in the pit of my stomach and, rather than beating myself up about it, I took myself off to the doctor's and got back on the meds. It's rarely pleasant at first. The side-effects can be hard to take and my sleep pattern was all over the place. I was in a general haze, my palms would sweat, but then gradually the chemicals started to work, my endorphine levels lifted and I began to feel better. I learnt to be much more compassionate to myself, but I was still dragging my feet a bit, so the doctor recommended I see a psychiatrist. It was good to feel supported and to understand the ups and downs of depression. I realised I had experienced these feelings all my life, but in the past instead of getting help I'd buried them under litres of vodka and self-hatred.

I believe I was sober five years when the fog finally started to clear. It is impossible to imagine that happening in the beginning, when you are taking it minute by minute, hour by hour. But when they tell you it's a process, that's because it's a process. I was more settled, more aware and more in touch with my real feelings. Now when I laughed, it was a true laugh from the belly, from the heart. I could feel the humour now. Not just mimic it.

And never more so than when we were with great entertainers, like David Walliams and Matt Lucas. We first met them in 2004 at the BAFTAs, then we saw them out and about a bit, and were lucky enough to see them on their *Little Britain: Live* tour in 2006, and luckier still to head backstage afterwards to meet Matt, David and David's wonderful mum, Kathleen.

'You must be so proud of your boy,' Bar said to Kathleen. Clearly, she was. We all got on and that night heralded the start of a beautiful friendship, cemented by our other mutual love, after pantomime, the Gooners (aka Arsenal FC). The absolute highlight of the year was being invited to Matt Lucas's wedding to his partner Kevin McGee. The theme? Panto, of course! I resurrected Dandini, Bar was her perfect Fairy Godmother self and David came as Biggins! Brilliant. The grooms were serenaded by Will Young and we all danced the night away. Now that was a wedding!

A few months later Bar was dressed in a tiny Fairy Godmother costume once again. This time folded inside a cardboard cake in Shoreditch town hall waiting for a jazz band to strike up a tune. Why? To jump out of Elton John's sixtieth birthday cake, of course, complete with a magic wand and her own cockney version of 'Happy Birthday'. David Furnish had set the whole thing up in secret. As the room got to their feet to sing along, I looked around and thought, *Scott, this is one of those pinch-me moments.* There was Sam Taylor-Johnson, Paul McCartney, Paul O'Grady, Sharon and Ozzy Osbourne, David Walliams, Jane Moore and Gary Farrow, Daniel Craig, the list went on. A few days later Barbara received a beautiful ruby, sapphire and diamond Tiffany bracelet as a thank you. It was an incredible and unexpected gesture.

'How about Mickey Rooney for Baron Hardup?!' I shouted across the office when my boss Kevin Wood told us we needed to think of bigger public figures for next year's panto season. I had heard on the radio that Mickey and his wife had been doing a two-person tour of the UK.

'Excellent idea,' said my boss.

Bar agreed it was a good idea, which meant a great deal to me. Now we just had to get him. He had a reputation for being difficult to work with, but he was a huge star, and had worked alongside Judy Garland and all the other Hollywood greats, so we thought it was worth the risk. Within a few days Mickey Rooney was booked for the panto in Sunderland. In fairness we did say it was just outside London, but I don't think that would have bothered him; it was the salary that hooked him in. He'd been married eight times.

'That's a lot of alimony, Scott!'

He sounded fun, so despite his reputation I was looking forward to meeting him. Bar and I took Matt Lucas along to see Mickey and his wife's show. Matt was a mega fan of the man and after the show we went backstage.

'Mickey,' I said, about to start on the introductions. But that was as far as I got. Mickey walked towards me, pointing his finger, snarling. 'You fucker! How dare you disrespect my wife, it's unprofessional.'

He reached out and grabbed me by the scruff of the neck, pinned me against the wall and went on swearing in my face. It was both shocking and hilarious at the same time.

'You don't think my wife is beautiful? How dare you use such a little picture of her on your fucking crap poster?!'

It suddenly dawned on me. He hated the promotional poster and thought I was the producer. 'Mickey, that's not my department. Let me talk to the producer, Kevin—'

I was trying to explain the situation, but he just went on shouting in my face. Behind me I could sense Barbara and Matt stifling their laughter as they watched the unexpected spectacle of me being pinned up against the wall by Mickey Rooney unfold. Eventually, he calmed down, met Bar and Matt, and we made a speedy exit.

'Thanks for coming to my rescue,' I said to them, walking back to the car. They were still laughing. 'A lot of help you were.'

'Honestly, Scott, that was the first time I've ever seen another man look up to you!' Bar said. They both doubled up in hysterics. Thanks, guys.

*

In August 2007 it was Barbara's seventieth birthday and BBC Radio 2 recorded a tribute show at the Hackney Empire to celebrate. It was an amazing evening full of family and friends, and an East End audience, all of whom had come out to celebrate their 'gal done good'. Bar was in her element as Bradley Walsh and Shane Richie took to the stage, among others, to each do a 'turn' and talk about her life and career. I hoped she could feel the huge amount of love people had for her.

Continuing the celebrations, we marked the big day with a party at the Royal Garden Hotel in Kensington. Surrounded by friends and cast mates, and with a cracking view of her beloved London, it was a wonderful evening. David Walliams turned up with a plus one, a young actor we'd met once before.

'Hello again, what are you working on now?'

'Oh, just a show for the BBC. It's something I've written with a friend about an Essex boy who hooks up with a Welsh girl on a stag night . . .'

'You play the boy?'

'Oh no, just his mate.'

That show was *Gavin & Stacey* and David's plus one was none other than James Corden.

I made a speech to my special wife, which of course I was terrified about doing in front of that stunning room full of natural show-offs, but I managed to get my point across, albeit in a somewhat shaky voice.

'The greatest compliment that I can give you, Barbara, is to say I like you. I really like you. It's easy to say I love you because that's what we're all supposed to say. And I do. But, mostly, I like who you are. I like the human being you are and I love being with you and spending time with you. And that means a lot more to me.'

How true that was for us. She was the person I wanted to be with more than any other human on earth. She was my best friend, my soulmate, my everything.

Life was great. We were happier together than we'd ever been. Bar was loving life back on Albert Square and my job was keeping me busy too, particularly looking after our American pantomime artists. After Bar's birthday party, and only three hours' sleep, I flew to LA to be a part of the photoshoots with Mickey Rooney, Henry Winkler and Paul Michael Glaser. I don't know if it was jet lag or just because I was surrounded by stars, but my nervous laugh started to re-emerge. The worst time – it had to be – was at Mickey's house. We sat down for lunch together, when Mickey suddenly went into one because his stepson hadn't brought any ice cream home. It unnerved me, I started laughing, and then pretended I was choking to cover it up, and my colleague Laura began hitting me on the back, which of course made it worse because it was all so ridiculous. Somehow, I managed to escape to the loo. The whole trip was really fun; it was nice to feel good at my job.

The only blot on the horizon was Bar's hours. They were getting unfeasibly long again and I was watching like a hawk for signs of exhaustion. As the landlady of the Queen Vic she was often in the background of other people's scenes, which meant she had to be there from the first shot to the last. I could see tiredness creeping in again, so I made a couple of phone calls to *EastEnders* asking them to be mindful. The thing was, she was fanatical about being prepared and would spend the whole weekend doing lines for the following week. She would also go over them the night before and sometimes again in the morning before each day, just to be sure they were fresh in her mind. Bar wasn't one to do things by halves and it was full-on.

In January 2008 I was six years sober and what better way to mark it than to be in the Sunderland Empire Theatre with Mickey Rooney and Les Dennis. I brought Barbara with me, which was a bittersweet moment for her, because it was on that very stage that Sid James collapsed with a heart attack fifteen minutes into his final show, *The Mating Season*. For a while, his co-star thought he was ad-libbing, but sadly not. A doctor in the audience tried to revive him, but he died on the way to hospital, three weeks short of his sixty-third birthday.

Bar had always felt guilty about Sid, who claimed, despite being married and a terrible womaniser himself, that Bar had shattered his heart when she ended their three-year affair in 1976. He had pursued her throughout the many films they had done together, and eventually she gave in. She thought, as Bar often did, one night won't hurt, he just needs to get his infatuation out of his system. But it didn't work like that. He was borderline obsessive, hurriedly climbing several flights of stairs at the Victoria Palace every night to watch Bar do her number in *Carry On London*, before hurrying back down to be onstage for his next scene. He would regularly flare up into jealous rages. Looking back on how he treated her, making her stay in to take phone calls at certain hours, you could say it was leaning towards what we'd now call coercive control. It was because he loved her so much, he said. But isn't that what they all say?

Bar put on a bright smile as usual and soon enough the audience spotted her and there was a buzz going around the theatre. You would always hear it first, the whispers, getting louder, spreading, people turning in their seats, leaning over; then you could almost see the news circulate around an auditorium. Despite her height, there was no hiding Barbara Windsor.

Backstage, Les took Mickey to one side. 'When you come on in the next scene, I want you to suddenly shout, "Get outta my pub!"'

'Why?' asked a very suspicious Mickey Rooney.

'Just do it. It will bring the house down. I promise.'

'This better not be a trick!'

Mickey walked onstage and, as directed, shouted out the words and, as Les had said, the audience went crazy, cheering and applauding Mickey. At first, he looked rather bemused, but then he smiled, looked quite pleased with himself and took a bow.

The next day I got a call from Les. 'Mickey shouted "Get outta my pub!" to complete silence when he went on tonight. He tore a strip off me after!'

Yup, I knew how that felt.

Life was busy. We were going from Ireland for a chat show up to Glasgow to see a panto, then back to London to do the Al Murray show, and then to another panto. It was relentless. And then back in London we went to Bruce Forsyth's eightieth birthday party at the Dorchester Hotel. With guests including Cilla Black, Jools Holland, Michael Parkinson and David Walliams, it was a proper, hands-down,

British showbiz extravaganza and, as ever, we felt privileged to be a part of it, but we weren't the spring chickens we'd once been and it was exhausting too. It was time for a break and some downtime.

Unpacking after a much-needed trip to Majorca, I looked out the upstairs window and saw a very thin girl with exceptionally dark hair sitting on the steps of the house opposite. Barbara came up the stairs. 'Scott, I think Amy Winehouse is outside.'

We opened the front door and she looked up, as if she knew we were going to open it. 'I knew you two lived around here somewhere,' she said, smiling. 'I know your mum and dad, Scott.'

'I know you do.'

'Want to come in?' Bar offered.

Amy got up off the steps, walked over and hugged us both. 'I've just checked myself into the London Clinic,' she said. 'I don't have to be there. I've just been overdoing it a bit.'

'I know how that feels,' I said. 'I've been sober six years.'

She looked at me. 'Yeah? It's fucking boring though, isn't it?'

'Come and have a cup of tea,' said Bar.

'You remind me of my nan Cynthia,' Amy said, linking arms with Bar. 'I really miss her.'

She looked so vulnerable, sitting on our sofa, a mug of tea in her hand, but soon the two were discussing life in the sixties and seventies, and she seemed to relax a bit.

Bar and I always liked listening to music and before long Ella Fitzgerald's voice filled the mews house. 'She's the best,' said Amy.

'You're the best, Amy,' said Bar. 'I mean it, you're that good.'

She shook her head. How could she not know she was that good?

She became a regular visitor to our house after that. Sometimes on her own, sometimes with a friend. I think, I hope, that's because she felt safe there. Whenever she came, I'd make tea and she would offer to help Bar learn her lines.

'Can I be Peggy now?' Amy would ask.

'Sure, darlin', you'd make a good landlady.'

This is my favourite photo. It captures everything we shared.

Just married. Gloria Hunniford's sixtieth birthday masked ball.

Another party. Fancy dress. Goldfinger and a Babs look–a–like.

Messing about on the *QE2*.

Dandini and Fairy Babs getting carried away.

hristmas card capers. Serious stuff,
ntil you open it up.

Beloved friend
Anna Karen.

Happy times with Paul, Dale and Cilla.

Off camera. Bar was devastated when Ross Kemp left *EastEnders*.

A brilliant friend to the end.

Biggins and Babs. The power of laughter and lasting friendship.

Trip to Venice with Biggins.

Danny La Rue in full
splendour, Brick Lane.

Lifesaver, our friend, the actor
Jamie Foreman.

Little, little and large.
Us with David Walliams.

The Best of British.
Elton and Bar.

GOSH . . . it's Arsène Wenger.
Bar in her personalised Arsenal strip.

Watching Arsenal at the Emirates
Stadium with Matt Lucas.

. . . And the lads.

We are amused. A royal visit to the set of *EastEnders*.

Catching up with Windsor business on the steps of the Queen Vic.

Sitting volleyball at the Paralympics 2012. As usual, Bar putting her all into it. Come on, Boris!

Catching up with more Windsor business . . .

13

Don't Let the Wig Fool You!

2009 started fast and furiously. Although I'd decided this would be my last panto season, we felt busier than ever. There were trips to Southampton to see Biggins onstage with Matthew Kelly and his son. We watched Steven Berkoff in *On the Waterfront* in the West End and he, as always, asked about my dad. Then we watched *A View from the Bridge* with David Walliams and his mum. Whatever the evenings brought, Bar would always be up again early in the morning to make her call time. It was mad. She was picked up at 6.30am and often didn't walk back through the door until 8.30pm. Bar never stopped and never called in sick.

Clearly my chat about cutting her hours had had an effect! So it came as no surprise to me when, in early March, Bar was sent home on doctor's orders and signed off for two days. But even that didn't stop her dragging herself out of bed the following morning for a photoshoot. The stress of us arguing about it only made things worse, but I didn't like it. I mean, really, she was nearly seventy-two!

In early April we went to visit Danny La Rue. He had sadly lost a lot of money in recent years after investing in a hotel and then being taken to the cleaners by bad management. Through it all his dresser Annie Braithwaite had stood by him and he lived with her now in Tunbridge Wells.

Annie opened the door. 'He's a bit poorly today,' she said as she showed us upstairs.

Danny was worse than poorly. He had a tumour and was fighting for his life. He opened his eyes when he heard Bar come in, saw her and smiled. It was clear he was thrilled she had come. Bar sat and stroked his forehead and hair. 'Cor blimey, we've been through some daft old times,' she said. 'Do you remember that man who heckled me back in Winston's? This was way back, late fifties, another world.'

Danny smiled.

'Very protective of me you were back then,' Bar continued.

'It wasn't that. The leery fella called me an old poofter.'

'I remember, you said, "Don't let this wig fool you!", jumped off the stage and knocked him unconscious.'

That became Danny's catchphrase and he used it for fifty years, which was how long that precious friendship had lasted. Danny meant the world to Bar and, as I sat listening to her retell all the old stories of their times together, I guessed she knew it would be the last time. Eventually he drifted off to sleep and for a long time Bar just sat there and stroked his head.

'He's still handsome you know, Annie,' she said, leaning over to give him a final kiss goodbye. Danny opened one eye. 'I suppose a fuck is out of the question?' He gave her the gift of leaving on a laugh, but she cried all the way home.

Danny died two months later, on 31 May 2009. When Annie called to tell us he had passed, Bar downed tools and took a moment. He had found his calling in the navy, putting on drag and impersonating women, and had forged his own path until the stroke, at age eighty, meant he finally had to hang up his feather boa. At the height of his career Princess Margaret was a regular at his club; at the end he was auctioning off his costumes, but he never stopped being generous, kind, funny and humane. Bar was devastated and was honoured to be asked to read a poem at his funeral, which she did, beautifully, despite feeling his loss acutely.

June 2009 saw the start of issues with pay cuts at the BBC and *East-Enders*. It wasn't across the board, but a couple of the actors were asked to take a 5 per cent reduction on their salaries and Bar was one of them. She was in the highest-per-episode salary bracket, but it was still nothing compared to the pay structure of BBC presenters and light entertainment stars. Also, presenters were allowed to do paid work elsewhere, whereas the actors were not. It felt messy from the beginning and stressful.

My gut reaction was, considering how hard Bar worked for the show and how successful her character had been, plus her age, that it was the wrong time to consider a pay cut. During discussions with the executive producer, Diederick Santer, he did at least agree she could have time off for panto in 2010. Qdos, a rival panto company, had approached Bar and I was excited that she was clear to at least hear what they were offering.

'I'm having a bad day,' Bar said on the phone. We always spoke three or four times a day, even when she was back-to-back filming. 'I couldn't get my lines out.'

'It's the stress of the pay cut,' I said. Another meeting with the financial controller had been inconclusive.

'I hate all of this. It's not just me, is it. Actors are vulnerable people and they know it.'

In the end we compromised on a one-year pay freeze that would take her through to the end of her contract. Two days later Bar wasn't home from filming until 11pm. And they wanted her to take a pay cut! I was glad we stood firm when a really nice job came in for Bar to do the September lottery. I gave *EastEnders* three months' notice to clear her for one day, but they said they couldn't. That irritated us both. We said there had to be more give and take. In the end Bar was cleared for the lottery, but she hated being a problem and didn't need the stress. I thought it was easy to take advantage of Bar because she was always so willing and also, despite all her outward appearances, she was scared of becoming redundant. Bar was conscious of her age and another birthday was creeping closer.

On Bar's birthday there was a constant flow of flowers being delivered, so many that by mid-morning the house looked like a Chelsea Flower Show stand. She'd agreed to go to Great Ormond Street Hospital that day to help Arsenal launch their 'Be a Gooner, Be a Giver' campaign to raise £500,000 for a new lung unit. Arsène Wenger had made her a team strip with Windsor on the back for the occasion; thanks to Matt Lucas we were regular guests at his box at the Emirates Stadium. Bar would do anything for that hospital, but an event like that is exhausting because you are there to cheer everyone else up. I think that's what Bar did best, actually. She cheered everyone up and then, when she was exhausted, I cheered her up.

The day after her birthday she woke up teary. She was more worried about becoming obsolete than she was about ageing. The pay cut business made her feel threatened. I got her out to the park to distract her and we sat and watched the world go by. When she was feeling a bit better, we talked about what was really upsetting her and she admitted that feeling tired frightened her. She'd got through life steamrollering through things, but at the age of seventy-two she no longer had the energy. The timing was terrible because the next day was the beginning of a week of late-night filming. It meant she didn't get home until 3am.

A few weeks later we went to see June Brown in *Calendar Girls*. Bar was asked to have a photo with the cast, including Anita Dobson and Jerry Hall, then we all went to J. Sheekey in Covent Garden. As soon as we arrived, Bar was mobbed.

'It's like the Beatles have turned up,' said June, standing back. She was spot-on; wherever we went now, it was pandemonium. It wasn't like that with all the other members of the cast.

'The difference between me and Babs is I am a soap person,' said June. 'But she's a star.'

June was right, absolutely, but my star was dimming. We went away to Majorca to give her a rest. Even then she worked on her scripts, but it gave us the chance to have some calm, honest chats about how she really felt about the future. The pace was taking its toll, but the thought of leaving made her sad. It was never about the pay cut. She felt grateful and guilty in equal measure.

'I don't want to upset anyone at the BBC,' she said. 'It changed everything for me.'

'True, but you've given just as much back.'

'What if I never get another job?'

She was as insecure as if she was just starting out. She had only just finished paying off the last debts, so she still needed to make money, but Barry and I had meetings about projects all the time and probably felt more confident than her. Only recently I had bumped into my friend Robert Campbell, an advertising executive, who was inventing a character called the Queen of Bingo for a company called Jackpotjoy. The pitch was: 'Think Barbara Windsor . . . but we can't have her because she works for the BBC.'

'I bet lots of people think that,' I reassured Bar.

'I hope you're right.'

So did I. I was relieved she was listening to me, but also nervous that she might turn around one day and say, *This is your fault. You told me to leave because you were always so worried.*

Bar resigned from *EastEnders* on 30 September and the producer seemed genuinely saddened. 'We will never be able to repay you for what you've done for the show,' he said, admitting she would leave a huge hole.

I think it was because of that, and protecting the brand, that they asked Bar to sit on the news until February. That was a real pressure on her because it meant lying to her closest colleagues and cast mates. I was doubtful from the beginning but respected their wishes. How did they think that news was going to stay quiet? There were always leaks from that set.

The first ones came just a few weeks later. So few people knew, yet it was impossible to work out where the story had come from. I thought it would have been better if the news was handled properly because she hated lying. It was upsetting her, which was an extra burden she could have done without.

'We still haven't cast that bingo advert, Scott,' said Robert Campbell when I bumped into him again.

'Call her agent now,' I said.

'What? Really? But what about . . .?'

'Just call him!'

Within days Jackpotjoy delivered a contract into Bar's lap that would put an end to her money worries. Period. Obviously that was tempting but Jackpotjoy is a gambling site, so we wanted to know what safeguarding regulations were in place before we put Bar's name to it. They showed us how they regulate their players by freezing people when they overspend and follow this up with a call to check on their welfare. In the end, we decided the Queen of Bingo was a character much like Peggy was a landlady. Peggy couldn't be held responsible for people going into a pub or ending up with a drink problem. In the same way, the Queen of Bingo wasn't responsible for gamblers. It was a role and in the eight years that Bar played it there were only a tiny handful of comments about the 'wrongs of promoting gambling'. As I knew only too well, you won't stop gamblers and you won't stop drinkers. They can only stop themselves.

The bingo plans were firming up and it all sounded great – better money and a fraction of the work. That's what I was most excited about. She was emotionally and physically exhausted so we went for a mini-break to Henfield to see the family.

Crack! Thump! The unmistakable sound of someone hitting the sink then collapsing to the bathroom floor. It was the middle of the night. I ran through to the bathroom to find Bar, once again, collapsed on the floor. She came round quite quickly.

On the advice of our doctor, the following week I took her to a heart specialist, Dr Spurrell, who again put our minds at rest but ordered some more tests. 'I think this is probably stress-related,' he said. There was no doubt she was stressed. That night we sat at home and watched Pat and Peggy do the most fantastic drunk scene in the ice-cream van. *EastEnders* gold. No wonder the show didn't want to lose her. But she was working herself into the ground and I didn't want to lose her either.

Finally, on 22 October, Bar was told she was allowed to announce the following Wednesday that she was leaving the Square. She had a meeting with the executive producer Diederick Santer and admitted to him that she was really tired and wanted to leave earlier than they had first planned. He was shocked. They didn't want her to go at all, let alone earlier. Maybe they thought she was bluffing, but she didn't work like that. In many ways she kept that studio a happy place to work. The old guard were pros. She made it fun. She led that culture from the top.

'I wish Babs was still here.' I would come to hear that a lot.

We worked out a quote with the press team. Something about 'My old man's not getting any younger . . .' Haha, still the butt of the joke. I didn't mind. I just wanted the announcement out.

The day it came out we were up early anyway because she was recording a voiceover for Tesco – 'Every Little Helps'. That job was allowed because of its anonymity. But you know it's Bar without being told. We sent texts to our close friends and family just before the announcement was made.

My phone beeped. 'I'd really like to write something for Barbara.' That first text was from Tony Jordan, the renowned ex-*EastEnders* scriptwriter who now had his own production company. Then my phone blew up. Sky News was running it as 'breaking news' along the ticker tape. It was mayhem and, I couldn't help but think, a bit ridiculous. The producers were worried that the pay cut would be cited as Bar's reason for leaving but she would never have said that. She loved that show and the BBC, and was a phenomenal advocate for both.

The press were camped outside our house that day, so we checked into a hotel. That evening, with room service, we watched every news bulletin carry the section. It was even on the *Ten O'Clock News*. It still strikes me as crazy now; a fictitious character leaving a TV soap made headline news. The next day the newspaper coverage was even bigger.

I dropped her at the studio at 7.30am and watched her walk in. She looked back and waved. I remember thinking she looked a bit diminished. It was strange. When she got home at 8.30 that evening, she seemed a bit brighter, but still not quite right.

Matt Lucas and I were watching Arsenal play Tottenham when a Google alert buzzed on my phone. 'MORE FAMILY TIME? NO, BABS QUIT OVER £54K PAY CUT'. I stopped watching the football and read the *Daily Mail* story.

'I'm so upset,' Bar said on the phone.

Not only was it not true, but it created more of the stress we were trying to avoid. The papers always exaggerate the money, it's very dehumanising. Bar was no longer as sanguine about the press. She didn't like the pressure. I put the phone down. 'I can't wait for her to leave,' I said to Matt, as I composed an email to the *Mail* with the right tone of denial.

'That's another goal you've missed!' said Matt. At least we beat Spurs 3–0, so not all bad. As the year ended, a new chapter was starting.

14

Goodbye Queen Vic, Hello Queen of Bingo

'The way you've treated everyone here all day is breathtaking,' the dresser said to Bar, as she was helping her out of her utterly fantastic Queen of Bingo outfit.

The woman was right on the money. Bar was old school. We had spent a long day filming in the beautifully restored Wilton's Music Hall. Despite still suffering from the tail end of bronchitis, Bar had delivered pose after pose for the photographer. Whatever was needed, or wanted, or expected, she did it. And then she made sure she had time for everyone on set. Anyone who wanted a photo, got one. She always had time for a chat or ten. I admired her so much for that. It didn't matter how many times I saw her doing it. The way she conducted herself never failed to amaze me, though it did mean it always took quite a long time to leave anywhere. Or arrive, for that matter.

'That was a long day, Bar. You feeling all right?' asked a producer.

'Well, I'm not exactly in a war zone!' she replied, batting their concerns aside.

EastEnders seemed never to be out of the press. Nor did Bar, to be fair. One article announced she was returning to the show in 2012, which was news to us. The whole pay cut issue was troubling a lot of the cast. We were good mates with many of them and would often have lunch or dinner. My advice was the same to all of them: if you can't accept the pay cut, you should leave; if you do stay, you have to do it with a good heart. It's a terrific job, and guaranteed work in a famously precarious business, so if you're going to stay, stay with good grace.

There was also the challenge of an approaching live episode that was making everyone, Bar included, nervous. All the actors were panicking. On the day, 19 February, one of the actresses jumped a page and in that split second there was terror, then Bar calmly stepped back into the section of dialogue they should have been in and continued to the end of the scene. That was where her experience came in.

There was a knock on the door. It was all systems go at the mews because we were getting ready for the premiere of *Alice in Wonderland*. In an interview with the *LA Times*, Tim Burton had described Bar as a national institution and said how lucky he'd been to have her in the film. 'I'm the lucky one,' Bar said, putting on her new royal-blue suit that had been tailored for the occasion by Stephen Williams. Even I was dressing up in my first custom-made suit. For once in my life I hadn't had to send my new trousers away to be taken up!

I opened the door, expecting hair and make-up, but instead there was Amy Winehouse, with an inebriated pop star called Kavana on her arm. Never wanting to turn her away we invited them in, but even Amy realised that the last thing we needed to be doing right then was listening to Kavana rambling on. Bless her, she tried to keep him in check and was definitely the more sensible of the two.

'Sorry, Babs,' she said. 'You've probably got other stuff to do.'

'Just today, love. Come back and see us another time, okay?'

'All right, Babs, see you.'

Every time she left the house we worried.

'Would you mind standing behind Barbara for the royal line-up,' said a production assistant. We were at the *Alice in Wonderland* premiere. I stepped back and watched Prince Charles come down the line, past Matt Lucas, Michael Sheen, Alan Rickman. Then he got to Bar and stopped for a chat like they were old mates. The prince and the showgirl . . . albeit now with a few years on the clock! Finally, as he was about to move on, he caught my eye.

'I hope you're keeping an eye on her,' he said, leaning around Bar.

Shortly afterwards she was presented with a TRIC lifetime achievement award by Anita Dobson. 'National institution, lifetime achievement,' said Bar. 'Do you think they're trying to tell me something?'

Jackpotjoy wanted the new advert to start running from 23 July but, although Bar would have finished filming *EastEnders* by then, she would still be on screen as Peggy for a couple of months. I was fairly certain that it wouldn't have the same impact if it launched concurrently. In the end Noel Hayden, owner of Jackpotjoy, agreed. 'It would look like Peggy Mitchell in a fancy dress, not Barbara Windsor, the Queen of Bingo,' he said. He agreed to hold the advert until September.

Meanwhile, Bar decided to do a short panto run in Bristol. She was excited. Her first love was theatre. 'There is nothing like being on a stage,' Bar said proudly at the first production meeting.

'It's *Dick Whittington*, Barbara,' said Terry Parsons, the renowned and very respected set and costume designer. 'And you'll be Fairy Babs.'

Sixty years since her first line, 'Here comes the baron', when she was just thirteen years old, playing a tiny tot on the end of a long line of kids in Aida Foster's annual pantomime at the Golders Green Hippodrome, here she was, preparing to star in her own panto as Fairy Bowbells (we called her Fairy Babs) a character that said it all and needed no introduction. Maybe Paul O'Grady got it wrong, I thought. If you snapped Bar in half, it would say, 'She's behind you!'

Amy Winehouse turned up at the mews again on my birthday, this time with her best friend Tyler. He was a lovely guy and of all the people she brought over, he was clearly the best influence and the person who most tried to take care of her. Barry took me to the Wolseley for lunch that day, but when I got home Amy and Tyler were there again.

'Sorry I haven't got you a present, Scotty,' Amy said. Instead she ripped a piece of paper from a magazine and scribbled on it: '*Dear Scotty, I owe you a run around Fred Perry for your birthday, Lots of love Amy xxx*'. I still have it and often look at her swirling writing and wonder why it had to end the way it did.

For, just over a year later, on 23 July 2011, Amy Winehouse was found dead at her home. We'd been snuggled in the back row of our local cinema, a favourite pastime of ours, and when I turned my phone back on there was a flurry of texts. We walked home in rare silence, full of sorrow that the kind, talented, sweet girl we had got to know would never arrive unannounced at our door again. To pay our respects we went to Southgate to see her parents sit shiva, the seven-day mourning process that is part of the Jewish faith and culture. It is designed to bring friends and family in to help the next of kin in their time of need and pain. People were quite surprised to see Barbara Windsor there because, of course, no one knew about Amy's intermittent visits. No one knew she liked to go through Peggy's lines with Bar. We never took photos. We never told anyone. It was all the more precious for it.

'What a waste of a great talent and a lovely girl,' said Babs, over and over, mystified by how such a young soul could go like that. There but for the grace of God, I thought, there but for the grace of God. It was devastatingly sad for everyone. I still shudder when I hear her voice float over the airwaves.

Our life of TV dinners alongside moments of high glamour continued. One night we went with Pam St Clement and Matt Lucas to see Debbie Reynolds in her one-woman show in the West End and we were lucky enough to meet her backstage afterwards. She was incredibly gracious and generous with her time.

A huge highlight was being invited to David Walliams's wedding to Lara Stone. There were famous faces everywhere and being sat with James and Julia Corden, Dale Winton, Matt Lucas, Alan Carr, David Bradley, Jonathan Ross and Rob and Clare Brydon made us feel very special and welcome. There were always moments you felt you had to pinch yourself; this was one of them.

During those last few months of *EastEnders* the storylines ratcheted up. Phil had a crack problem at the time and Peggy dared him to light the Molotov cocktail he'd made. Bar was knocked off her feet in one of the explosion takes and fell on Steve. It was constant night-filming and Bar was frequently getting home at 3am. In the end we limped to the finishing line, and when we got there it was tough.

I was clearing out Bar's dressing room, when she walked in and burst into tears. 'It's going to be okay, Bar,' I said, fervently wishing and hoping that was true.

'I love this show so much,' she said, sobbing. 'It's the very best show ever. What am I going to do, Scott?'

July 16th was Bar's last day filming. I went to the studio with her that day as they were laying on farewell drinks and a barbecue. Everyone went to the lot and applauded her as she walked out. She couldn't keep the emotions at bay. Every time I looked at her, she was crying, and so were most people in the room.

The producer John Yorke read a wonderful tribute. It was written for Queen Victoria after her death, the real one, but he said if you swap Queen Victoria for Peggy, and Great Britain for the Queen Vic, it was an absolutely fitting tribute to Barbara.

'To write the life of Queen Victoria is to relate the history of Great Britain during a period of great events, manifold changes, and unexampled national prosperity. No Queen in the annals of our history can compare with that of the late Sovereign; and to her, whose personal influence helped in a large measure to make this epoch one that will be ever gratefully remembered, we owe more than to any of our former Kings and Queens.'

People were openly crying now. He went on to say her departure would leave a void in the show. 'You will be greatly missed in every way,' he said. Bar cried even harder.

I knew that was true, she was so much more than a colleague. Looking around the room I found myself counting into double digits the truly wonderful friends we had made over the years, many of whom would step up in unimaginable ways in the years to come.

We packed up the car with her many gifts, including an actual Queen Vic bust, which still sits proudly in our living room, and drove home together, knowing the curtain had finally come down on the matriarch of Albert Square. I think, secretly, both of us were still praying it was the right thing to do.

Not only had Bar left a void in the show, the show had left a void in her, so it was good for both of us to be busy, and one of the first meetings we had was with the Mayor of London's office about becoming involved with Team London. Boris Johnson and Bar had met in 2009 when he'd done a brilliant walk-on cameo in *EastEnders*. Now he was offering her a voluntary role to support neglected or under-represented communities in London.

'You'd be a great asset,' Boris said, with a tiny flicker of humour. Cue the Sid James laugh . . . This was politics and showbiz. The Big Lunch had been launched the previous year by Tim Smit, founder of the Eden Project, to reignite community spirit with anything as small as a cup of tea over the garden fence to full street parties. Boris Johnson was now pushing the project into its second year with a London launch in Tufnell Park. By coincidence, it was on the street where Damian Lewis and Helen McCrory lived and they came out with their kids. Boris and Barbara made a very funny couple – infectious, larger-than-life characters with matching bleach-blond hair and wicked sense of humour. It was a happy Sunday. Fancy cakes, gallons of tea, egg sandwiches and a lot of chat . . . it suited Bar down to the ground and she was delighted to be a part of it. I watched her chat to everyone she met, as usual, and noticed one woman shaking with the emotion of talking to her. I saw this many times, the impact my wife had on people ran deep. I think she took them back to times and places in their own lives that triggered powerful memories, perhaps of people now gone. It was always striking to see.

On 10 September 2010 Bar's last episode on *EastEnders* aired. The closing scene saw Peggy walking past a burnt-out pub, sad but resolved; walking into an unknown future with one glance back at all that had been before. It felt very fitting and Bar had made sure everything was perfect, right down to including a last scene at the dry-cleaner's to pick up her one surviving outfit, which gave her the added benefit of a final scene with June. She even ensured the wig she wore made it clear that Peggy had done what she could with her hair, while it was still a bit of a mess. It was really poignant and beautifully handled. As the closing credits rolled, the production team added a specially written edition of the theme tune called 'Peggy's Theme', which was softly orchestrated and moving. Bye bye, Peggy, Queen of Albert Square.

We watched it together and cried. Then we turned over to *Coronation Street* and, in the first ad break, up popped Bar, fresh as a daisy and bedecked in jewels as the Queen of Bingo – Babs was back and the Jackpotjoy website crashed from the surge in visits. Everyone agreed we'd been right about the timing, which made me happy since my number one priority was taking care of Bar.

And after that the offers and invites came in thick and fast. Jackpotjoy signed her up for another year, with an increase in salary, and we swanned about going from book and magazine launches to film premieres. Café de Paris, Grosvenor Place, wherever we went we were blinded by camera flashes. By the time we came to filming *Piers Morgan's Life Stories*, we were both confident we'd made the right decision and, for the first time in years, Bar had energy to spare. For a little bit of time there, we hit the sweet spot.

She did a cracking job with Piers. She was on great form. Sending herself up as usual, painfully honest as ever. 'How would you like to be remembered?' Piers asked, as the interview came to a close. 'Best cleavage, best laugh . . .?'

'No,' she replied, serious for once. 'I'd like them to say, "She was a good bird."' It was the first time the audience had stood up in unison.

Shortly after that she was asked to host the Lionel Bart special edition of *Friday Night is Music Night*. It was full of great acts singing Lionel's best numbers: Russ Abbot, Bradley Walsh, Bernard Cribbins, Emma Barton, Sam Womack, Lee Mead. But the moment Bar got up to sing the last part of 'Sparrows Can't Sing', I swear Hackney Empire fell silent and a collective shiver went through the audience. It was one of those special, unforgettable, theatrical moments.

From reverence to a roasting on Jimmy Carr's *A Comedy Roast*. 'I don't like this,' said Alan Carr, 'roasting Barbara Windsor is like being told to kick a puppy.' But he needn't have worried, Bar took it all in good spirits, of course. She had awards being presented to her left, right and centre. There was the Lord Delfont Outstanding Contribution to Showbiz Award at the Variety Club Awards, presented by Bill Kenwright, which was swiftly followed by the *Sun*'s Spirit of London Award. But, by far the most fun, and funniest event, was the National Panto Launch Day at the Piccadilly Theatre. David Hasselhoff, the

Hoff, dressed as Hook threatening Babs, as Fairy Bowbells, has got to be the most ridiculous photo of all time.

But with the highs, as ever, come the lows. Bar kept losing people she loved. The saddest for her that year was Sue Carroll, a proper powerhouse of a journalist from way back. She suffered a stroke after fighting cancer and was now very frail. She was staying with a mutual friend and, when we visited, Bar tried to help her do her rehabilitation exercises, but it was a struggle. Sue had been part of our life for a long time and the professional had crossed over into the personal. Bar was hit hard when we left Sue's house, because, once again, it felt like a farewell and they were getting unnervingly frequent.

To our great delight, Paul O'Grady brought Sue Carroll to the *Daily Mirror* Pride of Britain awards. The famous faces were there but only to honour the true stars – the men and women of the public who'd shown extraordinary compassion, grit, determination and resilience. Sue embodied the entire event, in a wheelchair but dressed up and looking great, facing death with a stoical smile. I often wondered if, faced with that level of challenges, I could be as brave.

'I keep forgetting my lines,' Bar said, when she called me from the rehearsal room ahead of her panto in Bristol.

'You'll be okay once you're here, rehearsing onstage,' I said.

But the thing was, this wasn't the first time, and it wouldn't be the last. It was a bit concerning because she used to be so good with her lines.

I had travelled ahead to Bristol to turn our suite into a winter wonderland as a Christmas surprise for Bar. She walked in and burst into tears. 'That is the nicest thing anyone has ever done for me,' she cried. I doubted it was, but she was really moved.

But things didn't get easier once in Bristol. In fact, I saw her behave in a way I hadn't seen in a very long time. She got angry about something in the opening dance scene and stormed out. We talked and she settled, but it felt a bit odd. Not her.

Once the show was up and running, she relaxed and started to enjoy it. Every night kids were brought onstage holding hands. One night one of those kids was Matt Lucas, he was a real sport! And Bar was back to signing autographs every night at the stage door, even in temperatures of minus twelve, then falling into bed, exhausted but happy. The Christmas Eve performance marked her sixtieth anniversary of life in showbiz and at the end of the show, Andy Ford, the excellent local comic, and Eric Potts, the Dame in the panto, presented Bar with flowers onstage and the audience rose to their feet. Bar relished the applause and remembered with gratitude how lucky she was to work in an industry she loved.

As things had got busier towards the end of the year, I'd started going to my AA meetings less frequently. I wasn't worried. I no longer feared what would happen if I didn't go. In fact, at a few of the many events we went to I saw people close to the state I used to get into and I watched with relief that it wasn't me any more. Perhaps all we need to do is see our drunk selves through sober eyes.

I was always told AA was a bridge to normal living without alcohol. Well, I had done nine solid years and many, many meetings, and I felt that the compulsion to drink had gone. I knew some old-timers said it was not a good idea to distance yourself from the fellowship, but there was another school of thought that everyone had a different journey. The friends I had made were still my friends. But the thing was, I had another reason to pull back from the meetings. I was quietly concerned about Bar's health and that was something I couldn't share in meetings.

AA is a forum that asks for honesty, and I had in the past shared things about my wife when there were a hundred unvetted people in a meeting. But this was different. These were confidences I could not break, so I chose to see a therapist in a one-to-one setting rather than risk a leak. I am not saying there would have been one, but my fear of it happening would have held me back from honestly sharing and I didn't want to be there and not participate. I will always hold AA in the highest regard. It helped save my life and for that I will always be grateful.

15

Babs Bombs Hollywood!

After appearing in the BBC comedy series *Come Fly with Me* with our good friends Matt Lucas and David Walliams, I was happy to be taking Bar away. We flew to Barbados for sun, sea and . . . rest.

'You all right, Bar?'

'What?'

'You seem a bit low.' I said. 'Are you feeling okay?'

'Tired, I guess,' she replied.

It was easy to put it down to tiredness or age, but really it wasn't that. She seemed distant, withdrawn, and that wasn't like her. She would come alive for all the community events we were doing with Mayor Johnson when we got back home, culminating in the big one for the royal wedding, of Prince William and Catherine, which we followed with another one in Downing Street. At that event even the No. 10 armed police insisted on having pictures taken with Bar. I had now met David and Samantha Cameron, Prince Charles, John Major, Boris Johnson, not to mention a myriad of showbiz stars all because of the lady smiling with the armed No. 10 coppers.

'I'm the lucky one,' I told her, over and over. Sometimes she grinned at me, sometimes I would catch a fleeting absence.

'What are you thinking about?' I'd often ask.

'Nothing,' she'd reply.

But when she couldn't shift the jet lag, I booked her into the doctor's. The tests came back with nothing to be alarmed about, but I couldn't stop thinking that she didn't look well. No one else would have known a thing, but for me it was the beginning of living in a twilight zone. I had no one to confide in and I couldn't discuss my worries with Bar because I didn't want to alarm her. All I could do was help her pick and choose jobs so she didn't tire herself out. She loved sitting in for Elaine Paige's Radio 2 show, and she turned on the charm for BoJo's projects, but when it was just the two of us . . . she often fell quiet and despondent.

'Just a bit tired,' she'd say. That's what we both fell back on. Tiredness. But I knew deep down it wasn't just that.

'I don't feel I'm doing nearly enough for the money,' said Bar, as we headed off to a special garden party at Ragley Hall, near Stratford-upon-Avon, for Jackpotjoy.

'Bar, you've worked sixty years to get this gig, enjoy it.'

'I feel so guilty,' she said.

We were shown through the fairground attractions to a special marquee full of selected bingo players. 'Excuse me,' said one woman. 'Are you Barbara Windsor's husband?'

That's nice, I thought. I tended to be overlooked most of the time. 'I am,' I replied proudly.

'Oh,' she said, turning away. 'I thought he was younger than that!'

I nearly spat out my water.

'Would you like us to unpack your luggage, Ms Windsor?'

Bar and I exchanged impish grins. This was one of our favourite routines.

'No thank you,' said Bar. 'I don't want some stranger rummaging through my underwear.'

'Why? It's never stopped you in the past!!' I replied. Bar filled the reception area with her *Carry On* giggle and I would respond with my Sid James laugh. I have no idea what the hotel manager of the Wynn Towers in Las Vegas thought but it sure amused us. We were shown into the most ridiculous suite with its own massage room. What were we, two tiny tots, going to do in this massive place. Neither of us gambled. We were there courtesy of Jackpotjoy and when the boss and his girlfriend flew out we were able to thank them by taking them to see Elton John in concert.

It was very exciting. We were met by his tour manager and taken to the green room, along with Elton's entourage. And then within ten minutes of his phenomenal show ending, we were taken to Elton's dressing room where the five of us had a chat.

'So how long have you been sober?' Elton asked me.

'Nine years.'

'And how are you doing?' Only a recovering alcoholic knows you are always in recovery.

'Grateful not to be a drunk.'

He was charming to our guests too. He invited Barbara and me to his apartment the next day and when we arrived we were taken in through a private entrance. The nanny brought baby Zachary to meet us; a nine-month-old bundle of joy.

'What a nosh,' Bar said, perhaps a little wistful now.

'You'd have been a great mother,' I said.

'I'd have been so bloody strict!' she replied.

Hard to top that, but we managed it when we took Biggins and his partner Neil Sinclair to Venice, our treat. When we got to the hotel we discovered that Biggins and Neil had a lovely big room, and Bar and I had a shoebox. Of course, Biggins being . . . well, Biggins found the whole thing hilarious and offered to swap.

'No way, this will suffice for us two munchkins,' we insisted, but I instantly sent Biggins a text with a picture of a contortionist cramped in a small box, with a note saying: 'Here's Barbara in our bathroom getting ready to go out tonight.'

That set the tone for what would be a fabulous five days of laughter and ice cream on a busy tourist trail. I think we only saw a tiny number of the famous landmarks because we were constantly stopped by British tourists abroad. Biggins and Babs were a brilliant double act and they hammed it up for everyone. She looked fabulous and in every photo oozes star appeal, but then when we went to Dubai not long after, there were two days when she didn't leave our room at all.

'Not feeling up to it, love, you go on,' she said.

I worried privately, then one day when she was doing a Q&A for a small Sky project, I noticed she looked a bit awkward and uncomfortable. I could almost answer questions for her by now, so I knew she wasn't coming back as quickly as she usually did. Something was not right. She was anxious. I kept watching, worried now, and sent her for more tests, but they also came back okay. Maybe I'm being a bit overprotective, I thought, because then just as quickly she would snap back into full Babs mode. ''Ello darlin's, we are here for a brilliant cause and you are all brilliant for supporting it . . .'

It was the NHS breast screening campaign and my wife was giving it her all. 'Now some people would say my breasts are my greatest assets. But I will tell you, ladies, we all love our best assets, don't we, girls? Who here remembers *Carry On Camping*?' There was a big shout from the crowd.

'We were the good girls of Chayste Place finishing school on a camping trip. We were outside doing an exercise class . . .' And she was off. The story of the fishing line, being dragged through the mud, and then the flash of nipple that had controllers scratching their heads . . . And there it was, the *Carry On* giggle.

'Thank you so much, Barbara,' said one of the organisers when we went to sit down and take stock.

'Please, call me Babs. It's been a wonderful event . . .' She paused, went quiet. I watched her disappear into her thoughts.

'Would you like a cup of tea?' the organiser asked.

Bar turned and looked at the woman as if she hadn't seen her before.

'Bar, shall we head home?' I said.

'Thank you so much. It's been a wonderful event,' she said again. 'They all work so hard in the NHS, so hard . . . Sorry, what did you ask me?'

In early February 2012 we were at Headley Court, near Epsom in Surrey, surrounded by servicemen and women who'd come back from Afghanistan with life-changing injuries. Bar was given a hero's welcome. 'Don't be daft,' she said. 'I've done nothing. You're the real heroes. I've come here to thank you, all of you. You're the best of British and I am proud of each and every one of you.'

'That was a long day,' I said to Bar when we got back home after lunch in the Officers' Mess and a training session in the gym.

She looked up at me. 'What was?'

'Seeing all those brave people who'd lost their legs. My God, it makes you think.'

She blinked at me a few times.

'You okay, Bar?'

'I'm so lucky to have you,' she said.

'I'm the lucky one.'

I was starting to get really worried, but the only person I could talk to about my private fear was my therapist, Ashley Conway. 'You need Dr Angus Kennedy,' he said. 'He's a brilliant neurologist. Make an appointment today.'

Bar and I sat in the waiting room outside Dr Kennedy's office in the Lister Hospital. Opposite, a couple sat either side of an older lady. The couple were talking quietly across the lady while she stared off into the distance with a terrifyingly familiar faraway look. I'd seen that look. I knew that look. Panic rose from the pit of my stomach and in that moment I knew. I left Bar with Dr Kennedy so they could do some one-to-one tests.

'Barbara did really well,' he said when I went back in. Before I could feel any relief, he went on. 'I would like to do some further tests, but I'm not worried about anything now.'

'What sort of tests?'

'A simple scan and some blood tests. Nothing to worry about now.'

He made it sound as if there was nothing urgent to worry about, but in the car on the way home Bar became more anxious. 'Do you think there is something wrong with my brain?'

'I think you've exhausted your brain, learning all those lines for all those years.' I was hoping to reassure her, but I had spent every minute of most days with her for the last twenty years and I knew something was wrong. When we went back to Dr Kennedy he seemed pleased with the test results and said he would monitor her every six months. I was relieved, nothing was going to happen quickly, but I also knew something was going to happen. Even if Bar didn't. Or wouldn't.

'Look after yourself,' Dr Kennedy said. 'Perhaps take on a little less.'

How many doctors had I heard say that?

The next six months continued mostly as normal, as I tried to convince myself that Dr Kennedy was right and that I had been worrying unduly, as ever. We went from being surrounded by fifty Boy Scouts in the quadrant of Buckingham Palace to a packed pub in Bermondsey for Freddie Foreman's birthday. There was more work with Jackpotjoy, Radio 2 and as much charity work as Bar had the energy for. It wasn't the schedule of earlier days, but it was still quite a lot for a 75-year-old woman. Others were not doing so well.

'Here they are,' said Victor Spinetti, when we went to see him in hospital in Monmouth, 'Tarzan and fucking Jane.' He had cancer. He was looking better than we feared, but was high on drugs. That amount of morphine meant the end was near. He was a bit confused but still had the philosophical outlook on life that I remembered him for. It was hard saying goodbye to another lifelong friend. Four days later his sister called to say he had died. Another great, gone. Bar was very sad.

'We're so lucky to have our health,' she said.

Seeing Bar leap about during the London 2012 Olympics as she, along with the rest of the country, watched 'Super Saturday', punching her fist as Mo Farah took gold, once again made me rethink. She was as full of beans as ever. On her feet, pink with the exertion. Then, during the Paralympics, Bar and Boris, the blonde bombshells, tried to play sitting volleyball. Not sure either of them were real athletes.

After another decent break in Dubai, Bar took on some filming for Comic Relief in conjunction with Jackpotjoy.

'It's going to be centred around kung fu,' explained the production team.

'As long as you don't expect Bar to do difficult physical routines in her bingo outfit!' I said.

Despite reassurances, on set that is precisely what happened and Barbara was asked to do the action with a prop over and over again. Apparently, she couldn't get it right. 'Scott, you should get over here,' said Ian McIntosh, her alternative make-up artist. 'She got shouted at and she's really upset. No one knew where to look.'

The Bar of old would have given as good she got, but not now. She was more timid, less sure of herself and simply not as strong. It felt like a reversal of sorts was taking place. But it was confusing to see because it wasn't linear.

'Babs! Babs!' the paps called out. Bar, looking spectacular on the red carpet going into the opening night of the stage show of *Charlie and the Chocolate Factory*, found herself alongside Sarah Jessica Parker and Uma Thurman.

The British press were making a fuss of her and Bar was loving it. These two leggy Hollywood superstars were trying to work out why this tiny elderly lady was getting all the flashes.

'Can I have a picture with the three of you ladies?' asked one of the paps. Suddenly all the camera lenses pointed towards them so they couldn't say no. Uma and Jessica linked arms with each other and sort of blocked Barbara out. But Bar was having none of it and popped out from behind Uma Thurman's shoulders, pulling a funny face.

'BABS PHOTOBOMBS HOLLYWOOD!' said the headlines the next day.

I was upset. 'As if you ever would.'

'Honestly, Scott. Who gives a fuck?' said Bar. 'You think that's annoying? I met three people at the Robbie Williams concert who told me they'd just met my son!'

It was true. Some bloke had been going around saying he was Bar's son. 'Maybe they thought I was your son?' I said. 'It's happened enough times before.'

'You look more my age these days!' she chuckled. She could still pack a punch. We fell about laughing.

Bar had been asked back to do an episode for *EastEnders*, and though she was a bit disappointed it was only one, I was relieved. I read the script and spent the day worrying whether Bar could retain the lines. Dr Kennedy reassured me it was good for her.

'I tripped up a few times,' she said, when she called me. 'But I got through it.'

'It's not surprising,' I said. 'You're just out of practice.' But I worried that it might be something more. 'How did it feel being back?'

'It was lovely seeing everyone, but . . . I don't have a burning desire to go back. I don't need to go back.'

Thank God. I knew it was good to keep her brain working, but life was easier when she wasn't being exposed to the changes in her abilities.

For Bar's birthday in 2013 we just went for dinner with a few close friends, but I kept noticing brief moments when she looked around the table, anxious and lost. Then she would seek me out, see me looking at her and relax, then carry on as normal, as if reassured. I recognised that sensation immediately, I'd been feeling it my whole life, but it was out of character for Bar to be uneasy. If anyone else noticed that night, they didn't say.

A slower pace suited Bar better now. We would often walk to Regent's Park and just sit and watch people. We would make up stories about the people walking by.

'She's a Russian spy who infiltrated the British aristocracy—'

'And is now the mistress of the US ambassador . . .'

'That man used to be the greatest flamenco dancer—'

'He taught Princess Margaret to dance . . .'

It was a fun, silly game, but it also meant we could chat, and laugh, as we always had without raising questions that might set off Bar's increasing anxiety. I thought maybe it was because she hadn't been sleeping well, so we went back to the doctor's and changed her pills. I put it down to sleeplessness because that was easier than the alternative. In truth, her memory was going.

Tiredness made it worse, though, I was sure of that. She'd been up early to do *Daybreak* to promote her imminent return to Albert Square, then we went to the Black Cat pub in Camden to do some filming for the Amy Winehouse Foundation, a charity set up by Amy's father Mitch to support and inspire young people in her memory. It was dimly lit and there was no autocue.

'Barbara, we've written a few lines for you to say, if you wouldn't mind.'

She looked at me, a bit panicked. It was just a couple of sentences. She could have done it standing on her head a few months ago. I knew how much Bar wanted to support the foundation and also how important keeping active was for her health. But that day she fluffed the lines. So a runner wrote out the words on a card and held it up for her to read. But the room was dark and Bar was getting increasingly anxious, which made the situation worse. My stomach twisted watching her clawing her way through these few lines. I felt terrible for her and decided there and then that having an autocue was going to be a deal-breaker from now on. I took my exhausted wife home. She was quiet on the journey.

'You've changed your pills,' I said to her. 'They're bound to make you feel a bit . . .' – I was always trying to alleviate her worries, and maybe my own – 'foggy.'

'So how about getting Barbara back full-time?' asked the *EastEnders* producer Dominic Treadwell-Collins. I was having a meeting with him about getting my new client Lacey Turner back to *EastEnders* playing Stacey Slater along with a full series of *Our Girl* which the BBC also wanted.

'We'll see,' I said. I was wary after what had happened at the pub. I didn't want to commit her to something she wasn't able to do, but I also couldn't tell anyone what was going on. I didn't even know myself.

When her scenes were aired there wasn't an inkling of difficulty in her performance. They were strong and moving, all this despite being told by another actor that she'd struggled. I had three clients in the show at that time, Lacey, Steve and now June, who'd exhausted herself writing a memoir and wanted someone else to manage the employment side of things. They were friends as well as clients, that's how I've always worked, and it reassured me knowing there were good people on set keeping an eye out. By now Jessie and Bar were good friends too and being there felt like being with family to Bar. All this gave me hope. I was willing to believe it would all be okay.

'Bar, another email has come in saying how much you're missed,' I shouted out to her. 'And another saying how good you were.'

'You're just biased, you silly sod,' she replied, but she was smiling.

For a while now Bar, Barry and I had made an annual trip to New York to take in as many shows as we could fit in. This year our visit marked the beginning of a period of ill health. Not just Bar's, but my dad's too. On our second day in the Big Apple, Bar was bent double in agony, barely able to leave the bathroom. The doctor suggested it might be food poisoning and ordered antibiotics. Barry continued the trip without us, while we traipsed round medical centres seeing specialists, getting scans, X-rays and a procedure that involved a general anaesthetic. 'Hope you have medical insurance,' said a nurse, just as Bar was going under.

Thank God we did. I just wanted to get her home, but until they gave her the all clear to fly, we were stuck in a hotel room with her in pain. She got stronger once we were home, but then I received the news that my father was having trouble swallowing. I cancelled everything and made doctor's appointments with Bar's usual team, then went to see Dad. He'd started choking when he tried to swallow; it was awful to watch. Although he tried to shrug it off, I was worried about them both. To see two such strong characters appear so vulnerable was hard to bear.

'I know who Barbara Windsor is. Everyone knows who Barbara Windsor is.' Barbara heard that a lot, but not usually from Prince William. It was the launch of the Poppy Appeal, the Royal British Legion's annual fundraising campaign, and she went from filming live in Covent Garden for *Daybreak* to visiting No. 10 to meet David Cameron, and then finally William and Kate, the Duke and Duchess of Cambridge. All in a day's work for Bar. Charity work lifted her spirits. It is one of the greatest levellers and was a welcome distraction from everything else we had going on. I think one of my fondest memories is at another charity event seeing Bar and Camilla, the Duchess of Cornwall, shrieking with laughter, closing deals on ICAP Charity Day. They raised a staggering amount of money.

By the end of the year Dad had been diagnosed with myasthenia gravis, a chronic neuromuscular disorder. Although there was nothing in his throat, they didn't want to take the chance of him choking to death. He was hospitalised. Then he was intubated. It broke my heart seeing my lovely dad, my hero, so scared. I had never seen him scared before. It reduced me to tears. Sometimes Bar came with me to visit him in hospital, but the longer he stayed, the worse his mood got, so I started to leave her at home in London.

'Bar, I'm home,' I called out as I got back after a bad visit.

She emerged from the sitting room, looked at me blankly, then returned to the sofa. Then she got back up to watch me in the kitchen but didn't ask me a word about my dad. She appeared oddly disorientated for a person so at home being at home. It gave me a very uneasy feeling.

I was not looking forward to Christmas but we set off for the hospital to deliver presents to Dad and fake some seasonal cheer. Bar went round every single patient, sat down and had a chat. It was truly remarkable to watch; this diminutive Mother Christmas cheered everybody up, even me, because seeing her on form was the only thing I wanted for Christmas.

16

Seesaw

I could hear her crying as I walked up the stairs. She was sitting on our bed, her head in her hands. 'What is it, Bar?'

She just shook her head and cried. It is one thing forgetting the odd thing, it was quite another *knowing* you were forgetting things. She didn't forget she was forgetting and it terrified her. There was nothing I could do or say, so we went back to Dr Kennedy and, as soon as she sat down in his room, she burst into tears again.

'We'll do some more scans, Barbara, to put your mind at rest. Make sure we know what's going on. There are other tests and good medication these days. Don't worry, we will get on top of it.'

It was no good telling me not to worry. I felt for her, for us, and, if I'm being totally honest, for me too. Then a charity event for disabled children run by London cabbies seemed to snap her out of it. The event was loud, hectic and fun, and she loved it. Focusing on other people helped and I decided we should do as much of that as we could. It was good for her, for us, for me.

'*Listen with Mother.*'
  '*Housewives' Choice.*'
  '*Family Favourites.*'

Elton and Bar were competing over how many radio shows from their childhood they could remember. She was beating him. She had a list as long as the table we were sitting at – which was long! Our host, Evgeny Lebedev, the owner of the *Evening Standard*, had invited us to dinner along with Elton John and David Furnish, Liz Hurley, Jasper Conran, Janet Street-Porter, Hugh Grant, Keira Knightley, Felicity Jones, Nigella Lawson, Graham Norton and Harry Enfield. It was quite a table.

I drew comfort from that night as we drove to the imaging centre in Queen Square for the first follow-up brain scan. Bar was distressed and it took a lot to coax her into the gown. 'It's just to rule stuff out,' I kept telling her.

I'm not sure either of us believed it. The scan was loud and cramped, as scans are, and she was understandably tearful on the way home. The following day a neurologist arrived at the mews and did three hours of further tests with Bar. I went upstairs to work, but before she left we had a quick chat. 'Scott, it's clear there are some significant memory problems. I can't tell you anything specific at the moment, but I will go through everything with Dr Kennedy.'

Bar was utterly drained. I switched on the telly and we sat quietly, absorbing little, lost in our own thoughts and fears.

Incredibly, the result of the scan showed no significant change from a couple of years ago. 'That's great news, Bar,' I said.

'It is,' she replied.

'What a relief. It's better than the alternative.'

We were going through the motions together, but the relief was thin and our positivity felt precarious. Things weren't right and we both knew it. We thought it best to write to Dominic and tell him Bar would not be returning to Albert Square, and then I booked her in for the lumbar puncture that Dr Kennedy had recommended.

'Peggy!' screamed a nurse as we came out of the lift on the fifteenth floor of the hospital. She headed over to reception. 'It's Barbara Windsor!' she said loudly. So much for patient confidentiality. Barbara didn't mind, people responded to her like that all the time. She smiled sweetly, but behind the smile I could see fear. The lumbar puncture was at 3pm, then poor Bar had to lie flat, not moving, until 6pm.

The seesaw tilted again. Bar was having a meeting with UK Gold about a *Carry On* project and she was on fire. ''Course everything had a double entendre,' she said. 'Even in *Carry On Henry*, I played

Bettina of Bristol, and Bristol, as you may know, is slang for breasts. I was Henry's mistress and I say to the Queen . . .' – Bar did a full curtsy – 'Your Majesty, it is a great honour. The King has done me.'

'Sid is frantically waving his arms . . .' At this point she switched to Sid James's voice, which she delivered perfectly. '"No, no, no," he says, "there's no full stop."' The anecdote sank in. Bar waited and then everyone started laughing. No full stop. Listening to her, even I forgot about her waning memory. Those nine films made in the sixties were easier for her to recall than the breakfast we'd eaten two hours earlier.

After our meeting with UK Gold, we went back to the Defence Medical Rehabilitation Centre, at Headley Court, for a *Carry On*-themed evening in the new state-of-the-art MediCinema. Bar did a Q&A and then handed out popcorn like she was an usherette.

'My dad was in the Eighth Army in World War Two,' she said, immediately linking herself to the injured men and women before her. 'I feel a special connection to our armed forces. You are the bravest people I have ever met.'

'Who was the best of them?' asked one soldier. He looked about twelve to me, his wheelchair just beside him. Bar breezed up to this young man, a double amputee, without a second glance.

'Sid was the head honcho, but in my opinion Charles Hawtrey was the comic genius. He was also the most tragic figure in the gang.'

I was looking at all these young men and women with life-changing injuries, thinking, *Please don't tell them that Charles Hawtrey was tragic*. His wounds were self-inflicted, whereas these kids had suffered at the hands of others for the greater good. I almost wished she'd start telling the Fenella Fielding story. Once again, Bar proved me wrong, her enthusiasm for the story won out and everyone loved her. They always did.

'If anyone asked him for an autograph, instead of getting his signature "Oooh, hellloooo", he'd take the paper, rip it up and tell the person to eff off.

'Sid would play poker during the breaks. Hattie would do the crossword. And Charles would sit alone and drink, sometimes out of a teapot. I offered him a bucket once, when it was clear he was about to be sick. He told me to eff off too. "You're always trying to be so kind and good to everyone."' Her imitation of him was perfect too.

'You knew when he'd really tied one on because he'd come to work with gallons of R. White's lemonade. Deep down I think he was an exceptionally talented comic actor and felt a bit wasted being typecast in the *Carry On* films. But you had to be good to be in those films. Never more than two takes. Six weeks to film, all our own stunts. You had to be hardy to deal with all of that.

'He brought his mum to work. She had dementia, poor love, and he'd lock her into his dressing room while he was on set. One day he forgot to lock the door. She was found in another studio asking Sir John Gielgud if he had seen her son because he hadn't made it back from school in time for tea.' Of all the stories to tell . . .

'Barbara. Scott. I am sorry to tell you . . .' It was 5pm on 22 April 2014, the day that changed the rest of our lives. 'It's Alzheimer's.'

Barbara burst into tears, but almost immediately inhaled them back in, reached over with her little hand and looked at me. 'I'm sorry, Scott.'

Heartbroken is what I felt in that instant. 'It's okay, it will be okay.'

'I will put you on specific medication, Barbara, which will slow the progression down, but I would like to tell you both that now is the time to put your affairs in order. This disease is unpredictable, so act now while you are in such a strong place.'

We nodded but I don't think it had even begun to sink in.

'You should keep working as long as you can. Don't make any radical changes,' Dr Kennedy said. 'In fact, doing what is familiar to you will help. For you, that's working. Just choose carefully and don't get overtired. Balance is the key.'

Alzheimer's. The word kept ricocheting around my mind. Alzheimer's . . . How was I supposed to balance Alzheimer's and showbiz?

Bar led the charge. The following night she was at Cadogan Hall hosting a concert for the Coldstream Guards. Every time she came onstage she lit up the auditorium and charmed the audience. Not a hint of confusion or disorientation. Not a hint of fear. She really was a remarkable woman.

Eight days after the diagnosis I made an appointment to see Dr Kennedy alone. I walked through Hyde Park thinking about all the questions I wanted to ask him, but when I sat down opposite him all I could do was cry.

'I'm really scared about what happens now.'

'Nothing will happen fast,' he said. 'You may begin to notice some disorientation. She might not know where she is.'

'I'm scared that one day she won't know who she is or what she's achieved.'

'It's recent memory that goes first. We are nowhere near that yet.'

'But it might happen?'

'It's a bit different for everyone.'

'Will she know me?'

'Scott, while that is a possibility with this disease, it could take years to get to that point. The two of you must try to enjoy what you have as long as you have it. There is no timeline.'

'What do I do to help her?'

'You support her by being there. And I will support you by being here. Any questions, any worries, I'm here.' He was the greatest support and friend right up to the end.

I took Bar to our lawyer and we updated our wills. Then I left Bar alone while she talked them through her last wishes. After dropping her home, I went alone to the pharmacy to collect her new pills for Alzheimer's. They knew what drugs they were handing over and the pharmacist took me downstairs for a chat. They were extraordinarily compassionate and I remain grateful to them.

I felt like everywhere we went we were being reminded of life passing us by, but the hardest was watching Jessie Wallace and Gary Kemp in a revival of *Fings Ain't Wot They Used T'Be* at Stratford East. Although everyone was happy to see Bar, it was incredibly emotional for her. Frank Norman had originally written it as a play, but Joan, Babs's Joan, had asked Lionel Bart to add music and lyrics. In 1960 Bar had performed in the same show Jessie Wallace was now appearing in, about a period that Bar personally inhabited in the fifties; the bars, the pimps, the bent coppers, the prostitutes. These are people she knew the first time round, yet all around her people were telling her how much they missed Peggy and Kat. Sixty years, compressed into one night. No wonder she looked overwhelmed at times.

''Course we're going to New York,' said Bar.

I was remembering how hard it was when she was ill the last time. 'Do you think you'll be okay to travel? It's quite an intense trip.'

'Why wouldn't I be?'

I should have stopped then. 'You're still adjusting to your medication. What if something happens in New York?'

'Like what?'

'You've been feeling a bit dizzy and a bit sick.'

'I'll be fine by the time we go.'

'What if you get a bit . . .' – forgetful, disorientated, confused, upset – 'lost.'

'Why would I get lost? You'll be there.'

I was trying to have a conversation about her deteriorating memory, but it wasn't going well. 'But it might get harder if you're in a new place.'

'New place? I was working in New York before you were born. I am fine. Stop making me feel worse and don't you go telling anyone neither, making out I'm not well. I'm fine!'

She was defensive and I was learning on my feet. Needless to say, I did not always get it right. I cancelled everything in the diary for the next two weeks to allow the side-effects to settle.

It didn't take two weeks. It took months. At first, I noticed she started tossing and turning at night. Then muttering. Then halfway through June the vivid dreams she was having became sweat-inducing nightmares. Her screams woke me up and then I would force her awake and she would cling to me, scared and confused and exhausted. I lay next to her, holding her hand. 'It's okay, Bar, it's just a dream.'

But it wasn't really. Dr Kennedy introduced a new pill for the nights, as he tried to find the right balance to suppress the anxiety which was building and decelerate the brain disease, without crashing her heart rate and making her so light-headed she would appear vacant. There were frequent changes to her meds: anti-this, anti-that, sleeping pills, patches, back to pills – it was a Molotov cocktail of meds. I changed the patches and it became a daily hurdle finding new skin because she reacted badly to them.

To make it more fun, I would introduce myself as a new doctor every time with a new silly name. Dr Nookey, eat your heart out. 'All your doctors sound the same,' she said, giggling. She was giving critiques on my doctors.

When we ran out of skin, we had to go back to pills. It was easy to feel impatient, but I had to remind myself we were dealing with the brain and this fine-tuning of an ever-changing disease was where we were at now.

'Best-case scenario?' I asked Dr Kennedy one day.

'Maybe an eighteen-month reprieve, possibly two years if we're lucky. But, Scott, we can only slow it down; we cannot reverse it and we cannot cure it. Do you understand that?'

Bar might have protected herself with a layer of denial, but I was beginning to see clearly what lay ahead.

'She's in a good place now. I suggest you get away, have a break.' So we went to Majorca. My sponsor Ian and his wife Bev stayed nearby, which was nice for me. I appreciated their company and Bar always reacted well to other people. Ever the inveterate performer.

Peggy was not happy to discover her nemesis Sharon had her claws into Phil and they were announcing their imminent marriage. Dominic Treadwell-Collins had contacted me to see if there was any chance Bar could do a couple of scenes to set up Ronnie Mitchell's return. Dr Kennedy said to do it, so I told Dominic that, as long as Bar had autocue available, it was a yes. I thought it would be good for her. When it came to filming it was a glorious sunny day, which made it easier to imagine that the location house near Borehamwood was Portugal and Sam Womack, who played Peggy's niece, Ronnie, was sunbathing, reading a novel, when Peggy slapped down the wedding invitation to Phil's marriage to Sharon.

'What am I supposed to do with this?' asked Ronnie.

'Burn it!' spat Bar in true Peggy indomitable magnificence.

She was great all day. She looked fabulous, she was steady on her feet and hardly used the autocue, except to refresh her memory between takes. I breathed a huge sigh of relief. She was equally good a few weeks later filming an advert for Jackpotjoy. Sure, she used autocue, but she was spot-on. No one could tell, whether at work or shining at a family wedding doing the usual round of photos with the guests. It was at home the anxiety started to build, alongside bits of confusion.

Dr Kennedy thought he saw some improvement, which I clung to as Bar set off for Stratford East to do an interview, but as soon as she walked through the door she started crying. 'I had a total blank, Scott. They asked me a question and I didn't know how to answer it. Scott, I didn't know what to do!'

'Maybe we need to consider whether live interviews are worth it,' I offered, as gently as possible. 'Perhaps we should give the Poppy Day Appeal a miss?'

'But I'll be letting everyone down,' Bar cried. 'Dr Kennedy said things were looking better. Don't tell me I can't do it, Scott.'

This was the other seesaw. Overworked and she risked getting tired, stressed and disorientated; not working and she risked getting depressed, anxious and disillusioned. Every time we changed the meds it caused havoc one way or another. In the end, I would say turning up, doing her stuff and being part of things held off the disease, but I will never know for sure. We did go to No. 10 in the end and there was a great picture of David Cameron with his arms outstretched, welcoming Babs in. It made front-page news.

In 2014 the Tower of London boasted 888,246 ceramic poppies, which spilled out of an arched window creating a sea of red in the dry moat. One hundred years since the start of the First World War, each poppy represented a fatality and the final one was placed as we stood alongside the British Legion while a twenty-one-gun salute ricocheted off the castle walls and rolled over the London sky. It was a great honour, but suddenly I noticed that Bar was looking a bit unsteady on her feet, so I stepped forward to assist just as a trustee ushered the dignitaries in the official line-up to move on.

'On you go, Barbara,' said the official. Bar hesitated.

'You too,' he said to me so I stepped forward, but I knew in my head this was not supposed to happen. Next thing, we found ourselves in the middle of the poppy field facing the world's press. I could see they were thinking exactly what I was thinking: What the hell is Barbara Windsor doing in this line-up?

'We shouldn't be here,' I whispered out of the corner of my mouth. 'It's too late now!'

We stood under the flypast while I just tried to hold it all together. 'Parade, right turn!' shouted the Beefeater.

Oh my God, I thought, I'm at the beginning of the line. I did my best impression of a soldier as I led the line and we all marched out. Everyone congratulated us, but I couldn't stop shaking. Only when we got home, as texts kept pinging my phone, did we collapse into fits of laughter.

As the year came to a close, I thought about the ups and downs. Bar had been awarded an honorary doctorate from the University of East London the same year she'd faced a diagnosis of Alzheimer's. My dad was getting weaker, my brother-in-law had a near miss after being diagnosed with a rare medical condition, we'd stumbled into a poppy field and then Bar had recorded a Christmas special of the *Jonathan Ross Show* with David Walliams, Ed Sheeran and Lewis Hamilton. It was a long day. I thought she looked fantastic in a red sparkling dress, tiny shiny red shoes and lipstick to match. But she was grasping at words, missing names and told the audience that Ross Kemp was still alive. She meant the actor who played Dirty Den. Watching, I could see the ever-professional Jonathan and David either side of her ready to catch her if she stumbled, verbally speaking, and smooth over pauses, fill in names when they didn't quite come to her. I don't think anyone in the audience noticed. But it was often all I could see.

17

Sod Off, M'Lady!

We had a nice day to mark my thirteen-years-sober anniversary. Coffee with Ian, lunch with Barry, and in the evening we went to June Whitfield's house for canapés and drinks before heading out to the Wimbledon pantomime to see Linda Gray from *Dallas* as the Fairy Godmother in *Cinderella*. Bar loved June. She had been the leading lady in Bar's stage debut back in 1952. Bar was only fifteen and played a ten-year-old orphan in *Love from Judy*. Her talent notwithstanding, it was her diminutive size and childlike looks that cemented her the part. Keeping it for two years, however, required a bit of cunning. When June Whitfield saw Bar next, it was onstage at Winston's nightclub doing cabaret in a *Carry On*-esque costume that left little to the imagination. June was shocked to see how the orphan had *grown*. How had she managed to hide her 'assets'? June wondered.

'I used to bind them up,' replied Bar, with that famous impish grin.

'I'm just popping out to buy some food,' I said to Bar when we'd finished our coffee. Thirty minutes later she called me. 'Where are you, Scott?'

'Grabbing some dinner for us,' I told her calmly, but inside I was alarmed.

The doctor had said she may be okay for a long time and I had taken that to my hopeful heart, but that call reminded me that I needed to keep a very close eye on her. Mostly she was so on the ball and as sharp as she had ever been, but these little forgetful moments were starting to creep in more often.

At the end of January 2015, Bar had another brief return to *East-Enders*, which she really enjoyed, particularly filming with Danny Dyer, who she thought had a real charisma. His character had taken over the pub and after a face-off with Dot, Peggy went for a drink. Mick then kicked her out of the Vic after an altercation. Bar aced it. I think those small bits of filming suited her and the *EastEnders* team were happy to have her pop in and out, especially for big weeks, like the thirtieth anniversary of the show. I began to feel as if I was wearing two hats. One of denial, so she could keep just getting out there, as suggested by Dr Kennedy, and one of concern, because I was beginning to notice more changes.

For the live edition Bar did brilliantly as well. I told her the Peggy Mitchell story was trending and she looked at me blankly. 'What does that mean?'

This was a woman who'd never used a computer let alone an app, but she was happy and really proud of herself. Of course, not as proud as I was.

Another bonus was that Dad was now out of hospital.

On 14 February we went to our neighbour Nick Campsie's fortieth birthday celebration at the Bunny Club. It was a loud, packed party and Bar did brilliantly. She pulled a performance of proper mock outrage when I was surrounded by bunny girls. You could almost hear Sid James and Kenneth Williams laughing with her. One of the things I loved most about my wife was that she was always true to herself, her past, her abilities and her fanbase. She was never precious about who she was, ever. She took any opportunity to send herself up.

I quite liked auctioning my wife off for charity, but she liked it even more; the more she wiggled her bottom, the higher the bids. There were always interesting people at these big fundraising events and Bar liked hearing their stories and telling a few of her own favourites. I just crossed my fingers and hoped it wasn't the old Fenella Fielding anecdote.

It was people she loved. One day, when the mews was being resurfaced, I couldn't find Bar anywhere in the house. Then I caught a flash of blonde hair on the CCTV security monitor and she was outside on the road, linking arms with the workmen, having a cackle, and in her element.

It went on all the time. A couple of weeks later Barnet Football Club was having a charity do, raising money for underprivileged children. There she was having a kickabout with the kids, refusing to be extinguished. She was carrying on at her merry pace.

But then in April something changed. Bar seemed to be sleeping all day and talking in her sleep. When she woke, it was as if she was still in her dream, or her dream was so vivid she couldn't shake it off, and it gave me a jolt because I felt like we'd been doing so well.

'Have you just been here?' Bar asked, looking at me, perplexed. I had just arrived.

She was in hospital after a particularly vicious flare-up of diverticulitis and they'd kept her in overnight. Immediately I searched for excuses. Was it the change in environment? The pain? The medication? Perhaps it was dehydration?

'Are we leaving now?' Bar asked.

'Let's just wait for the doctor.'

'Dr Kennedy has been, he says I'm doing well.'

I just smiled. We weren't under the care of Dr Kennedy here. We weren't at his hospital. We were at the London Clinic. The specialist Mr Mudan had sent her here after a CT scan revealed a deterioration in her colon. 'He's worried you're losing weight,' I said. 'I'm sure he will be here soon.'

'Have you just been here?'

I turned away so she couldn't see the concern on my face.

Dr Nookey, aka Bar's fellow *Carry On* actor Jim Dale, was doing a one-man show at the Vaudeville Theatre in the West End. It had been decided that they would recreate the famous stethoscope scene, this time with a little bit more clothing on Barbara than three strategically placed red hearts. Bar was well up for it and as we approached the theatre she was mobbed by hundreds of *Carry On* fans. It took ages to get in. I stuck like glue to her left shoulder, talking her through it, keeping her safe. The following day there were photos everywhere.

The show was superb and the party afterwards at the Waldorf was brilliant. It was a high. I think it reassured Barbara that, although one day she might forget, they would not.

The best party of the year without doubt went to Paul O'Grady, who turned sixty in June. There was a big bash overlooking the Thames enjoyed by the best of British showbiz. Paul is much-loved, so the atmosphere was a joyous one, and it was a night to catch up with old friends and hear all those salacious stories I could never put in print. Sorry! Bar was great that night; she hit the dance floor and laughed uproariously as only she could. Sadly, it was the last time we would see Cilla Black. She died in August that year and we were both devastated. Another gem gone.

Then, just a few weeks later, we were at an event for the Royal National Institute of Blind People and I noticed Bar was not as good at recalling the stories she had told a million times. I wanted to unsee what I had seen.

In August we had another request from the producer at *EastEnders* to do some filming. Bar and I discussed it but sadly came to the conclusion that the occasional filming days would have to end. Good days felt precarious at best. We thanked him and suggested Peggy probably needed to die. He texted back that he understood but was very sad. I wondered if they might just kill her off, off-screen.

'Cheer up, Bar. We're off to see *Legend*, the Tom Hardy film about the Kray twins.'

She looked at me blankly.

'The premiere at Leicester Square,' I prompted.

'Where's Leicester Square?'

Another heart-stopping moment.

You've got to hang on to the good moments because living with dementia is like living in quicksand. One minute she didn't know where Leicester Square was, the next we were doing a radio commercial for Heinz. Bar did it so well they asked her to do a Christmas advert as well, even though it was only September. She agreed, they wrote it there and then, and, hey presto, the pro was back.

She could perform at will, but she couldn't remember at will. Later that same day I found her crying at home. She'd lost something but she'd forgotten what it was and where it was. She stopped fretting, looked me right in the eye and said, 'I don't want to live any more.'

I was horrified.

'Bar . . .' Immediately I tried to cajole her, cheer her up, but I was reeling inside. Those words were so shocking.

As Bar and Pam St Clement sat in Pam's garden near Oxford, they put the world to rights. Pat Butcher had been killed off against her wishes and I think it spurred the Peggy in Bar to end things with *EastEnders* her way. True to character, in charge. She wanted to go back and finish off Peggy herself and she sent the producer a text telling him as much.

Shortly after this we met Ross Kemp and his wife Renee and their baby Leo. They happened to be in Majorca at the same time and we had a lovely lunch, laughing and reminiscing about Bar and Ross's ten years being mother and son on TV. Theirs was a beautiful friendship. I had warned Ross in advance that Bar might get a touch repetitive, just so he was prepared.

'Is she all right?' he asked.

'There's a slight memory problem going on,' I told him, not wanting to divulge the truth of the situation, but also not wanting to lie to someone as important to us as Ross. He looked concerned, but was lovely, and just kept rattling through the stories and scrapes they got into over the years.

'She's thinking of going back to *EastEnders*,' I said, hoping to plant a seed.

'Oh, Ross,' said Bar, with a twinkle in her eye, 'wouldn't it be great to go back together? We could get Pat back too.'

'Bar, Pat's dead,' Ross said.

She waved a hand. 'There's always a way. You'll see.'

She had always wanted her friends with her for the ride. I get that. Showbiz can be cut-throat, so when you find good friends, you hang on to them.

'So what does this Freedom of the City of London actually mean?' I asked Bar, who'd been made a freeman in 2010.

'It means that if we get drunk, they have to give us a lift home.'

'That would have been more useful a few years ago!'

'It also means I can't get arrested.'

'Shame your pick-pocketing days are over then!'

'And I get to herd some sheep over London Bridge in full ermine robes and a hefty gold chain.'

'That sounds much more you!'

She was not joking and, honestly, watching my wife exercise her ancient right to cross London Bridge with a flock of sheep was heartwarming and hilarious at the same time, which sums her up perfectly. The image still makes me smile. It also inspired a couple of my favourite classic red-top headlines: 'IT'S BAA BAA WINDSOR' and 'CARRY ON BLEATING'. They are clever.

She was so proud of being given the honour because she was, in her bones, a self-proclaimed city girl. 'I can handle the country for a couple of days,' she'd say. 'But then I want to get back. I'm a high-heel girl and frankly I've never much liked the mud.'

I wondered if it went all the way back to her first *Carry On* film. It was midwinter, they had sprayed the grass green, and Babs was in a bikini which was attached to a fishing line. The first take took her off her feet and landed her in the mud. They rinsed her down and got ready to shoot the scene again.

She shouted at the director Gerald Thomas, 'My feet are sinking into the mud!'

'I'm not employing you to look at your feet!' came his quick retort.

As Bar said many times, 'You couldn't get away with it these days. Young actors, they don't know they've been born.'

Kenneth Williams was aghast and kept shouting at the director not to be so beastly, but it didn't land. Take two. The bikini flew in the air, Bar covered her boobs, but Hattie Jacques was stronger than she realised and when Kenneth yelled the line 'Take them away!' she grabbed Barbara's arm and, in a flash, the boob was out.

They went for a rare third take, but the director wanted the second take, so off it went to the censors. 'I don't think Barbara Windsor's right breast will corrupt the nation,' said the British film censors, thrusting *Carry On Camping* into British film history.

*

The conversations about killing off Peggy continued and Bar felt happier knowing she could use an autocue to refresh her memory between takes. Dr Kennedy had no concerns. 'Why not?' he said. 'You can only see how it goes.'

So we kept going in the hope that it was the right thing to do. I still believe that if we'd stopped, she'd have gone downhill faster. But despite all my hopes and prayers, she was going downhill. Promoting this year's Poppy Appeal, Bar did an interview on *Good Morning Britain*. I watched from home and she was pretty good. But then later in the day she did another with Sky News that didn't go so well. She had been up for many hours and been chatting nonstop. I wasn't sure she could hear that well and she was really concentrating on the questions.

'It isn't hard to give,' Bar started off. 'It's our armed forces.'

'Does it matter what kind of poppy you wear?'

'I've got a glittery one,' she said, 'but it doesn't matter. It's a pity we don't see the poppy sellers any more.'

'What do you think about people who don't wear poppies?' asked the presenter.

'Well, they can sod off for all I care.'

It was like for a second she'd forgotten she was live on TV. The presenter apologised for her language and then it got a bit confusing. Bar started talking about mud and dirt, she was trying to explain the word 'sod'. I knew what she thought about people who didn't support the armed forces and was glad she hadn't said anything worse, but I also knew the old Barbara would never have said that live on air.

The backdraught was intense. I wrote in my diary:

Thursday, 29 October 2015: Time to stop live interviews.

'Bar, you should open this.'

On 27 November 2015 the postman handed me a stiff brown official-looking envelope from the Cabinet Office. As Bar read the letter her eyes filled with tears. 'The Prime Minister has recommended me for a damehood.'

'Oh, Bar, I am so proud of you.'

The Queen's Honours List is a sacred secret until New Year's Day. I did confide in the two people who had been instrumental in the process, her agent Barry and our friend Gary Farrow, Jane Moore's husband. It's never public knowledge at this stage, but still rumours started to fly. Story of our life. The *Sun*, *Mirror*, *People* and *Mail* all ran stories about the damehood, but we were safely tucked away in Sussex for Christmas with no intention of responding.

When at midnight the news was made official, Bar said what was in her heart: 'If only my mum was alive to see it.' Seeking her mum's hard-won approval had been as much of a driving force in Bar's life as her father's rejection had created a deep wound. You can stop striving now, Barbara, I thought.

'Who'd have thought it? Me, a dame?'

'Me. I'd have thought it. Can I get you a cup of tea, M'lady?'

'Oh, sod off!'

'Yes, M'Lady,' I said, bowing deeply, retreating from the room backwards with a flurry of arm-waving. I was rewarded with that famous giggle.

18

Enter the Dame,
Exit the Landlady

Bar was unusually quiet; I suspected she was finding the damehood overwhelming. I understood that. Bar always had an underlying feeling that she wasn't worthy.

'You okay?' I asked.

'Are people going to think I've got ahead of myself, being a dame? People like me don't become dames.'

I sat down next to her. 'You have given yourself up to entertaining this country since you were seven years old. Your honesty, your graft, your hard work and all you give to people makes you more than worthy.'

She looked at me with those childlike eyes and I knew she was finding it hard to take it all in. Or I hoped that was what that lost look meant.

We busied ourselves with the storyline for Peggy's exit. The executive producer Dominic came to the house with the excellent writer Sarah Phelps, who would oversee the script. Sarah had some lovely ideas. Unlike mine. I thought Peggy should put a gun to her head and take her life in a final shocking, dramatic and bloodthirsty scene. Luckily no one listened to me.

'I thought I'd never see you again,' Bar sobbed into my arms.

I'd been out for a work meeting when Bar called me to say she didn't feel well. I had rushed back. The distress seemed to come from nowhere. I managed to calm her down and that evening felt she was well enough to join friends for a dinner at Scott's in Mayfair to mark her departure from the show. It was a lovely fun evening, but even though we were with close friends, Paul O'Grady and his husband Andre Portasio, Gary Farrow and Jane Moore, Ross Kemp and Renee O'Brien and Dominic Treadwell-Collins, I could tell that Bar was nervous. Nervous was not something I attributed to my wife, especially not with such good mates. That dinner marked the beginning of things happening more regularly.

I was by the pool in Majorca when my mobile rang. It was a reporter from a national newspaper. 'We've heard Barbara has early symptoms of Alzheimer's. Would you like to comment?'

Bar was still not able to fully accept the diagnosis. I knew it would destroy her if it was made public. I managed to talk my way around it and never confirmed or denied the rumours, then we left the villa for the last time. My sister and brother-in-law had sold it. It had been a real bolthole for us over the years and we were sad. At the airport a huge gust of wind nearly blew us over. Was it time to leave the island or were we about to be knocked off our feet?

Dominic was being a real star for Bar and was making her exit as easy as possible. They knew she had problems with her lines and were happy for her to use an autocue. Wardrobe came to our house to choose outfits and then Dominic and Kris Green, the script editor, came to go through the scripts with Bar, day by day. Everyone was aware this was a big deal for her. Dominic always said she taught him so much. 'I started out as a story editor and ended up as executive producer. And when I got to that level, I came to work wearing jeans and a T-shirt as I always had. Bar took me to one side and said, "Go home, put on a shirt and come back looking like a proper guv'nor."' He loved telling that story.

On 21 March 2016 Barbara went back to the set for the first day of filming. The feedback was that she had done well and they were ahead of schedule, which was a relief because the following day there was the small matter of her investiture. East End one day, Buckingham Palace the next. A perfect summary of Bar's life.

Up at 5.30. Hair, make-up, dressmaker, Barry, photographer. It was go, go, go.

Nerves were running high. You had to do things in the right order, but I was worried that Bar might not be able to remember all the instructions and she would have hated to get it wrong. The Bentley arrived, which had to be searched and swept before we could drive through the world-famous gates of Buckingham Palace. Bar was whisked away by a palace official and the Queen's Piper told me it would be Her Majesty doing the honours that day. Cherry on the cake for Bar, of course.

She was the third up. She looked fantastic, top to toe in mauve lace, hat and gloves, and as lovely as ever. Bar chatted to the Queen then did the sweetest curtsy, which set a little giggle off around the room. I breathed a sigh of thanks and relief. Her performance was perfect. The whole thing took an hour, but it was so memorable that in a way time stopped, or certainly slowed. Out in the courtyard there were more press pictures.

We arrived at Fortnum & Mason for a celebratory lunch laid on by the then CEO Ewan Venters. Richard Young, the king of the paps, was there to catch the moment and the atmosphere was joyous. A small group of our family and close friends were there to raise a glass to Dame Barbara Windsor. Not sure you ever get used to that! I am not sure what the rest of the diners thought. It looked like they were mostly tourists and, for once, they had no idea who anyone on our table was. This was extremely rare and meant Bar was left alone to relish the moment and celebrate with her friends.

'There's nothing like a dame . . .' sang the super-talented cast as they presented Barbara with a surprise cake on set the next day. She made a heartfelt speech which she meant every word of. *EastEnders* was a big reason why she'd achieved the profile to do the charity work that had won her a damehood. Bar, as always, oozed gratitude for the show that had changed her life.

'You would be so proud of the work she's doing,' Dominic said when he rang me with an update. 'Best ever.' Ross texted me a similar message. He had agreed to return to the show just for her departure. Our cunning Majorcan plan had paid off. As he said in an interview, 'I mean, how could I say no to Babs?'

Various work offers still came in, but I was getting choosier as I noticed a further progression of the Alzheimer's. Perhaps that was why the same newspaper that had contacted me in Majorca came back to me that they had heard from other sources that Bar was unwell. I rang our lawyer. 'Don't stand it up,' he said. Which meant don't say yes. It would have been detrimental to her wellbeing. Bar preferred to continue life as best she could and only ever mentioned her illness when she had a moment.

Eventually we reached the last day at Elstree. I was allowed to go to the lot where Bar was shooting her last scene. Dominic was also leaving; this was his last storyline, and what a storyline. The cancer was back. Peggy didn't want to be a burden, slowly disintegrating. She would go out on her own terms. Her great frenemy Pat Butcher with her to the end. In spirit. Bar nailed it once again. It was very emotional and a few of us went to the bar for a drink afterwards, but it was hard to take in. Twenty years. It was over. Bar was exhausted by the time she got home. I think a lot of that was relief, but there also was no denying Peggy's ending was inextricably linked to her own.

Bar and I were out doing errands when she suddenly slipped again. Although I broke her fall by holding her arm, she still ended up on the floor. There was a bit of a commotion. She wanted to get up and leave. I wanted to make sure that wasn't going to make it worse. I got her to our doctor's that afternoon, where we would later find out that she had osteoporosis in her hip.

'Poor old cow, I'm falling apart.'

The jungle drums were getting louder that there were health problems and the original paper was now hounding us despite repeated attempts by me to shut it down. In the end I had no choice but to instruct my lawyer, Henri Brandman, to send them a legal letter saying everyone has a right to medical privacy. Bar was not ready to accept her diagnosis, let alone talk openly. It was not my job, the newspaper's, or anyone else's to hit her over the head with her condition until the time was right, for her. After seeing her do a Q&A onstage with the boss of Jackpotjoy recently, where she'd had all the staff in the palm of her hand, I thought that would be years from now. The paper responded to the legal letter saying if she ever wanted to talk, there would be big money on the table.

'Look at that silly little bird . . .' she whispered in the dark. We were at a private screening of *Carry On Camping* at One Aldwych. I watched my wife watching her younger self. David Walliams had invited Joan Collins and Percy Gibson, Steve Pemberton from *The League of Gentlemen*, Neil Tennant, Barbara Broccoli. These days Bar became more emotional watching those films because of all the people she'd lost, especially Kenneth and Sid, Bernard, Hattie. A cab driver once said to Bar, 'It's a shame you're all dead now.' It wasn't until she got into the house she realised what he'd said and had quite a giggle.

After the film we went to the Savoy for dinner in a private room. I sat next to Joan and we had really good chats. She wanted to know if Barbara had changed her passport to Dame Barbara. We hadn't got round to that! In fact, if people called her Dame Barbara, she would say, 'Just call me Barbara.' And if they called her Barbara, she'd say, 'Call me Babs.' I don't think she ever wanted to feel separated from her fans – class and titles can do that.

The first episode of Bar's return to the Square aired on 10 May. Top brass were right. I was proud of her and really pleased for her as well, because I knew how important it was that she went out on a good performance. She had sat down for weeks learning the lines for these scenes. Really. It meant the world to her.

'It's not good news I'm afraid,' said the oncologist.

Peggy sat stock still, the camera on her face, so poised all you could see was her eyes slowly fill with tears, just a blink or two while she listened to the dire diagnosis and ever so slightly raise her chin. Defiant. Brave.

'I'm sorry to tell you there's been no response to your recent chemotherapy. The recent scan shows the cancer has spread to your brain . . . There are drugs, but at this stage I have to tell you they will only prolong the inevitable. And there are side-effects, most not very pleasant.'

'How long?' asked her niece.

'Months, which is why it might be time to decide, Mrs Mitchell, if treatment is really what you want.'

She was my Mrs Mitchell, you know, in real life, and in real life the drugs did have side-effects and would only prolong the inevitable. The episodes continued all week and I had never been so proud, not just because I knew what was going on, but because her delivery was so damn good. Ronnie tried to hide Peggy's return to the Square but Aunt Sal, the wonderful Anna Karen, knew by the scent in the air that her sister Peggy was back. Anna performed a phenomenal scene.

'Let me tell you something about Peggy. She has had to fight, the whole of her life, to keep the show on the road, every time a problem presented itself she'd put on a smile and work that bar as if she didn't have a care in the world. Peggy Mitchell taking on the world single-handedly. Only this time she doesn't have to cos we're her family, we're here for her, this is her last fight. I know she's here . . .'

'You always was an interfering old cow.'

'And you've always been a stubborn old goat.'

'Are you ready to come home.'

'I am home.'

It was a brilliant episode and they kept ratcheting up. Grant appeared. Phil had to keep his mum's plan a secret. Peggy justified her decision.

'It's your mum deciding what happens next, like what I've always done. What could be more ordinary than that?'

By the end of the week, as the fans were glued to Barbara as Peggy, my Mrs Mitchell was up all night in the bathroom in pain. Her specialist admitted her into the Princess Grace where she would be for the next four days, on a drip and having endless scans, which were making her tired and weepy. The doctor told her the only option was surgery but, like the *EastEnders* doctor, he advised against it. He said it was better to learn to live with her diverticulitis condition and be careful about what she ate.

And then we were back, the final episode. There was Pat, on the stairs, with her earrings rattling like 'Marley's bleedin' chains'.

'I think you look smashin',' said Pat, back from the grave.
   'I don't. Look at the state of me, like a little old bird that's fallen out of its nest. Shift yourself, you mad old tart, I've got stuff to do.'

Upstairs, all dolled up and looking exceptionally good, she threw open the window of her room.

'My nan used to do this, open the window to let the soul out . . .'

She looked over the square.

'I've loved it all so much.'

Bar came home on the night the finale aired. We were both speechless and moved. Dominic called from America to thank her, and texts and emails flooded in. I knew Bar was happy with how it had gone. She'd been a trouper to the end. She was pleased for Peggy, I think, even if she herself was sad. To have a long-term character like that dominate two decades of your life, well, no wonder life and art had intertwined. I think by the end they were almost one.

I just wish I'd had the privilege of editing *our* script because ten days after leaving hospital, Bar was back in for another five days. The hospital visits left her more confused, which meant she'd be tearful, anxious and perplexed. Dr Kennedy came in to see her and sat with her for a while. When I entered the room, she said in a very loud stage whisper, thinking he couldn't hear, 'I can't get rid of him!'

That stage whisper was normally reserved for cabbies, when she thought they were taking the long route, forgetting the mic was on from a previous chat. 'He's taking liberties . . . no idea where he's going . . .' I would break into a sweat.

She was getting frailer with every hospital visit. We didn't go anywhere for three weeks because she was so tired when she got home. Eventually I did manage to get her out for a walk, which was tentative, but I was relieved to be out. It was quite nice to watch the Soap Awards together. My client and friend Lacey had won an award and she thanked me personally, which I appreciated. It was good to be reminded I was more than a carer.

A few weeks later Peggy's funeral was broadcast. We decided not to watch; it would have been too macabre. Instead I read out the texts I'd received, which were mostly saying the same thing: 'It wouldn't be the same without her.' We took ourselves out the following night, to our local around the corner with Barry and our close friend Paul Bennett, but Bar had a scared look in her eyes. A few days later I went down to see Dad.

'Scott, where are you?'

'I'm with Dad, in Henfield.'

'I can't open the front door. I think it's stuck. Can you come and help?'

'Bar, I'm in Sussex.'

'Oh. Okay.'

Feeling a bit irritated, I was about to get back in the car when she called again. 'It's all right, a neighbour helped me.'

The annoyance soon turned to fear. She was vulnerable, simple things were becoming confusing, and I was too far away. I made another appointment with my therapist. I had to be able to keep a handle on this, especially because she started to get grumpy herself. It was so unlike her, especially at work, but it was happening, and I had to be able to cope. When, at a lunch, she cried in front of our friends,

I knew, despite Dr Kennedy's continued support for getting her out and about, things were speeding up.

The next day, though, was the total opposite. We went to see the Pet Shop Boys with David Walliams and Bar danced away in the box. She had done a film with the band many years before and chatted to them after the show.

Then a few weeks later she walked onstage with Diversity and, in a dramatic entrance, she flipped Ashley Banjo and Perri Kiely into a somersault and the audience loved it. There were 20,000 people on the Blackpool promenade that night, jumping about to loud rave music, as Barbara turned on the lights.

'It is such an honour to be here,' Bar said. 'You see, I was evacuated here during the war. I was so tiny the couple told me I was too small to go on the bus—'

Oh no, I thought. This is the wrong crowd for that story. But, you know what, all 20,000 fell silent and listened to her story about how she had barricaded herself in her room and screamed blue murder when the man tried to get in. How the neighbour's kid had heard the shouting and taken her to their house. How the couple were in fact siblings and seven-year-old Babs had a lucky escape. And how she first went to dance classes all those years ago in Blackpool. 'So, thank you, Blackpool, for starting me on my seventy-year career!' she said. 'Not bad for a four-foot-nothing shrimp from the East End!'

Way back then, the dance teacher had told Bar's mother that in Barbara Ann Deeks she had discovered a natural-born show-off. In many ways, as the Alzheimer's crept in, I watched the years peel away, until I saw glimpses of that little girl, standing her ground, fighting her corner, to the end a natural-born show-off.

Back in London Paul O'Grady welcomed Barbara to the stage. A room full of clapping and cheering soap stars were there to congratulate her for winning Outstanding Contribution to Television at the TV Choice Awards in September 2016.

'Please sit down, darlins',' Bar said as she came onstage. 'You make me feel so little when you all stand up. I never got telly. I was always a bit much. I was always being fobbed off, we'll let you know, and then

I got *EastEnders*. What a lucky lady I was. I loved it so much I wanted to be in it all the time, but I'm of an age now . . .'

I could see she was shaking and behind her Paul was watching her closely.

'I'll be ninety next year . . .' Paul looked away. I could see him gathering himself, holding in the emotions. 'Or is it eighty? It's eighty, isn't it . . .' She covered her mistake well enough.

Paul came and sat with me afterwards and got a bit tearful. 'She's looking frail.'

'Paul, today was a good day.'

I was seeing her every day, so I hadn't noticed the change, but Paul was right. The tummy troubles and hospital stays had taken their toll. Whenever we were anywhere there was press; I stuck to her like glue.

The highlight of the year was being involved in the former *East-Enders* scriptwriter Tony Jordan's creation of *Babs*, a BBC biopic about Barbara's life. Samantha Spiro would play the older Babs – she was more like Barbara than Barbara – and Jaime Winstone, Ray's daughter, would play the younger Babs. It was an exciting project and some of Bar's clearest days were working with the production team and designers. It gave us something to talk about. Better still, it was a heartfelt look at her youth, her childhood and what had been left unsaid between her and her father, who would be played excellently by Nick Moran.

Between those good days, there were long, quiet days and endless nights. Night after night watching telly, trying to keep Bar's anxiety at bay. The read-through was electric. It was worth cancelling a planned trip away. It must have been a bit nerve-racking for the cast to have Bar there, but for me, meeting my younger self, Charlie Archer, was surreal. I instantly liked him and we are still in touch. I appeared at the start and end of the show, and we joked that there could be a spin-off, *Better Call Scott!*

Bar played herself in *Babs*; her present-day self watching her younger self. It was strange and poignant to watch. On the last day of filming Bar performed 'Sunny Side of the Street' onstage in front of an audience of family, friends and fellow stars. I watched it on the monitor and couldn't help feeling emotional, as I knew it was likely to be the last time Barbara would stand on a stage and perform a song. Her eyes had a lost quality to them, her voice was a little shaky, but saying all that, as ever, my lovely lady pulled it off.

Mid-chat to switch on the Christmas lights in Borehamwood, the organisers accidentally switched them on. Quick as a flash Bar quipped, 'Well, what the bleedin' hell am I doing here?' The crowd loved it. Her intelligence and quick-witted sense of humour held firm.

There was another charity event a few days later, this time for the homeless in Canning Town. I begged her to do less but she insisted because it was helping people. I didn't argue with her because it was also helping her. We were on a roll.

Next, she offered to do the honours for the flower stall in Marylebone High Street. No one knew it was taking place. The 'lights' were a couple of strings of fairy lights, but watching people clock it was her and what she was doing was hilarious. 'Forget Regent Street, this is where it's all happenin',' she called out.

Never too grand, never one to consider herself above anyone else and always ready to laugh at herself, some things never changed. A week later, though, she caught a cold and I cancelled everything, including the charity events. From now on, nothing was more important than her health.

19

Happy Valentine's, Happy Anniversary, Happy Birthday, Happy Christmas – Not

Bar was being very forgetful, an inauspicious start to the year and, sure enough, rather than flying off to Barbados, she was admitted to hospital with a terrible cough that often left her gasping for breath. Happy Valentine's. She was in for three days and the day she came home my dad was admitted to hospital with fluid on his lungs. Six days later Barbara was back in hospital, on a drip and a nebuliser to ease the breathing difficulties. For four days I went back and forth as much as possible because, while she seemed fine when I was there, she was increasingly distant every time I went back. I could see the thread thinning and it was terrifying.

At June Brown's ninetieth birthday, the contrast between the two of them was clear. Where once they matched each other, now June could still tell a story with precise detailing, clarity and confidence whereas Bar looked a bit lost.

The private screening of *Babs* was fantastic, her life portrayed exactly as she wanted it. They did an amazing job and, as the credits rolled, Bar slipped quietly out of the room. When I found her she was having a good cry. I mean that: it was a good cry, as opposed to the frequent tears I'd witnessed that seemed to come from nowhere, over very little. These tears were real. How would anyone of us feel watching our whole life on screen knowing that the scenes being played would soon be lost to the person in them?

'And June Whitfield said, "You knew when Barbara grew up because she went from smelling like carbolic soap to Chanel No. 5 . . ."'

We were at the Grosvenor House Hotel for the 2017 TRIC Awards. There were lots of tables of actors and the creative teams behind hit television and radio shows. Bar was presenting a lifetime achievement award to June Whitfield, her friend of sixty-five years. This was the second time she'd told that story during her introduction and I'm sorry to say people had started to chat among themselves.

'Oi, shut up!' she called out. My insides twisted in panic.

She could get away with telling the audience to shut up normally because she would have said it in her sweet, jovial, jokey way, but this time she sounded cross. June Whitfield came to the stage and, while she was making her acceptance speech, Bar joined in. Twice. The old Bar would have hated it because it went against all her professional ethics. The signs were there. Things would get harder to hide. Later, people said to me that was the very first inkling they'd had that Bar wasn't one hundred per cent.

Dr Kennedy came to see Barbara and said he felt her mood was calmer than last time. He was always balancing the meds, adjusting dosages, trying to get it right. I told him I had rebooked our holiday to Barbados.

'Look,' he said, 'just call if you're worried about anything.'

Packing for that sixteen-day trip was more stressful than usual, and usual wasn't great. At one point I did snap slightly. 'I don't have time for us to stress,' I said firmly. Of course, by now, my own nerves were starting to fray. I thought I was doing okay but I challenge anyone in that position, when they're constantly dealing with someone else's wellbeing, not to wither a bit. I needed the holiday as much as she did.

On our first full day at the hotel, we went to sit on the beach. Both of us were very tired, Bar had no make-up on, we had just flopped on to a sunbed and were staring out to sea. It was a beautiful beach. Within ten minutes a hotel guest had come over to Barbara for a photo. 'Do you mind if perhaps you could ask again tomorrow or the next day? We need a little time to relax.' I said this as politely as possible.

I wouldn't say the guest was happy about it, but she agreed. I was totally used to this type of thing happening, but Bar was so tired and not looking her best and I wanted to protect her. The guest did return the next day and she sat with Bar for over an hour asking her questions about her life. I can remember propping myself up from my sunlounger every ten, fifteen minutes or so, joining in or just looking at the woman to try to make the point. But Bar, being Bar, patiently and graciously went on answering questions. Then the woman's husband came over as well. Maybe he was trying to retrieve his wife, since she wasn't picking up my signals. No doubt I was more conscious now but there was a growing part of me that just wanted everyone to leave her alone.

As we got to the beach the following day Barbara started crying. It was so unlike her to cry in public. I got so concerned I took her back to the room in the hope it would calm her down. It didn't, so I texted Dr Kennedy. 'See if she relaxes,' he said. 'It might just be the change of scenery. Hopefully she will settle down.'

I cancelled the restaurant booking I had made and hoped he was right. He wasn't. The following day it seemed to be getting worse. The crying was now accompanied by awful anxiety and I didn't know how to ease her distress except to basically stay in the suite and eat there. So now we were in Barbados and looking out of the window at this beautiful beach, but stuck indoors.

On day five I spoke to Dr Kennedy. 'I think I should bring her home now as it's getting too distressing for her. There's no point in staying here.' He agreed, so I arranged for the earliest possible flight back to the UK. The tears started as soon as she saw me packing.

'I'm sorry, Scott.'

'Don't you ever say sorry to me,' I told her.

'I'm scared of losing you.'

'I will never leave you, Bar.' I told her this over and over.

The anxiety and tears continued, even when we were home.

'I'd rather not put her in hospital because this time it would be on the psychiatric ward,' said Dr Kennedy.

I agreed; that sounded like a terrifying prospect for an older lady with dementia. It was better for her to be at home, but it did mean I was dealing with her on my own. My poor Bar was so scared and, now, so was I. On our seventeenth wedding anniversary, instead of flowers and a celebratory lunch, we picked up anti-psychotic medication. But still the tears flowed. The anxiety spiked, and the repetitive questions continued. I felt powerless.

'We've got a new business partner and they think it might be time for a change in image.' Bar was being politely let go by Lee Fenton, the CEO of Jackpotjoy. Not a day too soon since earlier that morning I had returned home from the gym to find her hysterical at the top of the stairs. She'd spilled coffee on the carpet and was trying to scrub it out. After seeing her in that troubled, distressed state, the thought of going to a big meeting to talk about the job she was supposed to be doing was preposterous. I wonder now if he'd heard chat about her recent public outings. Bar took it well and was very thankful. It was an absolute godsend that she'd been able to earn serious money just when she was going to need it the most.

After that Bar's stomach problems got so severe that Dr Kennedy stopped her new meds and readmitted her to hospital. It was my birthday. I was going to cancel going to my niece Charlie's wedding, but Bar insisted I go, so I did. But, as would now so often be the case, I wasn't really present. All the time I would be worrying about Bar. The guilt would hit me in waves. It was the beginning of a bleak time. There is no other way to describe it and I would be doing anyone else in the same position a disservice if I tried to pretend it was anything else.

I took Bar for a follow-up MRI on her tummy. I always had to be with her now because otherwise she panicked. I started talking to a guy in the corridor. He told me his wife had cancer and they were there for her scan. His phone kept ringing. 'Sorry,' he said, 'my mum has dementia. She gets worried when I'm not there.' At that moment Bar came out to say she was going to get changed. The man stared at her and then realised who she was. 'My mum loves you, Barbara,' he said, then he broke down in tears.

The nurse took Barbara to get changed. 'I know how hard it is,' I said. I sat with my arm around this stranger, hugging him, and let him cry. I never told him about Bar's illness, but I could really feel his pain. It was a powerful encounter, realising I was one of many going through this, even though I felt horribly alone at the time.

On 25 May 2017, Barbara, dressed in a fabulous colourful dress and red patent peep-toe shoes, pulled a square of red velvet off the pavement outside the entrance of the Hackney Empire to reveal a brass plaque with 'Dame Barbara Windsor' on it. Now when she made a speech, she kept to the script. Her ad-lib days were over but she still looked every bit the star. After the formalities, we drove to Sussex for a little break. I think mostly it was a break for me. I didn't have to cook, and there were other people around who could answer the constant questions and hold a repetitive conversation. It was a relief for me because my family knew what was going on, which meant I could relax, a bit.

'You know I've got a bit of a memory problem,' she'd say to whoever was in the room.

Sometimes she would fixate on something. 'I've got something, but I'm not sure what it is.'

'I've got something to do next week . . .'

'What am I doing next week?'

'Have you booked that thing next week?'

'I'm worried because I've got something on next week and I can't remember what it is. I've got a bit of a memory problem you see . . .'

It was like she was stuck in certain phases, certain conversations. Sometimes it was the hairdresser's, or nail salon, or doctor's. She would ask me if I had booked her appointment every few minutes. It would vary. During the day it would tend to be every ten minutes, but at night the gaps got shorter. Sometimes she'd be asking me the same question every three to five minutes. I would sit next to her and she would keep asking. Inside my head I would scream, but I always tried to keep a smile on my face as I answered for the umpteenth time. The trouble was, although she couldn't always pick up on the tone of my voice, often she could see it in my eyes.

'I can see I'm pissing you off,' she'd snipe back.

Then I would very gently try to explain to her that because of her memory problem she was asking me the same thing over and over. I always tried to answer her as calmly as I could. 'Sometimes, if I'm tired, I may get a bit irritable with you. I'm sorry, it's not your fault.'

She'd look at me, a little lost, but also recognising the truth of it and then she would apologise, which made it worse for me because I knew she couldn't help it. She wouldn't have done it if she could help it. There would be a short pause when we would be in it together, as we'd always been, back-to-back against the world, fighting dementia and then she'd fade off . . .

'Have you booked that appointment?'

'Yes, Bar.'

'I have an appointment, but I've forgotten what it is.'

'Nothing to worry about now.'

'Tomorrow, have I got something tomorrow? I've got an appointment. I can't remember what it is. You know I've got this memory problem . . .'

I'd keep answering gently, gently, gently and then . . . for a brief moment, I'd grit my teeth or sigh a bit too loudly. 'I can see I'm pissing you off . . .' And it would start again.

There were times when I felt like I was going a little bit crazy. There were other times I can vividly remember sitting there thinking, *This is never going to end*. And then there were fleeting moments when I just wanted to run out the front door and keep on running. Of course, I never did, but that was the feeling in my head. Please let me escape this just for an hour. When I was in Sussex, I could. It was a lifesaver, especially since Bar felt safe there too. A home away from home.

Wednesday 7 June was Ronnie Corbett's memorial at Westminster Abbey. Bar and he had played nightclubs together in her early career and they both appeared in the famous musical flop *Twang!!* by Lionel Bart, which was directed by Joan Littlewood. She had a line in the show: 'I don't know what's going on . . .'

To which she was regularly heckled by the dwindling audience: 'Nor do we!'

She always said, 'If you're going to have a flop, have a *Twang!!*'

After the service we went to Scott's for lunch with David Walliams and Bar seemed more at ease. With the medication and dosage now settled, I hoped we could buy a period of time with no further deterioration. But a week later we were at the Actors' Church, St Paul's, in Covent Garden for another service – this time to officially open the church's new toilets (you couldn't make it up – 'Carry On at Your Convenience'!). Bar said a few words in a video for the church, but by the time she got to the end of her speech she had totally forgotten why we were there. And so it advanced.

A few weeks later Barbara and I were strolling around Marylebone High Street summer fair. There were lots of people, which meant there were lots of pictures taken. It seemed to do her good. But ten days later, just as we were due to leave for an Age UK charity event, she said she felt faint and got anxious about leaving the house, even though her make-up artist had been and she was dressed and ready to go. It didn't matter, I called and cancelled instantly. I hated letting down a charity, but from then on everything would depend on her wellbeing at that precise moment. Nothing could be in ink. In my head, everything was pencilled in – a possible outing, hopefully we'd make it. More and more we did not.

Even so, I kept making plans, because there were some good days and they were just as important. Although things were more difficult, I still wanted Bar to feel part of her normal world when she was well enough.

We were at the summer party of our friend Evgeny Lebedev. As always, there was an incredible guest list – Dame Maggie Smith, Michael Gambon, Joan Collins and Percy, George Osborne, Vince Cable, Charles Saatchi and Hugh Grant, to name just a few. Usually Bar would be in her element at an event like this, but I noticed that being in company like that was now a struggle. She would hang on my arm and go quiet. I'd never known her to be introverted, but that is what she was becoming.

'Scott, I keep having these odd moments when I don't know where I am.' It was the middle of July. I called Dr Kennedy.

At Tony Jordan's sixtieth birthday Barbara spent most of the afternoon chatting to June Brown. I think June was aware that Bar wasn't herself, though I hadn't said anything. Lots of lovely familiar faces took turns to come over and say hello, old comrades like Shane Richie and Jessie Wallace. As we left Barbara told me that she was upset that one actor had not bothered to come and say hello to her and it confused her. It was sad and it was probably the last time they could have had a decent chat with her, I thought.

It was on a walk in the Lake District with Biggins that I first told anyone outside our immediate circle. 'We had noticed the repetition,' Biggins said. 'I'm so sorry.'

'Please keep this to yourselves,' I asked. He and Neil did.

'What do we say to her?'

'Just be your wonderful, usual self. She loves being with you, just keep doing that.'

For Bar's birthday we had a small dinner with her favourite people, who we could rotate as the evening went on. It was a smashing evening and Bar was on great form, except for the moments when she wasn't talking. In those instances, that faraway look would pass over her, but if anyone else noticed they didn't say anything. My little lady was eighty. I just wanted God to protect her. I was going to need help from a power bigger than me.

'Sorry, Barbara, could you do that again please?' Bar had now forgotten the directions twice.

'So where do you want me?' She'd already asked that several times too.

I felt sick and I knew in my mind that these two days for the final Jackpotjoy advert marked the end of her working life. I wouldn't let her be seen struggling after a career of always being the ultimate professional. On the second day she wasn't on until 8pm, as they'd got behind, but I needn't have worried. She did her last scenes perfectly and I was delighted it had all ended well for what had been a wonderful job. We headed home.

'I'm worried about you, as a man,' she said, as we made our way. 'We don't have a sex life any more.'

I was a bit taken aback. 'Please, Bar, don't you worry about any of that.'

'It's not right because you're still a young man.'

I was fifty-four, so not that young, but I guess it's relative. 'Please, Bar, let's not talk about this.'

'No, Scott. You must do what you have to do. Just please never leave me.'

'Bar, I will never leave you.' She seemed reassured by that.

'Right then, we never have to talk about this again.'

That was so Bar. Even at eighty. As I mentioned earlier, when she was married to Ronnie Knight she told him she was fine if he found a bit on the side while she was away. She never thought twice about it, knowing perfectly well she was likely to do the same. Whereas before she never confused sex with love, I think she only thought like that because she'd never truly been in love. Now it was different. Ours was a true partnership and she was thinking about me.

I was upstairs when she called my mobile. She'd only been out a few minutes. By this time, if I needed to go out, I would make sure Yvonne came over. But occasionally Bar decided she wanted to whizz round to the dry-cleaner's. Independence was good, so I let her. She'd been going to the same shop for years.

'You okay, Bar?'

'Will you come and get me?' she asked, sounding shaky and confused. I ran.

'I didn't know where I was, Scott,' she said. She was so sad.

'I'm so sorry, Bar, that must have been frightening. You're okay now. We'll go out together from now on, okay?' Bar nodded and we walked slowly home.

'What's that car doing there?' she asked, as we turned into the mews. Our neighbour had parked in the resident parking space outside our house. 'That's our spot.'

I tried to explain it wasn't 'our' spot exactly, just outside our house, but she got cross and tore a strip off our neighbour. It was so unlike her.

'It's the illness,' explained Dr Kennedy. 'It's getting stronger, Scott, and it will distort her feelings. She may become irrationally irritable over little things, but you still want her to be able to do the things she can.'

God, give me strength. The stress of it all was catching up with me but, in the sea of worry and sorrow, she stood surrounded by drag queens in Victoria Park, starting the run for World AIDS Day. It was a great morning and a lovely memory for me. She also managed a reading at a carol service perfectly. Precious moments I hung on to.

'I don't take pills at night, apart from my sleeping pill.'

This was how our nightly routine would often start. How well and calmly those negotiations would go depended on my own tiredness or stress levels from that day. Sometimes I could calmly explain, as many times as it took, that she did take the pills I was holding, but at other times, if she kept on refusing, I could be guilty of getting into arguments with her, losing my patience and telling her she had to take the pills and that was the end of it. I knew it was all part of being a carer, but I still felt bad. It wasn't her fault, I knew that, but I had to remind myself it wasn't mine either.

She was also increasingly argumentative during the day. 'You don't look after me.'

When she first said that, it felt like a punch to the stomach.

'You got a memory problem, Babs?' shouted a journalist from the press pack.

I was swift to manoeuvre her away, but she heard. I thought she could manage events and award ceremonies, but it was getting more difficult. There were press everywhere and by now I knew they all knew. I cancelled everything for the rest of the year, except the opening night of *Hamilton*, and worked out what to do. Eventually, I emailed the paper. Nothing had changed. I was not going to be dictated to about going public. That was going to be our choice and our choice alone.

We lay low until Christmas and then went to Sussex, as we had been doing for over twenty years. As we walked in, Bar said, 'I've never been here before. Where are we?'

That was the first time I cried. Happy fucking Christmas.

20

Breaking News

'Do I have a TV in my room?' We were at home. It had been a quiet day.

'Yes, Bar, you have a TV in your room.'

'That's good,' she said, and went back to watching the TV.

I can't remember what we were watching. I couldn't focus anyway. The fact that Barbara didn't think she was at home felt less like a punch to the stomach than before. It is amazing what you can get used to.

A few days later Barbara followed me upstairs. 'Where are you going? Always off, leaving me.' I was only going to the office to do a few emails. I tried to placate her with the usual routine. 'Come on, Bar, we're a team. You know I've got your back.'

'I don't know anything of the sort. You don't bother looking after me.'

I was too stunned to react calmly. 'Bar, I'm with you all the time!'

'You just leave me here alone. You don't care, coming and going whenever you please.' She unleashed a torrent of accusations that I was neglecting her. Her face twisted with deep fury.

'It's all right, Bar, I'm here. I'm not going anywhere.'

It was true. I couldn't even go to the kitchen without her getting anxious. I had a sense that Barbara now expected me to devote every minute of my life to her, yet I felt I already was. If she sensed for a minute that I was preoccupied with something else, she'd home in, because that too counted as me neglecting her. It's one of the hardest things about being a carer of someone with Alzheimer's. If I left the sitting room for a moment she would follow me or call after me. 'Where are you?'

'What you doing?'

'Come and sit with me.'

'Scott?'

'Scott!?'

There was little let-up and even less escape. She was totally dependent on me. I think I made her feel safe, so long as I was paying her attention and always on hand to look at her and say something that reassured her in that second. But there are a lot of seconds in a day. By the end of that first week of the new year we were both struggling.

'I'm sorry, Scott. I'm just so scared,' she spluttered through uncontrollable sobs.

We both could feel it getting worse. I held her as she cried. Honestly, I'd never heard her sobbing like that before, and I felt just as terrible because there was absolutely nothing I could do. It must be such an awful feeling.

The changes were daily, sometimes hourly. One day we were supposed to be going out for dinner, but Bar got very panicky as soon as she woke up. She'd recently had a change of meds, which may have been the reason, but she simply said she couldn't face going out. She appeared very nervous, so I cancelled dinner and told her we'd have a nice evening in instead. I was learning that it was all about taking the stress away. There was no point trying to work through that stress.

But when we did get out, I could see it did her the world of good. We went to see *Everybody's Talking About Jamie* with Gary Cockerill and his husband Phil Turner and Bar loved it, she was transported by the show. So, capitalising on the moment, we went to Joe Allen's for dinner afterwards. As I took in the familiar surroundings, I knew outings like this would become rarer. I could see the acceleration. So I grabbed the moments I could, for her and for me, and I cancelled the ones she couldn't cope with. My advice to anyone in the same position is to grab the moment. Moments matter.

*

'Scott! Scott!' I ran upstairs. I could tell she was distraught from her voice. 'What's happened?'

She was standing in front of her wardrobe crying. 'I can't pick an outfit out for myself. I've forgotten how to choose.'

'That's okay, Bar. I can help.'

We were only going to get a blood test, but she liked to look good whenever she went out because to be honest she was always on parade one way or another. From then on, I tried to be on hand to help her choose her clothes. That's what I did for my nephew Harry's birthday lunch at Scalini's. I took a gamble, hoping that a daytime event would be better, because Bar was definitely worse in the evenings. I knew tiredness was a factor.

She leant across to me. 'I don't know where I am.'

'It's Harry's birthday. We're at Scalini's, your favourite Italian food.'

She nodded, but a few moments later I could see the lost look on her face. 'Harry's having a lovely birthday, Bar. It's nice to be out for lunch with family.'

I always had one eye on her in social gatherings and tried to keep pace with her withering memory.

'We don't go out much any more,' I told Dr Kennedy at our March appointment.

'Barbara, you're looking a bit subdued,' he said. 'How are you feeling in yourself?'

'My memory's not good, not good at all.'

I sat by her, nodding. She was distant and not at all herself.

'You both look a little tired,' he said. 'May I suggest it might be an idea to get some help in.'

'Not in my house,' Bar snapped. 'I can look after myself.'

The idea did not go down too well with Barbara. But Dr Kennedy stressed the point. 'It will be safer for you, Barbara, and Scott must be able to go out without worrying about you. He needs a little break from time to time.'

It wasn't until he said it that I knew it was true.

'But I need him,' she said.

'True, and he wants what's best for you. We all do. We are all here to look after you.'

'I don't like it,' she said.

It was all too heartbreaking.

A few days later we had a birthday dinner to go to and Bar said she was looking forward to it, so I asked Gary Cockerill to come to the house at four that afternoon to do her make-up. He always made her look so beautiful and now I was noticing that she seemed to be forgetting how to do her own make-up. When she attempted it, her hand would shake. At around six I went upstairs to get changed and found Barbara in the bathroom taking off the last bit of make-up with cotton-wool pads and make-up remover.

'What are you doing, love?' I asked.

'Going to bed.'

She'd completely forgotten we were going out.

I called Dr Kennedy. More tests, more scans. This time on her brain and heart. It was never-ending. Already this year felt long, but it was only mid-March. Another step into the abyss of confusion and another cancelled evening. I could not have cared less about going out. The thing that really upset me was how fast this bloody thing was progressing now.

I was in the office doing my admin work for the actors and had left Barbara downstairs watching TV. I could hear her sobbing and rushed down.

'Barbara, what is it? What's happened?'

She blinked through the tears. 'Oh, Scott, I thought you'd gone forever.'

'Bar, I will never leave you. I promise. I'm always here.'

'But, when I can't see you . . .' Her voice trailed off. 'I just keep forgetting.'

'I know, love, I know.'

I had to be ready to adjust to a new scenario at the drop of a hat. Another time I returned to the living room and Bar looked at me, a little bewildered. 'Everything okay, Bar?'

She looked at a framed photo of us and then back at me. 'Have you lived here long?'

I felt a rush of sadness go through me, but I held it together.

'Quite a long time, Bar, yes.'

'What? A few months?'

'Not exactly. Actually, we've been together for many years.'

She examined the photo, unconvinced. 'Are you sure?'

'Absolutely, we've been married for eighteen years. Look, that's our wedding photo.'

The photo appeased her fear and this time she settled back into her chair. I sat down next to her. It was difficult just popping out of the room for a minute or two and it made me afraid. I was becoming someone else to her. Not quite a stranger, but not completely known either. I think that terrified me more than anything else. Would Alzheimer's destroy what I had come to believe was an unbreakable bond?

We had a long-standing appointment in the diary with the Royal British Legion at the Seamen's Rest, which I always thought sounded like a *Carry On* film. Bar was on good form at the time so I decided to go ahead with it and we were rewarded with a great visit. At one point there was a singalong around the piano, which Bar loved, and in front of my eyes she slipped back into the role of the great music hall star Marie Lloyd. She may not have been able to recall getting dressed that morning, but all her roles were still inside her. Word perfect, she started singing the song I'd first seen her perform at Brick Lane Music Hall, 'My old man said follow the van . . .' It was rare these days to see her like that and it made me think, even if it's just once in a while, it's lovely to see her happy and in her element.

'You have a lovely home, Dame Barbara.'

Bar sat looking at the woman. She was trying to be polite. Well, sort of. This accomplished woman was the first carer I introduced Bar to and it wasn't going down very well.

'What sort of help would you like?' the lady asked.

'I don't want any help!'

'Well, Bar,' I said, 'remember Dr Kennedy said it would be nice to have some company when I go out.'

'But I have you.'

'Yes, but when I go out. Then you won't worry, and it'll be better for you.'

The woman was trying as well and made some suggestions about what she could do to help, but it was just making Bar cross. I knew Bar. It wasn't going to be a good match. I showed the woman out.

Bar was furious. 'You're trying to make out I'm ill! I'm not ill.'

'Bar, it was what Dr Kennedy suggested.'

'He did not. You're just trying to get rid of me. Well, good riddance. You shouldn't be saying those things.' She'd already forgotten what Dr Kennedy had said just two weeks earlier. This was getting harder by the day.

Then we had a lucky stroke. A lovely young lady called Ruby Baker, who was the niece of a make-up artist in *EastEnders*, came to meet Barbara. Although Ruby was not a carer, Barbara took to her. And so she started to come over on certain days. Just to chat, make her lunch and coffees, and generally be around to make sure she was okay. It gave me a little break to have the odd work lunch, do some exercise and, frankly, just have some time on my own. I was always home to take over by 4pm.

Ruby was excellent and it worked out so well that by mid-April she was helping Barbara bath and get changed. Barbara loved her and of course they would jokingly gang up on me. I was just so relieved that she was happy.

Bar watched a lot of telly, so when reports of Dale Winton's death came on the news she was really distraught and overwhelmed. We had not seen Dale in quite a long time, but it was still a shock. Bar had met Dale when he was a little boy because she had worked with his mother, another blonde bombshell called Sheree Winton. She had then met him again in 1979 at Radio Trent when she was doing promo work for *Calamity Jane*, and he said he wanted to get into television.

'Poor Dale, poor Dale. He never got over losing his mother. It's so sad. He was only sixty-two, Scott. What happened to Dale?'

Dale was as committed to showbiz as Bar was. He'd lost his mother on the eve of his twenty-first birthday and his close friends often said he never recovered from that, throwing himself into work as a result. Just after Bar and I met, she had bumped into Dale on the street. He was very excited about his idea for a quiz show set in a supermarket. Bar thought he was nuts, but *Supermarket Sweep* propelled Dale into the stratosphere he had set his sights on for so long. The news regarding Dale's death confused Barbara and she got upset. And then she would forget and go back to the news and get upset again.

Bar was almost hysterical from the moment she woke up. I cancelled Ruby, as it was not fair to put this on her, but as the morning progressed the hysteria and confusion got worse. I didn't know what to do. Sometimes this happened when the meds changed; sometimes it meant the meds had to be changed. I put in a call to Dr Kennedy. After lunch the house phone rang. I was expecting it to be Dr Kennedy, but it was BT telling me our internet was not performing properly. I listened with one ear because in the background Bar was constantly asking me how long I would be.

'It doesn't matter. I don't have time to deal with this.'

'We would like to offer you a rebate for poor service.' He went on about how quick it would be. Just a few minutes.

'Are you still on the phone? Scott? Scott?'

My head was scrambled.

'If you just sign into your bank account—'

'Scott! Where are you?'

'We can make the deposit straight away if that's easier? £600.'

He asked me to press two keys on my keyboard. When I signed into my bank the screen went blank. It crashed. I needed this like a hole in the head.

'How long are you going to be on the phone, Scott?'

'Don't worry, that will come back up—' said the engineer.

I was stuck on the phone in front of my computer in my office, calling down to Bar so that she didn't worry because I wasn't in the room. But she was worried.

'Where are you, Scott?'

'In the office, won't be long.'

'Oh no,' said the engineer. 'Can you see what we've done?'

I peered at the screen. A deposit of £6,600 pounds had been added to my account.

'We paid you too much. I'm so sorry, you're going to have to refund us now. I do apologise.'

I just needed to get this over and done with. I had Bar in one ear while trying to understand what the man on the phone was saying in the other. I just needed this done.

'Refund, sure . . .' I tried and failed three times. I was getting more and more stressed and had now been on the call for over an hour.

Bar was getting worse, agitated and upset I was still on the phone. As soon as it was over and I was back downstairs with Bar, I called my bank from my mobile. Bar was calmer now I was with her, but I was feeling really stressed. 'Why is my online PIN number not working?' I explained I'd just tried to make a refund to BT.

'Hold on, sir, I'm sorry, I cannot see anything on your account showing a deposit from BT. I believe you've been scammed.'

'What? Close the accounts,' I said, now really panicking.

'You need to come into the branch with ID so we can freeze your account before they take more.'

'Bar, I've got to go out.'

'Where are you going?'

'It's really important. You stay here, Bar. I'll be back.'

She was perplexed. I never ran out and left her. I never left her on her own. I pelted down the street imagining all the money draining out of my account. When I got to the bank, they asked me to come back in the morning to talk to the fraud squad, which meant leaving Bar again. I was at the bank by 9.30 and they told me that the scammers had already managed to get £18,000 from my account. They had taken a screenshot of my actual account, while it was blank to me, added the excess figure, which wasn't really there, and then had me send them £6,000 three times, while I was looking at a fake image of my bank account where seemingly nothing was happening. They told me it was a very advanced piece of technology. Thankfully, I was reimbursed, and as I walked out of the bank, I turned my phone back on and there were two voicemails.

'Scott, it's Anna Karen. Babs has been calling me. She asked if I knew anything about you. I'm so sorry, Scott, but I thought you should know.'

The second message was from Yvonne. 'Scott, Bar called to ask me how long you've lived at the mews. She was sounding very confused. Call me.'

I ran home. 'Bar! I'm home! I'm so sorry. I had to go to the bank, but I'm back now. I'm here, you're safe.' I was babbling, talking fast, trying to reach her.

Suddenly she started crying. 'Scott, Scott, I was so scared. I couldn't remember you. Oh God, this is awful. I hate this. I'm so sorry.'

We wept in each other's arms. I knew then, without a shadow of a doubt, I was not going to be able to leave her any more. Dr Kennedy came that evening. 'It's possible you may need a few days in hospital, Barbara,' he said. I think he said that for my sake as much as hers. During all of this I was also trying to make sure my own clients' work was running smoothly. It was a lot.

Saturday, 28 April was my fifty-fifth birthday but we didn't celebrate. I couldn't really feel enthusiastic and found it an effort even getting back to people who were texting to wish me happy birthday. Dr Kennedy said he would pop over, but I told him not to bother as there was nothing he could do. I was feeling quite low. Barbara had entered a continual, repetitive phase of asking the same questions.

'How long have you been at the house?'

'How long have we known each other?'

'How long have we lived here?'

'How long have you lived here?'

The stress was incredible.

By May I knew we could not hide the diagnosis any longer. I spoke to Dr Kennedy and said, with Barbara's blessing, it was time to go public. We had a good chat with Barbara and explained the reasons why it was best to tell people. I explained to her how honest she'd always been about her life and how it would help people with the same illness. She liked that. In that precise moment she understood, she took it all in and I could see her computing it and acknowledging what was being said. In that second, it was a good idea.

Five minutes later, it was gone. 'Don't you tell people I'm ill,' she'd say.

We would go over the reasons again. Again, she would agree. Again, she liked the idea of helping people. And then again, she would forget. What mattered to me was that I always had to have that moment of acknowledgement from her, however fleeting; it helped when the doubt crept in.

I reminded myself that if we didn't go public, I wouldn't be able to take Bar out and that would have been awful for her. No one wants to keep their loved ones hidden away. This way people would know what was happening if she wasn't herself in the street, they would understand why. This way I didn't have to keep it a secret any more.

So, on 4 May 2018, I spoke to Jane Moore. Jane is a panellist and anchor on *Loose Women*, but for a long time she has also been a journalist with her own column in the *Sun*. Over the years Jane had become a close friend and she and her husband Gary Farrow already knew about Barbara.

'I'm ready to go public,' I told her, and asked that the *Sun* make a decent donation to the Alzheimer's Society. I didn't have a relationship with the charity at that time. I chose it because it was one of the two big dementia charities. The *Sun* gave them £25,000, which was a total surprise to them and gratefully received. I certainly would not have accepted money for the story.

Jane and I met at my lawyer's office for what would be a two-hour interview. At times I cried so much that we had to stop. I think it was the relief of saying it all out loud. For four years it had been a virtual secret and now at least the stress of that part of it would be over.

I got home, packed our things and we headed down to Sussex. As ever I was able to relax a little there because my family stepped in and took it in turns to engage Bar so I could get some space, walk, be on my own, and make the most of the glorious weather. My niece Abbie is a beautician and she painted Barbara's nails, while my mum chatted to her about old times. My nerves were frayed and I was grateful for those moments, but really there was little respite. One night Barbara was so confused she asked me how I had got the job, she had no idea who I was or how we'd met. She started to speak about her husband in the third person.

'Is my husband coming to collect me?'

'Do you know where my husband is?'

I just listened and replied calmly, but it hurt.

Copy went back and forth between me and Jane. They took pictures of me sitting in Regent's Park looking forlorn. I still don't like my photo being taken.

The evening before the papers dropped, I sent out a text to various friends and loved ones to explain what they would read the next day. I got a flood of messages back. Some had no idea, others had heard something but didn't know for sure. They were all very upset to hear the news and said how brave we were, praising the love we shared. While I was apprehensive about what the story would bring, I was resigned. Still, I barely slept, worrying whether I was doing the right thing for my Bar.

21

Are We Nearly There Yet?

Thursday, 10 May 2018, seven o'clock in the morning, I turned on the telly and it was the lead story. Dr Hilary was in the *GMB* studio talking to the showbiz correspondent Richard Arnold about the disease and saying lovely things. It was on all the national news bulletins throughout the day and the big chat shows, *Loose Women*, *This Morning*. We sat and watched. There was a general sense of sadness, almost a little shock, that someone as effervescent and familiar as Barbara could have this illness. I received over a hundred emails and texts that day, just offering support and love, from as far away as America. It was a massive relief and gave me a much-needed boost.

At first Bar was comforted to know that people were being kind and supportive. She liked the clips of her famous films; the good old days put a smile on her face and it was nice for us to chat about them. But by the evening she was beginning to feel overwhelmed and bewildered. 'Why am I on the telly?'

'You've always been on the telly, Bar.'

'But they're saying I'm not well.'

I didn't have the energy to go over it again, so I turned the telly off and soon she had forgotten the day. For many months afterwards she would lean over to me and say, 'Don't you let anyone know I'm not well . . . I won't get any work.' She was always worried the offers would stop coming in.

'Don't worry, Bar, I won't say anything.'

'You better not. Swear you won't . . .'

'I swear, Bar.'

In the beginning I would try to change her perspective, but I learnt to just go with whatever she was asking me. Anything else was impossible and in the end pointless.

The following day the story was on the front of every newspaper. The Alzheimer's charity rang to thank me and asked if there was anything they could do to support us. By the end of the day the website had received double the hits, and donations were up by 30 per cent as a result of what became known as the 'Barbara Windsor effect'. It was wonderful that something positive was happening, but it wouldn't bring my Bar back.

Things got worse for a while afterwards. I don't know why, but Bar's confusion reached a new level. She was frightened almost all the time. I spent most of my days trying to explain to her that I was her husband and that we both lived in the house. I felt so drained at the end of every night. Eventually I was advised by Dr Kennedy to make a visual aid of our life, so I bought a whiteboard and put together a picture story of us through our years together. When we first met, wedding pictures. I also wrote facts like: 'Scott and Barbara have been married for 18 years. We live in Marylebone. This is our house.' I used to leave it in front of the television, but she would forget to look at it and still asked the same questions.

I would point to the board. 'Remember that those pictures are of our life.'

'Look, that was us fifteen years ago . . .'

I can't say which was more heartbreaking, the moments she recognised and remembered, or the moments where she looked back at me with that faraway look in her eyes that I came to dread.

The great thing about going public was that many of our friends rallied round us. We received masses of plants and flowers and my phone seemed to be going off nonstop with people checking in on us both. That wider support made a huge difference. I started to feel less alone. The Alzheimer's Society kept thanking us for the effect it was having and asked me to approve a couple of press quotes, which I found a bit embarrassing. I'd never been asked for quotes before, it was only ever Bar, so it felt odd, but looking back I can see that bringing purpose to our situation helped.

*

Dr Kennedy said he wanted Barbara to go into the Cromwell Hospital for some observation for a week. We were met and taken in through the back entrance and straight up to her room. Bar was confused and thought she was coming home so got distressed when I left. It was hard leaving her, so I was grateful that Dr Kennedy stayed to settle her in.

When I went back the next day, Bar got teary when she first saw me and then she got angry. 'I'll call the police if you don't get me out of here!' This flip between sorrow, fear and anger would happen fast and furiously and, though each moment would pass, they were stressful. It was hard to know how to be. It took a lot of patience to stay calm. Eventually she agreed with me that it was better to stay there for a few days. I was hanging on for the moments when her natural intelligence would win through and she'd recognise the situation for what it was. I was terrified about what would happen if and when that intelligence failed her. In the meantime, I grabbed on to those lucid moments like lifebuoys.

In the end, she was in hospital for ten days, which was the longest break without her at home. It was a rest of sorts, but not an emotional one because every waking hour was spent worrying about Bar.

While she was in hospital Dr Kennedy made some changes to her medication, and then observed her for any side-effects. She was more inclined to do as she was told with the nurses about, but she still argued with me during visits. 'Go and start a new life without me,' she said one day.

I made the decision to pay Ruby to go and sit with her when I couldn't, so she felt less alone. When she finally came home, she seemed elated, though I wondered whether that might just be the new pills working.

Sometimes I would catch her looking at me. 'Are we married?'

'Yes, Bar.'

She'd punch the air with her little fist, beaming. 'Yes!'

This happened many times a day, but I never tired of seeing it. To capitalise on her good mood and the effect of the new meds, I

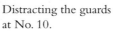
Distracting the guards
at No. 10.

Playing the pap game.

Hollywood superstars make the
mistake of trying to squeeze
Bar out of the photo. She's
having none of it.

'We're not supposed
to be here, Bar!'

Proud doesn't come close.
Dame Barbara Windsor, DBE.

Barry Burnett, agent and dear
friend, celebrating the day.

Never happier and more at
home than in a theatre.

Flying high at seventy-three.
Fairy Babs, Bristol Hippodrome.

...abs and me on our first date.'
...y Facebook post.

The picture the press had
been waiting for.

...home, Bar always had time
...a cup of tea and a natter.

Announcing Bar's illness.
My brave wife.

Magical day at *Mary Poppins*. The audience
gave Bar a standing ovation.

Hoping to make a difference for dementia
research. The beginning of the journey.

Doing the 2019 London Maratho
saved my sanity, though not my knee
The campaign went on to raise ov
£4 million – a record – with a little he
from my friends. And a medal to prove

Jake and Alison Wood, making her day.

June Brown pops in for tea.

Campaigning for social care, tea at Downing Street with the PM.

The gentle giant, David Walliams.

Last picture of us at home before Bar goes into the care home.

Care home, August 2020.
Bar's eighty-third birthday cake.
I couldn't get her to eat it.

October. 'This is my husband,'
she told everyone, pointing to
her badge of honour.

November.
Never wanting to let go.

In Loving Memory of

Dame Barbara Ann Windsor

6ᵗʰ August 1937 ~ 10ᵗʰ December 2020

Golders Green Crematorium
Friday 8ᵗʰ January 2021 at 2:00pm
Father Simon Grigg Officiating

Barbara: "That picture will follow me to the end"

Scott: "Yep!!! "Rest in peace my darling Bar, my love forever Scott xx"

Barbara's order of service. Stunning picture on the front, but on the back ... Barbara: 'That photo will follow me to the end!' Me: 'Yep!'

...aying goodbye to my ...ar. The hardest day of ...y life.

Just a few of the many wreaths sent by people who couldn't be there because of Covid restrictions.

London pays its respects to Bar in lights. I pay mine in stone. She was, indeed, a good bird. I miss her every day.

...dsor ~ Rest In Pea...

IN
LOVING MEMORY OF
DAME
BARBARA WINDSOR
6TH AUGUST 1937
10TH DECEMBER 2020
'BABS' - ACTRESS
ADORED BY HUSBAND
SCOTT MITCHELL,
FAMILY, FRIENDS
AND HER MANY FANS.

"SHE WAS
A GOOD BIRD"

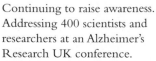
Continuing to raise awareness.
Addressing 400 scientists and
researchers at an Alzheimer's
Research UK conference.

Marathon 2021.
Forever pinned
to my heart.

We did it, Bar.

Live your best life.

made sure friends popped over regularly to see her. The faithful stalwarts were joined by new faces now that more people knew, which eased the burden. Jessie Wallace, Emma Barton, Kellie Shirley, Gaby Roslin, Jake and Alison Wood and, of course, Barry all came over.

One day I had lunch with Shane Richie and afterwards he came back to the house and spent ninety minutes with Bar while I did some admin upstairs. Her friends were the jam in the Ruby/Scott sandwich, and they made her feel part of the world. It didn't matter how many times they heard her stories, they sat and smiled, nodded and asked questions, or they just watched telly with her. But when they left the house, out of earshot, they used to say to me:

'How do you do it?'

The only answer to that is: You just do.

'Are you getting help?' David Walliams asked after a visit. 'You need to get some proper help.'

Reluctantly, eventually I agreed. It was clear it was getting close to the time we'd need to change the type of care we had for Bar. I couldn't go on relying on Ruby and friends to fill the gaps, so I met the owner of a care agency that had come highly recommended. I started mixing in the new carers between visits from Ruby. She had done an incredible job, but she was not a trained carer and it was getting harder to take care of Bar's growing needs. I also thought a turnover of new faces might be a good thing. Having people around her seemed to revive her spirits, she'd always been such a people person, just as long as she didn't get too tired, which then had a detrimental effect.

When the Alzheimer's Society came to the house to meet Barbara, she was amazing. We had an engaging, upbeat meeting with her telling them she wanted to do something to help. It was reassuring for me to see her not only openly discuss her illness, but also putting her positive personality to the problem of raising awareness. Supporting a cause was always the greatest reward showbiz status could bring. True Bar. I wish everyone had been so generous. I read a couple of articles from actors giving interviews saying how bad it was watching Bar's demise. Of course, I agreed, but the people saying it sometimes had not been to see her. I tried not to get wound up.

*

'Are we nearly there yet?' We were on our way to Sussex for a few days. It was June.

'I didn't realise this would take so long.'

Journeys were noticeably harder.

'I didn't realise it was this far!'

As soon as we got in the car she started repeating herself and I knew we had two and a half hours ahead of us. Sometimes we tried listening to the radio, but she wouldn't be able to hold her attention.

'Why are we not there yet?'

Every thirty seconds from getting in the car to arriving in Sussex, but it was worth it because as soon as we were there she'd perk up and she and Dad would start their playful squabbling, and I'd collapse in a heap. Mum and Dad were both sad to witness the decline in Bar. Each time we went they noticed it more acutely than I did, but I could see how bad things were getting through their troubled, concerned eyes.

In July I noticed a new breathlessness in Bar's chest, so I took her for some more tests. This time with a specialist in respiratory conditions. It was nonstop, a constant barrage of symptoms and tests. I seemed to function on autopilot, waiting for the next episode to reveal itself. I didn't have to wait long. Bar's stomach started playing up again and that was terrible because she was in a lot of pain and sometimes had accidents that really upset her.

The best day by far was when the Alzheimer's Society came to the house to do some filming with Bar. She looked fabulous. The house was busy. Camera, action, everything she knew and loved. Immediately became the true professional she'd always been. She was so good and I was very proud of her.

There was a cost, though. The following day, she was admitted for an overnight stay in hospital; the stomach issues were getting worse. They had her on so many lotions and potions, the poor lady was exhausted, not to mention confused. It was impossible to explain her pain and her symptoms; it all just frightened her. I felt beside myself seeing the demise, thinking this was it. But then, like the trouper she was, she would rally herself enough to go out for lunch with her great mate from *EastEnders*, Pam St Clement. We had lunch around the corner, sitting outside in the sunshine, and the reaction from the passing public, catching a glimpse of Peggy and Pat together, was heartwarming. I can't believe there had ever been a time when I'd begrudged it. Now I relished it. The public had been exceptionally supportive since the news broke. People smiled at her, made a point of saying hello to her without being too intrusive. It was like they were saying, *It's okay, Bar, we haven't forgotten you. We're still here. Still rooting for you.* She was quite chatty that day and could follow the conversation as long as we kept engaging her. Of course, she would be repetitive and if Pam and I started talking about something else she could quickly drift off. It was easy to lose her.

We were taking our seats to watch the matinee of *42nd Street* with Jake and Alison Wood when a few members of the audience started waving at Bar. She waved back. More waved, she waved back, and on it went until the houselights dimmed. It was sweet to see the smile on her face and she seemed so good we braved an early supper at The Ivy. Chris Evans was there and came over to wish her well. It was on one of those precious good days that I wondered if only I noticed how quickly she got out of breath when she walked.

Then one day I happened to walk into the bathroom just as Bar wobbled. I reached forward and just about managed to catch her as she collapsed, white as a sheet, to the floor. I laid her down, called 999 and within ten minutes the paramedics were there. She came round but her heart rate was way too low, and she was rushed off to UCH for immediate tests. What followed was lots of calls between the doctor at UCH and Dr Kennedy, which resulted in the decision to get her blue-lighted in a private ambulance to the Cromwell so that Dr Kennedy could oversee her care. He needed to work out what was going on with her heart and lungs.

It turned out that Bar's medication was making her heart rate drop, but she needed to stay on it, so the only option was a pacemaker. All the specialists agreed it was the best way forward for her quality of life. The next day she was prepared for surgery. I was allowed to go right down into the theatre with her and stayed with her until she was on the operating table. I did my best to keep her calm, told her I loved her and would be there when she woke up. Then I returned to her room and wondered what would be next.

'Where are we?'

'Hospital, love, you've had a small operation.'

She was groggy.

'My chest hurts,' she'd say, trying to rub the spot where they had inserted the pacemaker. I could see the lump through the dressing.

'Try not to touch that, Bar, it needs to heal.'

'What is it?'

'Just a little device to stop you fainting.'

'I don't faint.'

She drifted off. Then . . . 'Where are we? Why does my chest hurt?'

How could I explain that she'd had a small round flat battery inserted under her skin with a wire now attached to her heart so that when the rate dropped it would send a pulse of electricity to get it beating faster because the medication she needed to stop the plaque building in her brain dangerously lowered her heart rate. Thankfully, the doctor gave her a big dose of morphine and I noted as I was leaving that her colour was much better than it had been all week. The effect of the pacemaker was immediate, so I was pleased we'd done it, but I was a bit fearful of the next couple of days.

Why was she being made to walk around by physiotherapists?

What was she doing in hospital?

Why couldn't she come home?

Where had I been?

Where was I going?

Why was she here?

'Good news, you're being discharged today.'

Bar looked concerned.

'Home. You're going home.'

I knew what that look signalled. She didn't know what home meant. The tears sprang up and slipped down her face. 'It's okay, Bar, you're coming home with me. You'll be happy when you get there.'

She shook her head. Tearful and agitated. Somehow I got her back to the mews and watched her settle back into her bed and go to sleep. Her sleep was my respite.

'Flowers for Dame Barbara,' said the delivery woman. Several bunches arrived at once.

'Who are they for?'

'You, Bar, it's your birthday.'

'Is it? Silly cow.'

The doorbell rang again. Bar was concerned.

'Flowers for Dame Barbara.'

'Who are they for?'

'You, Bar, it's your birthday.'

'Is it? Silly cow.'

The doorbell rang again . . . The strain was starting to get to me and I felt drained, emotionally, mentally and physically, but what choice did I have? What choice did either of us have? We had to soldier on.

'But I can't even run!' I pleaded.

'You'll be fine,' said Adam Woodyatt.

'It's not that bad,' agreed Jake Wood.

'Twenty-six-point-two miles – not that bad?'

And so I ended up signing up for the 2019 London Marathon. How could I not? The Alzheimer's Society had joined forces with Alzheimer's Research UK under the umbrella 'Dementia Revolution' and had been made the partner charity for the 2019 marathon. They asked if it would be okay for them to approach the *EastEnders* cast and see if any of them would run the marathon in support of Barbara and, of course, being the fabulous people they are, a team – who would become known as Barbara's Revolutionaries – signed up immediately. Joining me were Adam Woodyatt, Jake Wood, Tanya Franks, Natalie Cassidy, my client Jamie Borthwick, Jane Slaughter, Kellie Shirley, Emma Barton and John McIntyre, all *EastEnders* cast, past and present. Plus a couple of others: Bev and Sam Woodyatt, Liz McGill, Hayden Heath.

I rather naively wrote in my diary:

Wednesday, 8 August 2018: I better go and buy myself some trainers!

'Roll up, roll up . . .' I cried out in a silly voice.

'I'm not going on that.' Bar eyed the new stairlift with a mix of fury and disgust.

'Welcome to the best ride in town. Fasten your seatbelts and scream if you want to go faster.'

Eventually Bar relented and allowed us to harness her in. 'Silly bastard,' she said, but at least she was smiling.

I had to do it, the breathlessness was better but still there, and it made it harder for her to go up and down the stairs. That made her unsteady, which made me nervous. Every time she went up, there had to be me or a carer directly behind her and, when she came down, directly in front of her. Even then I wasn't sure we could save her from a fall, so while she was in hospital I'd had a stairlift installed.

'It's good to be back in Finsbury Park,' Bar said as we drove over the Westway.

'My mum left me this house,' she said, as I unlocked the mews house she had worked so hard for.

'It's in Stoke Newington.' We were in Marylebone.

I just went along with it until it passed and she realised we were back at home.

Just another day.

Up until this point we'd kept the heart scare under wraps, but Biggins let it slip on an evening out. The *Sun* called me, so I had to confirm it. Biggins was mortified. The next day it was a front-page story.

Just another day.

I knew they would keep coming.

Occasionally I would be thrown a lifeline, although I was particularly nervous about this one. I was asked to be part of a video for the Dementia Revolution. I met a number of people who were involved in Alzheimer's one way or another. One lady was a senior researcher, which was fascinating; another young lady told me that not only did her mother have the disease, she herself had the gene. We all told our own stories, not dissimilar to AA in a way. Everyone had a different experience, but we were all affected by the same disease. It was a relief to feel supported because, honestly, the bad news kept coming.

Bar's health went up and down and then my dad was admitted back to hospital.

Just another day was now a bad Groundhog Day.

Towards the end of September lovely Ruby told me she had to stop looking after Barbara. I got it. It was not her chosen profession and she had done such a great job to get this far. Bar and I would miss her but wished her nothing but health and happiness on her journey.

'Who are you?' Barbara looked at me blankly as I was helping her out of the bath. I had been dreading this day since the diagnosis. It was 23 September 2018.

I was dumbstruck for a moment.

'Who are you?' she asked again.

Now she looked frightened. It was like she was looking at a stranger. She was vulnerable. Scared. Usually I could find the recognition in her eyes. This time there was none. My heart sank. When she snapped out of it, she started crying, realising what she had done.

'I'm so sorry, my memory is awful.'

'It's okay, Bar,' I said gently, and got her out of the bath, wrapped in a towel and safely in her room.

'I'm so sorry, my memory is awful.'

'It's okay, Bar,' I repeated, but inside my guts were in knots. The experience was as painful as I'd always thought it would be.

A sad day.

I left Bar with a carer and drove to Sussex to see Dad in hospital. He was on a grim ward. One man looked like he was going to die any minute and another had Alzheimer's and was being abusive to a nurse. Dad was being stoical and putting on a brave face. Driving back to London I thought, *This is a living hell*. There was no escape.

With them both ill I was struggling, but apart from my therapist and a couple of friends to confide in I just ploughed on.

*

The Virgin Money Giving page for Barbara's Revolutionaries went live and I kicked it off with my own donation. I would never ask others to do what I wouldn't do myself. The Alzheimer's Society asked me to go on *Loose Women* to announce the team for Barbara. I was nervous but Jane Moore, Stacey Solomon and Linda Robson made it easy and the audience were lovely, so I soon calmed down. Which made recording an ITN bulletin for the evening news a bit easier.

Jeremy Joseph, the owner of G-A-Y and Heaven nightclubs, emailed me to say he'd seen me on *Loose Women*. He's a keen marathon runner and knew I was a novice so offered to help me get started. Once a week for the next seven months he took me running. He was very patient. The first time we went out I was so slow and gave up, thinking I was going to be sick. But he gave me his time and encouragement, and slowly I found I was huffing and puffing less, and liking it a bit more. I will always be indebted to Jeremy for that. He is a kind soul and a very funny man, which helped me get round the park.

Otherwise, time crawled, with days much the same. One day Jonathan Ross paid Bar a visit and sat and chatted with her for a couple of hours. It was extremely kind of him, particularly because, while they knew each other professionally, they weren't great mates. Which made it all the stranger when friends much closer to us than that never visited. I never got my head around that.

'Queen Barbara,' said Adam Woodyatt, opening the door to the royal box. We were back at *42nd Street*. This time Bonnie Langford was starring. Barbara had worked with Bonnie several times over the years and loved the show. I suspected she had forgotten about the last time we went. The audience spotted her and started applauding and cheering her. Bar did her best royal wave to the crowd and it made my heart sing. After the show she performed a little tap-dance of her own on the stage. My Babs, she's still got it.

*

On 9 November I got my running distance up to 2.1 miles. Only another twenty-four to go – would I ever manage this? But donations were slowly starting to come in, so there was no backing out and, over time, I started to like the runs. They cleared my head, which was a good thing because I was aware I was struggling. I felt numb and detached. Low and tired. Thank God for the carers, as they allowed me some hours in the day to do things that were good for me. I think I was lonely. I didn't have a partner any more and I missed that connection.

By 10 December I hit the five-mile mark. Progress. Bar had a regular team of carers who she liked and it meant I could pop out occasionally. Not guilt-free, but taking less worry with me for a while. The runs were helping. And I was still always home by 4pm to cook the evening meal. Even that was tricky because Barbara was constantly looking for me or following me into the kitchen wanting to know what I was doing.

'What are you doing, Scott?'
'Cooking dinner.'
Wait.
'Where are you, Scott?'
'In the kitchen.'
Wait.
'What are you doing, Scott?'
And so on . . .

Matt Lucas and I took Bar to the Palladium panto. A rare and special evening out. Bar and Matt were mobbed by the audience and paps alike. I was worried Bar might get scared, but in fact she enjoyed it.

I got together with Barbara's Revolutionaries to do our first group training session at the track in Mile End. It was great. We were coached and filmed by Martin Yelling, the London Marathon head coach. It was particularly lovely to chat to Tanya as her stepdad had Alzheimer's, so she knew as well as I did what it's really like living with this terrible disease.

By Christmas I was doing 6.2-mile runs. I was feeling stronger, but it was a strange Christmas Day.

25 December 2018: Bar was not really with it.

I brought her home from Sussex on Boxing Day. It felt easier for everyone. New Year's Eve was a bad day. It was truly heartbreaking to watch Bar disappear more and more from the world. It was all just too much.

22

Marathon Man

'Barbara doesn't want to get up today,' said the carer, as I returned from my training run. This was getting more regular and it was tempting to let her sleep, but routine was important, even if she didn't remember it. The trouble was the meds made her drowsy, so getting her up was a battle; it was like trying to get a pubescent school child out of bed.

'Ten more minutes.'

'Leave me alone.'

'No.'

'Go away.'

There was a battle to get her up. A battle to get her to eat. A battle to get her to take her pills. We couldn't wear her down; she would either change her mind, or not.

'Ladies and gentlemen, may I present to you Dame Barbara Windsor,' I called out as she sat in the stairlift, finally bathed and dressed.

Sometimes she'd laugh. 'Silly sod.'

Sometimes there would just be a faint smile. 'Hello darlin'.'

Other times she'd gaze at me with a particular look in her eye. 'I'm not good . . .'

'I'm not good' meant different things: I'm not good right now. I'm not good in my bones. I'm not good compared to what I was . . . or, simply, I'm not well. I knew when we were looking at a bad day, she'd be shaky and breathless.

Starting every day was hard because it was boring, difficult and repetitive. All I could do was my best and keep clocking up the miles.

'I'm having one of those black-outs,' she cried. She didn't know where she was, who she was, who I was. She would look around, terrified. I held her hand and talked to her softly to try to bring her back. It became instinctive after a while. I've never been a parent, but it felt to me like looking after a baby. A lot of it was trial and error, finding what worked for us. I was on high alert, all the time, even when I slept. I would spring awake, every hour; hour after hour. Until I was chronically sleep-deprived myself.

'I'm sorry you have to look after me,' she said on one of the many evenings we stayed in watching telly. Going out in the evening was too hard for both of us.

'You'd do the same for me,' I told her. Though in my mind I jokingly thought, *No she wouldn't, she'd be out on the town with Biggins!*

There was no quick fix for dementia. For how long would this be our way of life? Months? Years? What I came to enjoy was the publicity campaign for Dementia Revolution. Bar made a promotional video and she owned it. 'You're very handsome, darlin',' she said to the cameraman.

She switched back into pro mode as soon as the autocue started running. It was a delight to watch, as ever. Later she got tired and, as the crew were wrapping up, she looked at me. 'Who are they?' Dementia experts call it 'sundowning'. Things always got worse when the sun went down.

Having the *EastEnders* cast involved helped me enormously. As did becoming part of something that was bigger than us. The positive effect gave me something to think about and definitely helped me cope with the stress of Bar's illness. Anything was better than sitting at home watching my wife decline.

The Virgin Money Giving page for Barbara's Revolutionaries went public. 'Hey, Bar, Kellie has come over to go running with me.'

Bar was sitting on the sofa. 'Oh, look at you. You haven't changed a bit.'

'Bar thinks I look ridiculous in my knee supports, but I tell her it's all for a good cause. Barbara's Revolutionaries are raising a lot of money for dementia.'

'I've got that,' she said to Kellie.

But sometimes my feeding her information like that wouldn't work and she'd get cross. Whispering loudly, 'Don't you tell them I'm ill. I'll never get any work.' Her perennial fear.

Kellie and I got papped on that run. Me huffing and puffing around the park was hardly news, but the donations leapt up, so I did not mind a bit. Every news bulletin led to increased support. This was the press working at its absolute best.

Jane and Gary came over to take Bar and me round the corner to lunch at Fischer's. You couldn't help but notice Bar was leaning forward, so Gary and I took either side of her and I remember thinking how wrong I'd been to think she'd looked frail before.

That night she held her head and said she'd heard a loud bang. Could she feel her brain malfunctioning? 'I'm hungry,' she announced.

'Bar, we've eaten.'

'No we haven't.'

I took her into the kitchen and opened the dishwasher to show her the dirty plates. She would eye me suspiciously, thinking I was tricking her. 'How about a biscuit?' I offered as a compromise, hoping she'd forget that she thought she was hungry. It was a never-ending loop of distraction, subterfuge and exasperation.

Towards the end of January 2019 I did a piece with the *People* promoting the campaign. I went against my own code and looked at some of the comments following the publication. Foolish.

'Why is he selling stories?'

'This should be private.'

It made me doubt myself, but I remembered what I had learnt in AA: what other people think of you is none of your business. I wondered what these people who comment on the internet were doing for other people; probably very little. I was putting myself through 26.2 miles of running on my little legs to raise money and awareness for a disease that was stealing my wife, that was stealing a million lives.

Paul O'Grady popped over, which was lovely for Bar. She was in a good place, but it started to cost her more, faster.

'Sorry, love, I'm tired now.' It was always done in such a nice way, though my insides would twist a bit.

'I bet you are, Babs.'

And if our guest didn't take the hint and say a quick farewell, she'd add, 'It was lovely to see you. Where are you going now?' Brilliant.

The routine at home wouldn't really change. Carers arrived. Carers left. I cooked dinner.

'Scott, where are you? Come and sit with me.'

'I'm trying to cook.'

It reached a point where, although she could walk, she wasn't steady. I would bring her through to the kitchen and we'd sit in there and, despite always being hungry, she'd then pick at her food. Her appetite was declining. It was easier to keep the telly on and eat in there. Another distraction technique. I would try to get her up to bed around nine, help her get undressed, and then the nightly process of persuading her to take her medications would begin again.

'I don't take them.'

'You do, Bar, for your memory. To make you better.'

That was a lie, but I was knackered by this stage and just needed her to take the pills so she would drift off, finally, to sleep. We'd lie on the bed, watching telly, holding hands. Waiting, waiting, and then slowly I would start to pull my hand away, ever so gently.

'Where are you going?'

'Nowhere.'

And repeat . . .

Eventually the pills worked and she would be asleep and I would go to the spare room, look at my iPad, text a mate, try and have a laugh, maybe a chat, but I was also exhausted. I worried constantly about her falling so I slept with one eye open.

'You need an alarm mat,' suggested one of the carers. It was a blessing and a curse. When she moved an alarm went off in my room and I would jump up, heart racing, which was what the alarm was designed to do. Often she'd just turned in her sleep. Or sat up. But sometimes I would find her on the floor.

'It's okay, Bar, I'm here.'

Sometimes she made it to the bathroom on her own. Sometimes she didn't. The thing was, I would never know. I kept waking up at the slightest sound. I still wake up at times thinking, *Is she okay?* I open my eyes in the middle of the night, my ears straining and think, *Barbara*.

Bar was grinning like a child being offered a giant Mr Whippy. David Walliams had popped in to see her. He sat next to her. They would hold hands and he would ask questions about all the old showbiz times, this gentle giant of a man, swooping in and protecting my little bird.

Meanwhile, I kept clocking up miles round the park. Honestly, hitting double figures made me feel euphoric. I used to take cocaine to feel like this. Who knew?! People donated what they could afford (for some that was quite a lot, thank you!) and every pound made a difference. By February our Virgin Money Giving page had received just under £50,000. I was very happy to be part of such a dedicated team of runners.

Visitors distracted and exhausted Bar. Tanya would chat theatre. Jake would chat soaps. Barry would talk about the old times. Those special hours with friends didn't reflect what it was normally like, but even so I was relieved the pressure was off me for a moment.

I started to notice the visits were leaving her more tired and disorientated, though. One time she got a bit lost, in our very small mews house, and had an accident. I wasn't sure if it was because of having a visitor or a new decline, it was hard to know. Once, when Debbie McGee came round, we had such a lovely time, but the subsequent crash was intense. I started to wonder if the cost of the visits was getting too high.

'BABS' DYING WISH' read the front page of the *Daily Star*. Then, in smaller print, 'IS TO HELP PEOPLE'. She wasn't dying, she was at home, but it was a grabbing headline. *The One Show* followed up, asking me to take part in an obituary piece.

'Barbara is still very much alive.'

She was in particularly good form that day, ironically; alert, funny, and found the whole thing hilarious. 'That's me,' she said when her face appeared on the TV. 'They say I'm helping people.'

'You are. A lot of people.'

'That's good.' It made her happy in that moment, but ten minutes later she'd forget again.

'Why is my picture in the paper. Am I dying?'

'No, Bar, it's a positive piece about your memory loss.'

'There's nothing wrong with my memory!'

Training saved me, no doubt. I don't know what I would have done if I hadn't had that to get me up, get me out, get me going. One foot after another, just keep going. The training for the London Marathon gave me the strength to complete the marathon that was my life living with the knock-on effects of dementia.

'My ears hurt, Scott.'

Jeez, what now, I'd think, and I swear she could tell immediately.

'What's up with you?'

'Nothing.'

'I can't hear anything, Scott.'

Sometimes I'd snap back something mean. 'Not another ailment.'

'I heard that!'

I was sorry every time it happened. I am not making excuses, but I think anyone in my position knows how desperate it can get. Just going over and over and over the same thing; another complaint on a loop, another question on repeat. It can send a person mad.

'We'll take a break to play Barbara Windsor singing "What the World Needs Now Is Love",' said Jeremy Vine. The Radio 2 studio filled with her voice and I broke down. It was too much. She didn't sound like that any more. We continued the interview, but I got a bit emotional talking about her.

When I came out of the recording studio, Steve Wright was waiting for me and gave me a huge hug. It felt surreal being a guest, rather than waiting in the green room, as I had done for so many years. I was quite lost without her.

'It's not easy,' said Steve Wright, 'but you are doing a great job – raising awareness, starting a national conversation about something really important.'

Was I? It didn't feel like that. It felt like I was letting her down, but a flood of donations came in after that interview and it lifted my spirits more than anyone could imagine. The public are so generous in this country and we should be so, so proud. It is always the public not the government that keeps charities alive.

'Her ears are very blocked,' said the doctor. Now I felt bad. 'That might explain why her balance is so off too.'

So along with everything else, she couldn't hear properly and now she could hardly walk. It was becoming harder to get her up the road, so even though we were living in a medical epicentre I would still have to put her in the car. Everything was an effort for her. She was slow, unsteady and frightened because now she was aware her balance was off.

The team did some fun training on Primrose Hill with Olympian Jo Pavey. She put us through our paces. The class was filmed; more promo work, more donations. Now I was beginning to feel happy about it. Then I went home.

'I've got a bad back.'

And I'm back to reality. I put on the film *Bohemian Rhapsody* to distract her. It worked. We both cried. I don't know why; I guess because ultimately it's about what we have, what we lose and what we leave behind.

The number of the carer flashed up and immediately I panicked. 'Sorry,' I said to my fellow runners as I left the table where we were having dinner.

'Scott, Barbara is a bit distressed because she doesn't know where you are.'

Then she put Bar on the phone. 'Where are you?'

'You know all this running I've been doing.'

'No.'

'Yes, you do. You think my shorts are silly.'

'Your legs are too little to run.'

'Exactly, but I'm running for you, to help you get better. Remember, our campaign for Dementia Revolution.'

'To help people like me.'

'That's right. Well, tomorrow I have a big race and it starts really early. I need a good night's sleep so Gabriella will be with you tonight.'

'But I miss you . . .'

'I miss you too, my love.'

I couldn't explain not being there. I had barely left her side. How could I tell her I needed to get out a bit? I needed to breathe? I knew the real Bar would have understood and I had to steel myself and remind myself that I had to survive in order to be able to care for her. I sat back down and tucked into more pasta. My phone rang again . . .

Mo Farah took off like a bullet, then twenty minutes later we, along with 14,000 other runners, crossed the start line of the Vitality Big Half Marathon. I'd been talking to the crowds, had been interviewed, and as I set off I thought what a radical change I had been through in my life. For as long as I could remember I had been the person in the background. Now that I was standing on my own in the foreground, all I had to do was keep on running. Of course I started off too fast, like a greyhound out of the traps. Tanya asked our friend John McIntyre to catch up with me and tell me to slow down, which he did. God knows how he found me.

I finished it in two hours and forty-one minutes – I was over the moon. Six weeks to go until we did the whole thing. Could I really run twice that? Deep down I was very doubtful.

'Tell me all about it,' said Bar, when I got home. She knew I had done something, even if she didn't completely understand what it was.

I did a phone-in on Chris Evans's show the next morning. Chris said that he and his team would like to do something for Dementia Revolution, would I mind? Would I mind? Honestly, he is the most unsung hero of fundraising and he deserves an honour.

I was lucky enough to get a tour around the Dementia Research Institute with scientist Amanda Heslegrave. 'Dementia can start twenty years before the first symptoms show,' she said. 'It's a curve. There is no real understanding of how to prevent it, no cure and no understanding of the cause, but we are getting closer to ground-breaking treatment. That's where your hard-run money is going.' It was fascinating learning how the plaque around brain cells blocks the signals from the memory part of the brain. These scientists were the real heroes. I left with a sense of hope for the future.

The promo work continued to gather pace, even if my running started to slow. But I kept my aches and pains to myself and my running mates. It was all smiles for *The Gaby Roslin Show*, *Steve Wright in the Afternoon* and *Loose Women*.

I returned home to battles with Bar, who wouldn't undress for the osteopath who'd come to see her, but then Biggins popped in and within minutes she was shrieking with laughter and was all smiles again. We also had a surprise visit from Matt Lucas. Bar never forgot who Matt was – turns out he's dementia-proof. Pity we can't bottle him. Then David Walliams came over again with his new puppy Ernie. Bar had always loved dogs and spent a happy hour cuddling him.

Matinees were good for us. We went to see *Only Fools and Horses* at the Haymarket. Bar had a great time and they had asked if she wanted to go backstage and have some photos taken. She was led by Paul Whitehouse, whom I knew she felt safe with. The pictures made the next day's papers. The producer Phil McIntyre called me the next day to say thank you and made a generous donation to our page. He had personal experience with dementia, losing his mother, Joyce, to the illness.

Little acts of kindness meant a great deal. Once, when I came back from Waitrose, Jane Moore was having coffee with Bar. It was a silly thing, but this meant I could unpack the shopping without explaining everything to Barbara.

'Bar, guess what? I got up to eighteen miles today!'

'I'm so proud of you, darlin'.' But before I could appreciate the moment and feel the joy of her compliment, she said, 'Whose house is this?'

Care. Run. Care. Promo. Care. Sleep. Care. Repeat.

I did interviews with Chris Evans, the *Sun*, *Loose Women* again, *This Morning*, *Good Morning Britain* and Virgin Radio, and each time donations were made. The closer it got, the more we raised, but also the twitchier I became. What if I couldn't do it? What if I let everyone down? That critical voice never left me.

Bar was falling frequently when she got out of bed to go to the loo, so I thought it was time to get overnight care. There would be a break between 4 and 8pm, then a new carer would come in. I found myself going to bed at 8.30pm and leaving the bedtime routine to another person. This allowed me to sleep a bit better.

'Scott!' She'd appear at the top of the stairs. 'Where are you?'

The carer would try to distract her, guide her back into her room. Sometimes it worked. This dementia research couldn't be done fast enough.

The night before the marathon, Chris Evans invited some of Barbara's Revolutionaries to join him at a dinner for competition winners from Children in Need. Later that night we returned to our hotel and Natalie Cassidy's nine-year-old daughter Eliza donated all her pocket money to our page. Bless her heart. Every penny mattered.

The day of the London Marathon arrived. Sunday, 28 April 2019. My fifty-sixth birthday. I got up at 5am, and forced myself to eat porridge and a banana, even though I felt sick with nerves. My legs were like jelly, all I could think was, *Shit, this is not going to go well . . .*

'Next year we should—'

We were on the Virgin bus at 7.15. I was chatting to Chris Evans.

'What do you mean, next year? There won't be another marathon for me. Ever.'

'It doesn't work like that, Scott. You've started a cause. You're being heard. You're doing good. You can't just switch it off!'

I must have paled.

'Don't worry,' he said, patting my already sore knees. 'We'll talk about it later.'

No we bloody won't, I thought.

I managed to do an interview with Gabby Logan, but I can't remember much about it. We watched the elites from the balcony and then were taken to the start line at 10.15am. Eventually it was my turn to be fed into the sea of runners from the side. Our gang started together at first. I made sure we began at a slow pace so that somehow, when we'd lost everyone else, it was just Tanya and me, step by step, for the whole 26.2 miles.

I have never experienced a day like it. The crowds were amazing, calling out everyone's names. I wish Bar could have been there. We thought about it, but it would have been too much for her and I would have worried about her all through the run. I had enough to worry about with whether my little legs would get me round the course!

As I approached Buckingham Palace and turned into the Mall I could see the finishing line and the surge of emotion was volcanic. But also, the more I looked at the finishing line, the further away it seemed to get. Of course, it was painful at times but the music and crowds got us round in five hours and forty-one minutes. Tanya and I crossed the finishing line at exactly the same second. I felt like I'd won an Olympic gold.

'Bar! I've just run the marathon.'

'That's good, dear. What time will you be home?'

'Well, there's going to be a bit of a celebration.' I was coming off the call and going straight into interviews.

'But you've been out all day . . .'

Please, God, can this day not end with Bar and me having a barney. 'I know, I'm sorry, love. I've got some people to see then I'll be home and I'll bring my medal.'

'What have you got a medal for?'

'I love you. I've got to go now.'

We went to the Royal Society for the Dementia Revolution party. The CEO of the Alzheimer's Society was very complimentary about what Bar and I had done in terms of raising profile, and even produced a birthday cake for me. In the cab home I started to feel the come-down. That wonderful euphoria was beginning to wane. As I came into the sitting room I saw Lieze, the carer, help Bar up on to her feet and get her clapping.

Very gingerly Bar walked towards me and hugged me. 'I'm so proud of you. I'm so proud of you, Scott.' It was hard to know whether or not she knew what she was congratulating me for, or why she was proud. I'm sure she was, but probably not for running 26.2 miles and being part of a team that had raised nearly £150,000 to fight the disease that was incrementally taking her away from me.

'What's for dinner?'

That was easy. A few taps on the phone and I placed our order. Hamburger, chips and a chocolate milkshake.

'You shouldn't eat so much,' said Bar.

She was often ticking me off about my eating. She was right most of the time, but not today. Today I had well and truly earned those chips!

For the next three days I used Bar's stairlift to go up and down the stairs because when I got out of bed the following morning I fell into the wall. My legs had completely seized up. The come-down was hard; all that focus, drive, attention and whirlwind was suddenly gone. And then things got worse.

'Well done on your run,' said the lady at the café in the foyer of the Princess Royal Hospital. It was still alien to me. Without Bar I was used to being totally anonymous.

'I am so proud of you, son,' said Dad. He was breathless. He was weaker with every visit. It was scaring me. That this giant of a man, who had loved me so fiercely, could look so frail was gutting. I fed him some yoghurt. It was like feeding a baby. He didn't speak, we just held eye contact and I tried to be brave.

The next time I saw him I fed him lunch and he seemed a bit more alert. I kissed him goodbye. 'Thanks for looking after me, son.'

I pulled over on the way home and wept.

'Scott, a man came to the door and said he'd worked with Bar many times over the years. I'm really sorry. I didn't know him, but Barbara invited him in.'

'What? Who?'

Already I was running upstairs to look at the CCTV footage. I watched in horror. The man entering our house wasn't a person Bar had worked with, he was a paparazzo on the hunt. I could see him pointing out to the street and telling her to come outside. I watched

Bar go to the mirror in the hall because, although confused, she knew she wasn't ready to go 'out'; she had no make-up on and was dressed just in clothes that the carer could easily put on. Had he asked her to come outside for a photo? She couldn't remember, but I could tell from watching the footage that Bar instinctively knew something was wrong. So then he asked for a selfie with her, which he took, quickly, before she could really respond. Then he was out the door. He left his card, so I had his name and called the police but was told that legally there was nothing they could do because Barbara had let him in. I got my lawyer to alert the press editors to what he had done and sent him a warning letter. He showed no contrition.

What that man did still makes my skin crawl.

'Scott,' said my mum on the phone. 'The palliative care team are taking over.' She said it was okay if I didn't come because of the revolting invasion of privacy, but I couldn't keep away. Yvonne came over and stayed.

'Dad?' He was still with us but unconscious. 'It's me, Scott. I'm here.'

I sat alone with him and was holding his hand. The tears kept coming. My hero was leaving me. 'Thank you for being the most incredible man. I am so lucky I've had you as my dad.'

His eyes opened. I leant forward, hopeful, but there was no real recognition there. My sister's lifelong friend Gina was with us all day. She was a top nurse and her help throughout the day was invaluable. Everything that could be done to ease his passing was being done. At 11am they started to give Dad some morphine and at 10pm they were still giving him huge doses and couldn't believe he was still going. My dad, the fighter. Then at 10.50pm my father took his last breath. Mum, Marsha and I held him to the end.

'Why are you crying?'

'Dad has died, Bar.'

'What? Oh no, oh no, Scott, that's awful . . .' Every time I told her she burst into tears. Maybe that's why I took the car to get it washed. I was rinsed out. The carer Gabriella and I packed a bag.

'Where are you going now?'

'We're going to sit shiva for Dad. You remember, it's part of being Jewish. We bury our loved ones quickly then sit and pray and remember them.'

'Who?'

I wasn't sure I was able to do this.

'What are you packing? I don't know what to bring.' I took her downstairs and turned on the telly.

'Oh look, there's my mate.' Ross Kemp was on *Loose Women*. What were the chances? They asked him about Barbara.

'Well, Scott is having a really hard time. His dad passed away yesterday. They were very close.'

Dad would have loved that, but it set Bar off again and she was even more confused when I put her in the car with the cases.

'Where are we going?'

'How much longer?'

'Have I got an appointment?'

'Don't drive too fast.'

'When are we going to get there?'

I was so sad and utterly drained. How could it be that I would be saying goodbye to my dad?

We lowered my father into the ground, then my brother-in-law returned to the prayer house to check on Barbara. There he was met with the sight of Barbara doing a tap routine for the other older guests who'd stayed behind. Typical Bar – when in doubt, entertain.

'I think I need to go home now.'

'Why are you sitting on a small chair?'

The second night the electricity went off – Dad, the joker, up to his old tricks? Who knows, but we did the service by candlelight and it was beautiful. The men and women were in separate rooms and both nights you'd occasionally hear slightly inappropriate bursts of laughter. That was my wife, entertaining the troops. An evening with . . . Dad would have enjoyed the Fenella Fielding story.

I went alone for the last night of the shiva and stayed. In the middle of the night I was dreaming about Dad. Someone was going for him. I shoved them out of the way and woke up to the sound of a glass shattering.

The next morning I told Mum, 'I was clearing up shards of glass in the night and managed to cut my finger quite deeply.' The colour drained from her face.

'You okay, Mum?'

'Your dad cut his finger in the middle of the night on the last night of *his* father's shiva when a picture fell off the mantlepiece.'

I looked at the plaster and hoped the cut might leave a little mark when it healed. I returned home that day and was straight back into caring for Bar, dealing with the intruder and trying to stay strong for her, which meant there wasn't really time to grieve properly for my father.

A month after he died, it hit me. I was crippled by the pain of it. But I had to keep going, so I turned to humour. I found a great picture from the set of *Sparrows Can't Sing*. A very young Babs pushing a pram. I put it up on Facebook. 'Babs and me on an early date!'

Laughing made me feel less alone.

I came to life a bit during a meeting with the Alzheimer's Society. Every day I gave thanks that Barbara had earned enough money to be able to afford the care that meant I was not looking after her all alone. How does someone on their own cope? How does someone of the same age as their partner cope? How does anyone in a high-rise cope? I felt deep concern over the state of social care and the lack of funding for it.

Bar and I signed a letter asking the Prime Minister, Bar's old mate Boris Johnson, to meet and discuss it further. They sent a reply saying they were looking for a date. It was good to have something to look forward to.

On Barbara's eighty-second birthday it was officially announced that we were going to be ambassadors for the Alzheimer's Society and were backing their social care campaign. Then we went to Scott's for lunch, just the two of us. I loved every second of that lunch. Bar was in a good place. It was easy to forget in the wearing world of dementia that we had a great love for one another. An unbreakable bond. However hard that would be tested.

*

Chris Evans is a superstar. He secured fifty places in the Amsterdam Marathon and ran a live auction on his breakfast show that Tanya Franks and I took part in. The winners would get a place in the marathon plus an all-expenses four-day trip to Amsterdam, including travel there and back on a private plane. By the end of the show on 8 August a staggering £320,000 had been raised. We all went back to Marylebone for brunch. Tanya and I jumped on the tube, while Chris and his equally superstar assistant, Hiten (the frothy coffee man), ran all the way from London Bridge. As you do. An amazing morning.

How, oh how, had Bar and I become synonymous with a running race? She'd never even owned a pair of trainers, but I was grateful to have a new focus.

First I did an interview for *BBC Breakfast*, then half a dozen down-the-line radio interviews, each highlighting the need for the government to look at social care funding. It was on the floor. There weren't enough trained staff. There wasn't enough money. There was no provision for people with dementia in the NHS. No special wards. And if there was no one at home to do the caring, these patients stayed in hospitals, blocking beds. Our online petition reached over 100,000 signatures. This was something I could get my teeth into.

'Where are we going?'

'Downing Street, Bar, to see Boris Johnson. He's Prime Minister now.'

It was the eighth time she'd asked during the fifteen-minute drive. Please, God, don't let this be one of her confused days. But when she got out of the car and saw the bank of photographers, she knew where she was. She knew who she was and what she had to do. It was miraculous to watch.

'No bad behaviour,' she said to the paps, wagging her finger.

She had to hold on to my arm, her stoop was now quite visible. She looked like she was going to topple forward, but I held on tight and at one point I whispered that she needed to straighten up a bit. There was a tiny flash of defiance, but her back straightened and she put a smile back on her face. She posed on that famous step, in front of one of the most famous doors in the world, with a 'Fix Dementia Care' sign and I thought, *That's my Babs. A bloody trouper.*

Boris greeted Bar like an old friend. We took tea and chatted a while.

'You've done so much for London,' said Boris. 'Do you remember we worked together to help people look after their neighbours, their communities?'

'They all loved you,' said Bar, holding Boris's hand.

'Some of them didn't. It was pretty variable.'

The representatives from the Alzheimer's Society discussed building an NHS dementia fund. Bar listened intently.

'It's not good,' she piped up.

Boris said he would do the best he could. 'We're going to put this right.'

For the whole time Boris and Bar held hands. We paused for a photo halfway through. Not missing a trick, Bar leant in for a kiss.

'Did you get that?' Bar asked the photographers.

'Will you do it again?'

Well, she didn't miss a beat, and in came Boris for another kiss.

The pictures were everywhere the next day. It was all over the news and it was down to one person: Barbara. Not even the Prime Minister could say no to Barbara Windsor.

After a week away on my own, I felt strong enough to take over the nights again and decided to sign up for the Windsor half-marathon with Chris. It was really tough because it was so hilly, but each time I ran beyond my expectations I also found the strength to carry on caring for my wife while the disease metamorphosed her before my eyes.

Bar was getting more frail and I was terrified about her falling. I made some more adjustments to the house, like a gate at the top of the stairs. Apart from that we got through each day battling with the same symptoms. Confusion, anxiety, breathlessness, subdued mood. The odd good days were gradually being replaced by good hours.

Then she started to lose her grasp on words. I could see her visibly trying to think what the word was, but it wouldn't form and in the end she would give up and shake her head at me. That was unbearable to see. A sign that she was giving up, as if to say, *What's the bloody point, Scott.* It broke my heart.

The campaigning meant she was not being forgotten, even if she was forgetting herself. *GMB* named an award after her for the 1 Million Minutes campaign: the Dame Barbara Windsor award for helping someone with dementia. She was thrilled. Barbara's Revolutionaries were presented with a *Best* Magazine Heroes Award and then there was the Amsterdam Marathon trip. Bar recorded a special message to the fifty bidders who'd won a seat on our team plane. It was a hoot and I much preferred running on the nice flat roads alongside canals. Having sworn never to run again I found myself shaking hands with Hiten and Chris and Tanya as we committed to doing the 2020 London Marathon! What kind of madness was that?

As at every theatre, there was a monstrous queue for the ladies at half-time. We'd gone to see Matt Lucas in *Les Mis*. Jane Moore led Bar to the back, but the woman at the end of the queue ushered her forward, as did the next and the next and so on, until she was waved right through like the queen that she was.

'It was amazing,' said Jane, retaking her seat. 'Everyone helped, even with washing her hands, getting a towel. It was wonderful.'

'While you were gone a woman came and cried on my shoulder,' I said. 'She thanked me for raising awareness. She'd just been diagnosed.'

Jane hugged me. Maybe I did deserve the Champion of the Year Third Sector Award and the Spirit of London campaign award. Maybe I was making just a little bit of a difference for the millions of people directly and indirectly affected by dementia. The houselights went down and I saw the smile on Bar's face. She was at home in a theatre and I was at home wherever she was.

But the year wore on and as the days got shorter and the evenings got longer, and longer, Barbara got worse. We had interminable confused chats, which I would try to untangle sometimes. I wanted to help Bar make sense of what she was muddled by, but of course it was a thankless task and very tiring for both of us. They were long, relentless hours. So often we'd just watch telly.

There was an empty chair at the end of the table when we all sat down for our first Christmas without Dad. Bar's illness was taking her further away from me, but I still had so much to be thankful for. That I had my dad for as long as I did. That he was the man he was. That we were building an awareness of a crucial cause and that the money raised would make a difference.

To my knowledge, the Dementia Revolution was the most successful London Marathon partnership of all time, raising just over £4 million.

23

No Guilt

'No guilt,' John Suchet said to me at the *Good Morning Britain* 1 Million Minutes Awards ceremony in January 2020. He had met his wife Nula at a care home. They'd both been caring for spouses with dementia at the time. No guilt. It was easier said than done. I was there to present the inaugural Dame Barbara Windsor Award to Danny Brown, an exceptional man who'd thought about ending his life after being diagnosed with dementia but was turned to life-changing volunteering after contacting the Alzheimer's Society. We played the video that Bar had made earlier that month. Filming had been a long ordeal, even with the autocue it was a struggle. There would be no more personal messages from Babs.

Visitors would be next. 'It's lovely to see you, but I'm very tired,' she said to Richard Desmond, who never forgot her. He took his leave sadly.

Another time. 'Do you live here?' she asked Paul O'Grady when he came over, then turned to me and said, 'Who does he live with here?'

I knew better than to confuse her with corrections and details. It was best to let the 'black-out' moment pass. Paul gave me a huge hug at the door. For a moment all I could do was cling on to him. Then he looked into my eyes and smiled sadly. What more could he do?

When Dr Kennedy saw for himself that she couldn't quite get her words out, he asked me to come and see him for a debrief. 'It's time to start thinking about the next step,' he said. I felt sick inside. 'Not right now, Scott, but you need to start looking for a place for her to go.'

*

As we walked to our seats in a packed Prince Edward Theatre I heard the Barbara Windsor effect, before I saw it. Gary had made her up beautifully. She wore a wonderful bright red coat and, although we were being helped by staff, she held herself up. I was exceptionally proud. A few people noticed her and began to gently applaud. Hearing this, the rest of the audience looked around, noticed Bar and started to stand and join in with the applause. Bar waved. It was impossible not to feel the love for her that day and I will never forget it.

'I've been here sixteen years,' said Roger, the theatre manager, 'and I have never witnessed a celebrity receive a welcome like that.'

I thank every single one of you who was there to see *Mary Poppins* but gave a standing ovation to the fierce little lady in red, because she felt that wave of love. It gives me goosebumps now just thinking about it.

'What have you done?' said Bar, looking at the boot strapped to my foot. There was £30,000 worth of reasons why I had to do the 2020 London Marathon, but I was really worried I wasn't going to be able to get through it.

'Strained tendon,' I said. It had happened on a twelve-mile training run with Tanya. The injury meant I could not respond as fast as I needed to in the night and Bar was still often falling when she tried to get to the bathroom. It was time to get the night carers back in.

When Ross Kemp asked me to take part in his documentary series called *Living with . . .*, I was happy to do it for the millions of voiceless carers out there who have it far, far worse than us. Also, I didn't want her to be forgotten. That really worried me.

I have always been one to catastrophise. But with this thing called coronavirus spreading around the world, stock markets crashing, storms, floods and fires, it was beginning to feel like the end of the world to me. Italy shut. Broadway closed for a month. No Premier League for three weeks. No toilet rolls in Waitrose. When *EastEnders* stopped filming I knew it was serious. Shops started to close. It felt very eerie when I went out for a walk . . . where was everybody? On 20 March it was made official. We were in lockdown.

'What's happening, Scott?'

It was very hard trying to explain it to Bar. 'There is an awful flu going around, so we're safer at home.'

But, of course, she would forget and I would have to repeat it over and over. I would have loved to ignore it but there was nothing else on the telly so . . .

'What's happening, Scott?'

I went to bed shivering; I had a tight chest and was wheezing. I didn't have a cough but I had sweats that left me ringing wet. I spent nearly a week in bed and wore a mask whenever I went downstairs, which was infrequently as the carers left food outside the spare room for me.

'Where's Scott? Why is he wearing a mask?'

'He's not well, Barbara. He doesn't want to give it to you.'

Our system sort of worked, until there was no one available to come to the house and so, even though I was still not feeling great, I got Bar up.

'Why are you wearing that?'

I gave her breakfast.

'What's that on your face?'

It was a really long day. Thankfully, Gabriella came at six and I was able to get back to bed.

The next Thursday was the first evening we clapped for the NHS. Two days later we reached 1,000 deaths in the UK. By 3 April it was 3,000. Bar and I were doing what everyone else was doing. I was terrified she might catch it, so I didn't take her out when I went for a walk. Instead, we would go out into our little back patio for fresh air. We were ever so lucky to have that outside space. Deaths continued to rise. Our twentieth wedding anniversary came and went. I got her a card, she smiled and said how wonderful, but it wasn't registering.

'The problems always seem to happen between carer shifts,' I told Dr Kennedy. It was true. Sometimes I wanted to sit on the floor and cry. 'She's sleeping a lot and has trouble trying to explain things to me.'

'Have you thought about what I said?'

'Of course, but how can I put Bar into a care home now?'

'There is a good one in Chelsea, specifically for dementia patients.'

I knew he was right. I couldn't cope with the falls, the bathroom issues, getting her in and out of the bath. 'I'll call them,' I told him.

I returned to the sitting room.

'I was walking down the street yesterday when someone stopped me to ask me about Mummy.' She'd not been anywhere, of course, she had just imagined it. 'I'm worried about Mummy. I've not seen her for a long time.'

I must have looked upset because she studied my face. 'She's gone, hasn't she?'

'Sorry, Bar,' I said, nodding. She'd mourn her mother as if for the first time; it was impossible not to get emotional too.

I rang the home hoping for a solution but found myself faced with further problems and difficult choices. This place cost a staggering £4,000 per week. I wasn't sure how long the finances would last at that level, but I wanted the best for her, so I went to the accountant to work out if I should sell the mews. As far as I was concerned it was her money. What I didn't know was how long I would need to be paying. It was an emotional, financial, moral quagmire. Knowing about it and being in it are two different things.

I visited a couple of homes in full PPE and left feeling hollow. I saw dimly lit dementia wards with residents sitting around a table with no one interacting, and I glimpsed through open doors into rooms occupied by patients with severely advanced dementia. And I couldn't erase what I had seen. How could I leave her in a place like that? How could I make such an awful decision? What should I do? I was thinking about best worst-case options when Bar looked up at me.

'Scott, I'd be scared without you.'

No guilt? That was going to be impossible.

She grabbed my hand. 'You know how much I love you, don't you?'

Could she sense it? How could I do it? It was agony and the stress of it was making me ill. I walked for hours with David Walliams in the park. He was kind, patient and understanding, and I couldn't have got through those months without him and other close friends, but in the end I knew the decision was mine and mine alone.

I drove to Anita Dorfman House in Stanmore to meet the man who ran the care homes for Jewish Care, thanks to an introduction from Richard Desmond and Dame Gail Ronson. Friends were really stepping up to help give me options. I couldn't go in because of Covid, but I could walk around the outside and talk to them and look in. The building was modern and I could see immediately it was in good condition. Oddly, I liked the fact that I couldn't go inside. They were prioritising the safety of their patients.

'So how is she?' asked the manager. 'How are you?'

How could I answer that question? The previous evening between carer shifts Bar had complained of pains in her stomach. I had put her to bed at 6pm and lain with her until the carer arrived at 8pm. She was like a frightened little girl, holding my hand.

'I don't want us to be apart, not ever.'

It was crucifying. Was it possible that my turmoil and concern and fear and guilt were seeping through my skin to reach her? But it was a decision I couldn't put off much longer. Bar was so confused and it went on for hours.

'I fancy something, but I don't know what it is?' I'd make her a cup of tea.

'I'm hungry, Scott.'

I tried not to give her too much because she was so sedentary; she was gaining weight and her stomach issues were getting worse. She'd get angry. I'd snap back. I felt so wretched when I looked into her eyes. None of this was her fault. It wasn't mine, either. It was just a horrible, ghastly, miserable situation for the pair of us.

And as soon as I was able to go inside Anita Dorfman House, once the Covid rules had been relaxed, it felt right. The building was in good nick, the staff were proficient, and everything was neat and clean. Better still, the residents were well turned out, smiling, and, a deal-clincher for me, there was a nursing station on every floor. The rooms for the residents were large and had air-conditioning. Outside each room there were a couple of armchairs in the wide corridors, so even if the resident didn't want to go and join everyone in the common room, they could watch the world go by rather than being stuck alone in their room. It felt at last like a place that I could see Bar in. When I explained to them how she really was they said they were genuinely taken aback at how long I had managed at home.

My last care home option helped me make my decision. The dementia floor was understaffed. One resident had been brought out in her bed and left next to a table with people just sitting staring into space. I don't blame the staff, they were valiantly trying to care for too many people, but the system is broken.

My choice was made. I applied for a place at Anita Dorfman House and started the assessment process. I would have delayed this decision forever but I was not medically trained and, despite having learnt how to be a carer, I knew she needed more care than I alone could provide. Even with wraparound carers, our house was a hindrance now.

So much about what happened next was heartbreaking. I went to the little shoe shop and got her two pairs of slippers and one pair of pink loafers. Holding these doll's shoes in my hands tore my soul to pieces. Now to tell Bar.

'Dr Kennedy wants you to go to a place for a bit of time to keep an eye on you and work out the best meds . . .'

Until she was in and settled and we were confident she could stay there, we had decided to tell her it was for a few weeks.

'We're going to talk to them on the computer, okay?'

Bar nodded.

'How long have you been feeling unwell?'

She shook her head and looked at me.

'Can you tell me your address . . .?'

'No, sorry.' It was the 'sorry' that always got me. 'My mother bought me this house,' she said.

Bar was finally offered a permanent room at Anita Dorfman House on 5 July 2020. As relieved as I was sad, I snapped into practical mode to make her room feel as familiar as possible by the time I moved her in there. I got a TV. I bought her new bras, some simple wigs the staff could manage. I was trying to pack the clothes I thought most useful and kept them in the office until I could put them in the car without her noticing. The subterfuge felt horrific. Our relationship had been based on being upfront and honest and here I was sneaking about with her belongings.

I prayed the press would leave her alone and asked for a reflective film to be put over her ground-floor window. I was a bit paranoid after the pap tricked his way into our house, but I'm delighted to say that, to my knowledge, no picture was ever taken. Tony, the maintenance man, put pictures up for me. It was a nice spacious room and I tried to make it as homely as I could with familiar photographs and small items from home. Deep down I knew her home was in Marylebone with me. I was window-dressing, setting a scene for this final act, because, whatever I added, you couldn't take away the hospital bed, the red alarm chord, or the medical en-suite bathroom. This was hospital, not home, and I knew it was a one-way street. I told myself she'd adjust, create her own Barbara Windsor world, holding court and doing the odd tap-dance and telling showbiz stories. It was the only way I could find the strength to go on packing and driving and unpacking and driving and packing.

On 10 July they did a Covid test on Bar and on the 11th Dr Kennedy came to tell her again that he was changing her meds and that was why he wanted her to go into a place where there were nurses all the time to keep an eye on her. She started to look more anxious. I paid the first fees. She would have 24/7 care in the beginning, so she was never alone in that room while she settled. Paul O'Grady called to see how she was and I told him I was moving her but I never told anyone where.

'The car is ready, Bar. Time to go.'

'No, no, I'm not going. I'm not going anywhere.'

'Remember what Dr Kennedy said.'

'No.'

'A clinic with nurses. To keep an eye on you.'

'I don't need to do that. No thank you.'

'Dr Kennedy's orders, Bar,' I said, getting a bit firmer. In the end I would reason with her in the only way that ever worked, since you could never tell Bar what to do.

'You know I love you.'

She nodded, wide-eyed, leaning in intently.

'You know I would only do the best for you.'

'Yes.'

'You know I would never hurt you. So now we're going to get in the car and I'm going to take you to an excellent clinic with nurses who can check your meds.' I had to reach beyond the veil of dementia and to her heart.

She got in the car. Our carer Imola stood in the rear-view mirror. She smiled and waved, but I could see her crying. She knew that was goodbye.

'Where are we going?'

I explained again that Dr Kennedy was going to do some checks.

'I'm not staying anywhere!' she snapped.

I cajoled, reassured and, in the end, I lied. No guilt? Impossible.

24

End of Life

Bar and I pulled up at the smart modern building. Outside there were three uniformed members of staff waiting. Bar smiled and waved. For most of her professional life she'd been driven to events and appearances and a welcoming party would be on hand to take Dame Barbara Windsor through to her adoring fans, so the only unusual thing so far was that one of the staff members was holding a wheelchair. I helped Bar out of the car and into the chair; she did not complain about the chair. *Am I really doing this?* The staff wheeled her through the foyer and into the part of the building that, unbeknownst to her, would become her home. She waved at the residents sitting outside their rooms. A few waved back. She wanted to stop and chat, immediately switching into meet-and-greet mode, and kept trying to reach them, stretching out her hands. At one point she tried to hug a woman walking in the corridor.

'Sorry, Barbara, maybe we can hug everyone later.'

There was no point explaining the rules of isolation, the threat of Covid, the need for distance and hygiene, masks and personal protection, that we were in the grip of a global pandemic. All of that would have scared her and, by the time she'd reached the next resident, she would have forgotten it all anyway. Instead, the staff wheeled her into the garden, to the terrace overlooking the beautifully kept gardens. This was a distraction technique I had learnt well.

After a while we took Bar to her room. For several days now I had been ferrying personal belongings from the house we'd shared for twenty-seven years and placing them here, at Anita Dorfman House. Her bedside table clock would be where it had always been. Familiar photos of our wedding day. The pair of us dressed up as the Pearly King and Queen at Elton John's fiftieth birthday party. Her with Ross Kemp, her on-screen son and off-screen beloved friend. And with David Walliams, another favourite; he looked like a giant holding a sparrow. I had recreated her dressing table as far as I was able, but for all the photos and cushions, throws and personal items there was no disguising that this was a care home. The priority was care. Comfort came a close second, but it was second. I couldn't even look into the en-suite. 'Adapted' is the word they use. I could not adapt so effectively.

I'd assumed they'd have her ample and varied medications ready, but they didn't so I had to drive back to the West End to get them. I was never going to get everything right. I was so on edge, so sad and so scared, but all anyone would have seen was the benign smile stapled on my face. The smile I had mastered these last few years while caring for my progressively ill wife.

I got back around 6pm but Barbara wasn't in her room.

'We've said she can go into the restaurant,' said a carer. I would learn all their names in time, but for now there were just a few familiar faces. Bar was in the empty restaurant, sitting alone, a knife and fork in her hand, her food untouched, looking around, left, right, back at the food, left, right, back at the food. It ripped my heart in two. She had never eaten alone. I put the smile back on my face.

'Hey, Bar . . .'

I was rewarded with a beaming smile.

On the way back to her room one of the residents recognised her. 'Barbara, we're so honoured to have you here. What are you doing here with us?'

'Oh well, you know how it is. That's life.'

They brought her dinner through to the room and a plate for me, so we sat together at the small table at the window and ate. 'This is good.'

'I'm not staying here.'

'Do you remember Dr Kennedy said he needed you to have a few tests?'

'Oh yes . . .'

'The food is good.' She was picking at it.

'Are you staying here too?'

'For now,' I would reply. 'Aren't those flowers lovely?'

I had learnt to be adept at keeping to the absolute present. There were fewer demons in the moment, until the moment changed. And it did. A member of staff came in, indicating it was time for me to go. Immediately Bar was on it. So smart even when her brain was plotting against her.

'You're not leaving me here!' Her little face screwed up in fury.

'Don't worry. All these lovely people are going to take care of you until I get back.'

'Why are you going? Don't go. I'm not staying here. This isn't my room.'

'That's your clock,' I said. 'I'll be back tomorrow.'

Cajole, be calm, and sometimes lie. I would only be back tomorrow if Bar settled in. I'd known this lady for half my life. She was a fighter. I suspected she was going to fight. David Baddiel told me that the thing with dementia is that the person you love is always in there, somewhere. His father had the illness. This was both comforting and terrifying. My Bar would despise me for leaving her here, yet I lived for glimpses of my Bar.

Just when I thought there was going to be a scene, she smiled. 'I love you.'

'I love you too, Bar.'

I got in the car and broke down in tears. How I held it together when I was with her, I will never know. My diary entries are so full of anguish but they are unfiltered and honest and mostly desperately sad. Death is a lonely business.

Wednesday, 15 July 2020: It feels surreal being alone in the house. Please let my Bar be safe.

I pictured her, in that room, looking around and wondering where I was. I thought there would be some respite now that I knew she would be well cared for twenty-four hours a day, but instead I lay in bed wondering, *Is she okay? Is she okay?* She'd flash into my mind. *Is she okay?*

I had arranged for her to have one-to-one care for the two weeks she had to 'isolate' for Covid reasons, which meant she would always have someone nearby, even during the night. They called the following morning. 'Barbara woke in the night and was calling for you. She got quite distressed. It's probably better if you don't visit today.'

I got off the phone and sobbed.

I spoke to her instead.

'What am I doing here?'

I would repeat the same explanation. 'Doctor's orders, remember, Bar? They're just going to do a few more tests.'

'Then I can come home?'

'Let's get those tests done first.'

And then: 'Why are you talking to me on the phone?'

'Where are you?'

'Why am I here . . .?'

My sister called. I was ready to give them an update, but Mum had fallen in the garden and smashed her eye. FFS. Can anything else happen? Made me think of *Hamlet*. 'When sorrows come, they come not single spies, but in battalions . . .' Never was a truer sentence written, or so I felt today.

When I next visited, Bar was up, dressed and wearing make-up. I was thrilled that she was looking so well. She smiled when she saw me. 'Let's have a coffee outside,' I said.

She was happy about that, so the nurses came and helped her into the wheelchair. I braced myself for a bit of Windsor backchat, but she didn't object, not once, and I realised how weak and tired she'd become. All I prayed for was that this decision had been the right one. Seeing the team around her made me realise that I simply could not have gone on doing all this at home with one helper.

We chatted for about forty minutes about the people, the room, the garden. It was only when I said I had to go to work that she became anxious and kept saying, 'I love you.'

'I love you too.'

She didn't want me to leave, so I would change the subject. 'Aren't these women lovely taking care of you . . .'

'They're wonderful . . .'

'Aren't these plants nice?'

'They're lovely.'

Trying to keep up that positive spin was pretty tiring for the both of us.

I managed to leave her in the garden while she was distracted by a member of staff. It was hard but I felt she was happy enough. Happy enough was going to have to be enough.

'Perhaps give it a few days before the next visit,' the manager said.

After that I drove down to see Mum. Her face was black and blue. To ease the anxiety, I did a five-mile run with my nephew Harry, which felt knackering, but overall I was happy to spend a couple of days in a busy, bustling family home.

When I spoke to Bar it was clear she was not as happy as when I'd left her sitting in the garden. 'What is going on?'

Sunday: 'When are you coming to get me?'

Monday: Bar was more agitated. 'I'm waiting for you,' she said curtly.

I think the realisation was beginning to hit home, so on Tuesday I left Sussex and drove straight to the home. I walked in and Bar had no smile for me. 'I can't stay here.'

I smiled and said gently, 'You've only been here a few days, my love.'

'I can see that you think this is funny.'

I popped outside to talk to the manager. Bar followed me and saw me talking to them. 'Bollocks to all this,' she exploded in sudden extreme fury.

A wall of staff screened me off. 'We suggest you leave immediately.'

What? They insisted. So I did. I turned on my heel and left. It was awful. I understood Bar's anger. I would be angry too. But being angry made her difficult to care for so they needed me out, for both our sakes; she was still supposed to be in isolation. I fled, hoping and praying and trusting in their ability to care for her. Handing her over to them felt impossibly hard. While I knew they were right that me being there would only make it worse, God it was hard to leave. I sobbed all the way home.

Now she was in the home I did another interview with Jane Moore. She came to the mews house and I broke down a couple of times recounting those first few days and the decision to place her in a care home. When I checked in on Bar later, I didn't talk to her because they said she was doing okay and it was best to leave her in peace. I had been warned the settling in could take up to a couple of months. Every patient is different. Some like it instantly, some never do. I wanted to do what they recommended, but I also didn't want her to forget. The following day they phoned me to say she had picked up a bug and was on antibiotics. Then they organised a time we could FaceTime. I tried to be brave and smile, but it was so damn hard. 'I'm not staying in this place,' she said, over and over.

Thursday, 23 July 2020: Bar still wants out. I feel awful about it but have to stay strong. I am low today.

I forced myself out on a run. I managed to push myself around the park for three miles to clear my head. I waited for instructions. My life in limbo, almost more than ever before.

They called and said I could visit so I got her some flowers and arrived at 12.20. She was outside her room in a nice armchair, having a coffee with a carer. At first she was frosty but I did get her to smile eventually. It was a short visit.

Driving home I got a phone call – she was refusing to have a blood test. I talked her round and eventually she agreed.

Friday, 24 July 2020: Please, God, let her continue to trust me so I can continue to care for her.

I had hardly told a soul about Bar going into the home. I wanted to make sure she was settled. Jane was holding the piece until we were ready, which I appreciated and realised was a huge favour in the cut-and-thrust world of the red-tops. When I arrived to see Bar again they told me she was not eating well. I walked into her room and her first words, with that same look of pure fury, were, 'How could you do this to me?'

I knew she couldn't help it, but it felt like a knife going through me.

I started doubting my decision, even though I knew the reality was that she had to be there. I had taken her as far as I could. I reminded myself of the falls, the confusion, the incessant questioning, the accidents, the danger, the constant, constant vigilance. I tried to encourage her to eat by saying they had nice chicken Milanese on the menu for lunch.

'I don't like that.'

'You love it when I cook chicken Milanese for you.'

'Well, you can't cook!' she barked, quick as a flash.

'Yes, I can. I always cook for you.'

'Maybe so, but you can't cook,' she said with a serious face. So sharp. Still so sharp.

I was quite wounded. 'So you've waited twenty-seven years to tell me I can't cook.'

'Well, I never wanted to hurt your feelings.'

I knew what she was doing. She was trying to get me back for abandoning her. I just smiled at her. Wrong choice.

'I can't believe you find this all so funny.'

Ah, I thought, she mistakes my smile for laughter, but this was no laughing matter, unless you like your comedy really bloody dark. 'I'm not laughing, Bar, I promise. I just want you to feel okay. Let everyone look after you, please. For me. That's what they are here to do.'

She wasn't convinced. The food arrived. She pushed it away. Then the staff arrived to start getting her ready to go to bed. This was my cue to leave. They took her through to the en-suite bathroom, the door closed and I disappeared.

I called her the next day. 'Where the hell are you? I'm sitting here surrounded by old people!'

Pretty ballsy for an 83-year-old. You've got to love her.

'You better come and get me, Scott. I'm not staying here.'

From that day on it was a struggle to get Bar to eat. I knew what it was. She was protesting. She'd done it before as a little girl, aged about eight. She had refused to eat until her parents said she could have a dog. She got the dog. Maybe David Baddiel was right.

For a bit of light relief, I had to have two hours of root canal treatment the next day. At least my mouth could feel numb, but I couldn't sleep. When I did get back to the home, I noticed our wedding photo had been damaged. The glass was broken. I could tell by the carer's face that Bar had done it.

'Oh look, it's broken.'

Bar looked at me in mock shock. 'What a shame,' she said, sarcastically. ''Course the real shame is I really loved you, but that's all going out the window now. There's no use you visiting me any more.'

'Now, Bar, that's not going to happen because I still love you and I will still visit you for no other reason than you have to see my miserable face. I will come just to annoy you.'

'You are annoying.'

'Yes. I am. I also love you very much.'

Inside it was agony but I did at least make her smile and a little of her anger and fear subsided, just for that moment.

The *Sun* finally ran the article. It was 1 August 2020. The headline was: 'MY FEAR HAS BECOME A REALITY'. This was true. My wife was in a care home and was never coming home. Jane wrote a beautiful, sensitive piece, but I didn't sugar-coat it. I admitted I was constantly in tears and that Bar was 'cross' about being in the home. I said that we no longer had the luxury of choice and I knew I couldn't keep her safe at home. I had incredible support from people and felt relieved not to be carrying yet another secret. Some people responded negatively to the fact I'd placed Bar in the home, but I do think that unless you've walked in the shoes of a carer, then perhaps, even if asked, occasionally 'no comment' will do.

Bar kept insisting she needed to leave whenever I visited, but she was becoming calmer when I had to go, so they advised thinking about reducing her one-to-one care, which we did, slowly.

*

Question: What is a suitable birthday card for a showbiz dame turning eighty-three who has forgotten most of her twenty years of marriage and her seventy-year career and more frequently believes herself to be a child waiting for a visit from her mother who died in 1981? I can tell you, there isn't one. Instead, I went to Selfridges with her long-standing make-up artist and bought her a full set of new products. I also got her a badge with a picture of me when I was thirty on it. The photo had been taken shortly after we'd met and Bar wouldn't take the badge off, telling everyone, 'That's my husband!' I'd been temporarily forgiven.

On 6 August we sat outside in the courtyard and celebrated Bar's birthday with a lovely cake the staff had got her. Everyone sang, we chatted over cake and coffee, and she smiled, but there was a bemused look in her eye. While she looked amazing, and still smiled for the camera and blew kisses to the staff and waved to the residents, I knew she was on autopilot. She was being the showbiz legend she knew how to be. In truth, she was diminished and needed help cutting her cake because she had so little strength. She still wasn't eating. Even that beautiful pink-iced cake, with her name on it, couldn't tempt her. She just pushed it away. The protest would continue and I left that day with a pit of emptiness in my stomach.

The next day I spoke to Dr Gould, the home's resident doctor.

They felt she was refusing to eat.

They were right.

Three days later we had a better visit.

Monday, 10 August 2020: Bar in an upbeat mood. A few tears but that is part of her condition now.

She'd say something, start crying and then say, 'I'm sorry.' It all happened in the blink of an eye. She'd remember I was visiting, not staying, and weep. Then that memory would vanish and she'd apologise for crying. It was heartbreaking to watch her go through that rapid range of emotions. Generally I thought she was in a better place, but it was impossible not to notice she was looking thinner.

Later the same day: Eating is still a problem.

I went to St Albans to meet Adam Woodyatt and we went for a walk in a park in temperatures of over thirty degrees. I was occasionally asked out now that Covid restrictions were being lessened, but I often cancelled. I didn't want to bore people or depress them and honestly I wasn't sure what else I could talk about; it was so all-consuming. She wasn't at home, but I was still negotiating my way through Face-Timed conversations where I tried to convince her to eat, just like the nightly routine we used to go through when I had to convince her to take her pills.

She looked so tired.

'I want to come home now.'

'I know, love.'

I was home to her. Though when she'd been at home with me, she often thought she was in Stoke Newington, where she'd grown up, wondering where her parents were. The carers told me that still happened.

'When is Mummy coming?' she'd ask, with that little girl look on her face.

Every visit I noticed the change in her face. The hollowing out. The shrinkage. Every visit she asked, 'Why can't we be together?'

I would always go back to the same thing. 'It's better for you here at the moment so they can keep an eye on you . . .'

On 14 August the stairlift was removed from the house. It was partly for my own psychological benefit. I had waited a month to see if she was coming back, but I knew deep down it wasn't going to happen.

'It's rude!' Bar said.

'What's rude, Bar?'

'Why we can't sit together.'

And again, how do you explain social distancing to a dementia patient? It was an impossible situation. The staff told me Bar was making her presence felt and when she didn't like the noise in the dining hall she'd yell, 'Shut up, the lot of you!'

'It's like having Peggy Mitchell with us,' they said.

Sometimes the language got much more inappropriate than that, but luckily the staff managed to see the funny side. Bar had been a touch filter-less during the best of times. That was why she was always such a laugh to be with. But the no-filter Barbara Windsor was an acquired taste. One time she told a member of staff they could do with a trip to the gym. This was reported to me by highly amused staff who I believe honestly did find her funny. Occasionally the comments would be laced with a *Carry On* giggle. But those got fewer and fewer. By the end only a silly dance by me would elicit that laugh.

Wednesday, 19 August 2020: She told me she doesn't care if she dies today. For the first time ever I see a little old lady near the end of her life. It was very sad to see.

Perhaps if I brought her home she would start eating again? This question went round and round in my head. I would beg her to eat. 'Please eat for me. You've got to have some energy in you. This isn't like you. You're a fighter, you're a trouper . . .' but it was to no avail.

And if I had taken her home, how long before she was back in a home? I couldn't fight the dementia and I couldn't fight my wife's choice of how she wanted to fight her illness. Perhaps she hadn't given up the fight. Perhaps this was her fight now.

The staff were aware it was a rapid decline and admitted to being taken aback by how quick it had been, but they were hopeful she would start eating eventually. But, once again, they didn't know my Bar. She was a fighter. This was her fighting. I truly believe that now.

One time I went up there and she wouldn't come out of her room, so they suggested I go to her. They were making allowances because she was still in the settling-in phase, but from the beginning they had told me they believed the family was as important as the resident when it came to end-of-life care. Everyone had a right to be with their loved one at the end, Covid or not. So they took me to her room. It brightened her up and I let myself brighten too. I told myself I was there because of the allowances in the settling-in period, not the end-of-life matter.

A nurse took me to one side. 'You have to relax more. Try to start living your life.'

I stared at her. What life? Bar was my life. Though she was being cared for, I never really switched off. Spouses were usually of a similar age. Clearly, I was not the usual next of kin.

I joined a meeting with Dr Kennedy and Dr Gould, and we discussed Bar's refusal to eat and the impact it was having on her health in general. But there was no way we would consider feeding her against her will and I was very clear about Bar's will and wishes being respected. Once I had established that, the conversation took a darker turn.

Thursday, 27 August 2020: Today end-of-life care was first spoken about. Not sure why it shocked me so much, but it did. I signed a DNR form.

Bar was brought in at the end of the meeting, like Liza Minnelli at Carnegie Hall; buoyant and chatty, in full performance mode. Typical Bar. I sign a DNR, she's working the room.

I went out that evening with *EastEnders* mates, but it was hard to be anyplace where people were laughing without feeling a sense of guilt.

The next day Bar was tired. She didn't want to get up and was telling everyone to shut up. Luckily, they didn't remember because later in the day they'd all be outside her room singing along to the radio. She had one particularly good pal in the room opposite. They would get into huge arguments about random things, like where a shop was going back fifty years, or who had a cardigan, or who hated hot chocolate more, but then within a few minutes they'd be drinking hot chocolate and hugging each other goodnight.

On 31 August I had to wait once again because Bar wouldn't get up. When she did come out to the terrace I noticed immediately that her face was getting smaller and her teeth seemed larger in her mouth.

'How you feeling, Bar?' I asked.

'Tired,' she said. 'I was working in cabaret all last night, after a full day's filming and that's why I'm so tired.'

'No wonder you're tired,' I replied.

'All in a day's work.'

'That's right, Bar. You're a hard worker. Always have been.'

I'd brought some photos from home. It was her onstage in *Fings Ain't Wot They Used T'Be.* 'Who's that?' she asked.

'That's you, Bar.'

She looked at the photo. 'Silly cow.'

The home offered me some counselling support if I needed it. It was very nice, but, honestly, where to begin? One time she was in bed, listening to her music on a loop, over and over. Another time she was in the garden with a friend, a well-dressed lady. I left soon after arriving. She didn't need me that day. I got home, exhausted, and once again cancelled the plans I'd made to go out.

On 4 September Anita Dorfman House went into lockdown. Two people had Covid: one resident and one member of staff. They also told me Bar was getting a bit abusive towards the staff, possibly brought on by a change of meds or maybe the fact that she wouldn't always take the pills.

Later that day I drove to Sussex. It was Dad's stone setting the following day. One joyful day after another.

I spoke to Bar and she seemed okay. Mum was okay. I was quiet. We ate a nice meal of veal and homemade chips, followed by trifle, followed by cheesecake and custard. I wasn't looking forward to the next day, but of course Dad had to be honoured. There were only twenty-five people allowed at the service. In another time it would have been hundreds, which was sad.

Back at the house I got a call. Bar had tried to punch a carer. I FaceTimed her. She looked different. There were dark circles under her eyes. There was so little of her, but still I fancied her chances in a street fight. Every change was noticeable now. The whole day thinking of Dad, and now this, sent me into an uneasy sleep.

Because of the Covid outbreak, all contact was screen-only. I was really missing being able to see Bar in person. The new meds were increasingly sedative, which made screen chats even harder. Her aggression was still there, however. She was arguing with people more and more, and was very up and down. I knew it was the illness, but I wondered if they might ask me to bring her home. Which, of course, I would do. But how?

A few days later Bar was in a slightly better mood but still Dr Gould said he'd like to bring the mental health team in to see her and assess how they could support her and the carers. She was by far the unhappiest resident and they didn't like to see her that way. I rang Dr Kennedy immediately. We always talked through the big issues and this was a big issue. Thankfully, on the 18th we were told we could visit so I booked in for the following Sunday.

Sunday, 20 September 2020: At last I can go and have a garden visit.

I was excited. I got there for 10.30am. One of Bar's carers, Patience (oh boy, if ever a name suited a job), told me Bar was refusing to get out of bed to come and see me. I FaceTimed her to show her I was there, thinking she'd change her mind.

'Sorry, love, you'll have to come back another day.'

I was bereft. I always had to remember at times like this that it was not my Bar. It was the illness. I felt more for her than myself.

Two days later she did come out, wearing her pink coat and sunglasses with white frames, looking every bit the Hollywood superstar. Her mood was lighter and she seemed more accepting of the fact that she had to be there. My God, she was thin. But I could sense the inner strength that I'd always known was still in there.

Towards the end of September, Bar was regularly not waking up until three in the afternoon, then she was telling everyone she'd been working late the night before. When I visited, I would sit outside, all wrapped up, and she'd sit inside an open doorway.

'Why can't we live together any more?'

'The doctors need to take care of you here. You've not been very well, Bar.'

Whatever reason I gave her, she didn't buy it. She gave me a little shake of the head in disapproval. More and more she was disappearing in front of my eyes, but her mood was generally more serene and that was all I could ask for. It's all any of us can hope for our loved ones when going through this confusion.

'Will you marry me?' I always accepted her offer.

Friday, 25 September 2020: Bar's visit cancelled and I can't see her till Monday because they have no slots for me.

I was sad, but then the following day they gave me a slot when someone else cancelled. Care homes in Covid times, it was difficult for us all. It was a nice visit. Bar was tired but calm, and had a new question. She fixed her green eyes on me. 'Am I your daughter?' Then she corrected herself. 'Silly cow.'

The light was getting dimmer. My sweet lady.

On 3 October I got a call from the head of Anita Dorfman House, followed by an email. To my utter disbelief, she told me Bar had entered her end-of-life phase and I could visit at will. 'It is imperative you spend as much time as possible with your wife now,' she said.

I was stunned. 'What? How? When?'

'It could take weeks,' she said, 'maybe months.' Weeks, months . . . I knew she would never get better, but she'd only been in there three months. I thought I would have her for years. I thought that she'd stabilise and I'd be able to visit her in this place that would begin to feel like home.

Perhaps I'd been naive, but the news still shocked me. Deep down I knew the truth of it and the reason for it. The staff could not have been better, kinder or more capable. It was an excellent care home. They were looking after Bar beautifully, but the choice that she had made to stop eating, and now not to take her meds, was her own. The real Barbara Windsor, deep within her, was controlling this to the end. It was impossible not to think of Peggy Mitchell's last scene in *EastEnders*. Dressed up to the nines, looking beautiful, powerful and very much her own person as she talks to the spirit of her old nemesis and friend, Pat.

'I'm like a little old bird that's fallen out of its nest. I can't, I can't wait. I'm being eaten alive and it hurts. I don't want to be that little old lady in the bed being looked after, people saying, "Remember her, cor, she's skin and bone and helpless." No. Not me. I will go out as I have lived. Straight back. Head held high. Like a queen.'

This was life imitating art and I was powerless to stop it.

25

I'm Going to Lose You

On 5 October 2020 the mental health team went to see Bar. They were really worried about her. When I got to her room, I received a warm but distant smile. She wasn't taking much in but once in a while she told me she loved me and that I looked well. I couldn't tell her enough how much I loved her, over and over. 'You know how much I love you, don't you?' She'd nod. The doctor took me outside.

'She's refused to have her flu jab, her blood pressure taken, and all food, even the protein shakes.'

I nodded, trying to understand. I went back in and attempted to get her to drink something, but she got cross. Desperately undernourished, but she still found the strength to fight. I had to admire the tenacity. Sitting at home alone in the evenings I felt so sad, picturing her, a tiny broken bird. I knew she was leaving me and was already grieving.

But then a lift. We had a better time four days later. Bar looked particularly pretty. I took her flowers and told her stories about our life and she laughed. When I took her back to her room, she lay her head back on the pillow and closed her eyes as her songs came out of the speaker set up next to her clock. She held my hand and softly sang along to 'Sparrows Can't Sing', word perfectly. I did all I could to conceal my tears and sadness from her, but in the end I just turned my head away and wept. Her voice sounded so sweet. It was torture to watch her fading before my eyes, but it was also a beautiful moment and I knew as it was happening that it scalded my soul.

*

I went for a walk with David Walliams the next day and told him the home had moved her into the end-of-life phase. I knew that I wasn't doing the moment justice, as I'm sure I'm not now, but at least he knew, as did my other close friends, that it was serious. I could not have done it without Ian, David, Matt, Tanya, Adam, Jake, Barry, Ross and my family. I saw them as often as I was able to, to give me the strength I needed to keep visiting.

Bar was sitting outside her room.

'Hello, you,' I said. She looked at me, eyes blank.

'Oh look, Scott is here to see you,' said the carer.

'I don't know him!'

'Sure you do.'

Instantly she got aggressive with the carer. Blaming her for the misunderstanding.

'I don't know him. Who are you to tell me? Leave me alone!' She looked scared and it was impossibly hard to see her so afraid and bewildered.

I didn't know whether to stay or go. 'I'll just keep you company,' I said quietly.

After a while she calmed down and we sat quietly, holding hands. At one point, tears filled her eyes. 'I'm going to lose you,' she said.

'I'm not going anywhere, Bar,' I said, feeling devastated inside. The visits were getting increasingly sad and I wasn't sure how much more I could take. I had a very emotional session with my therapist on Zoom. It was heavy but it did me a lot of good.

Dr Gould called and told me he'd spoken to Dr Kennedy and had agreed it was time to make Bar more comfortable if needed. More comfortable meant morphine. It was too soon, too awful, too much. The staff followed the call with Bar on FaceTime and suddenly she was there, in good spirits, smiling and chatty. That is dementia – unpredictable, unexpected and unkind. Just when I was about to give up, she reached me from deep inside the disease.

'I love you,' she said immediately when I next visited. I felt ten feet tall.

'I love you too.' We held hands. 'It has been an honour to have shared my life with you.'

She nodded. My queen.

'We've had a lot of fun,' I said. 'And we've been ever so lucky.'

'I'm lucky,' she said.

'No, I'm the lucky one. You're the star.'

Precious moments. I slipped away while the staff got her ready for bed. The carer called me that evening. 'She was a bit lost when you left but soon fell asleep. Also, we've been told there might be an increase in restrictions on the horizon. But it's okay, you can still come as often as you like.'

There was little to like about the visits but I felt worse without them.

On 16 November I met Zara, the palliative care nurse who would be responsible for preparing Barbara's end-of-life care, when the time came. I asked the question I suspect she is most often asked. 'How long?'

'Weeks, I think. Maybe less. She is very weak now.'

'Is she in pain?'

'We will make sure she is not. Think of the woman she was,' Zara told me.

'I do,' I replied. I thought about her and our life together all the time.

'It's okay to grieve for her. I assure you Barbara will be peaceful and comfortable at the end.'

Perhaps I imagined she would now drift off into the quiet night, so I was a bit unsettled when things got more turbulent.

'Get off me!'

I recognised the voice before I saw my diminutive wife swinging her handbag at a six-foot male nurse. Mighty mouse was not finished yet. I had no idea where she found the energy. She had no food inside her. I managed to intervene that time, at others I was not so lucky.

I was in her room when she looked at me and I knew I was a stranger to her.

'That's it. I'm leaving!' She got up and walked out of the room.

I had not seen her out of a chair or bed for weeks now and I was quite alarmed when she escaped past me. I tried to hold her arm.

'Get away from me!' she spat. Her eyes were wild, manic, deranged.

Two carers were immediately on hand, but she shooed them away. 'Get away from me, get away . . .'

She would swivel and hobble back the way she'd come. The carers walking close but not touching her, step for step. It would have freaked me out, but they had to stay close because she was so unsteady on her feet. She grabbed the railing along the wall but still looked like she was going to topple. She was furious and I knew deep down it came from a place of fear.

'It's okay, Bar, it's okay . . .'

But it wasn't. She didn't know me. She didn't know where she was. She didn't know why she was being followed, guarded, chased. It was utterly traumatic. Eventually Bar sat down in the chair outside the room next door to hers. Another resident, sitting opposite, looked alarmed. She was scaring the poor woman. It was scaring me.

'What are you looking at?' She looked through me, with pinprick, unrecognisable eyes. 'You've always been horrible to me.'

I thought later that she might have been talking to her father.

'Not me, Bar, I've always loved you,' was all I could offer.

She shook her head, getting agitated again. 'Get away from me . . . Who are you? . . . Where am I?'

'I think it's best you leave.' I knew they were going to have to sedate her to get her back in her room, but they had to catch her first.

Weeks, Zara said. I didn't want her to leave me, but also weeks felt like a terribly long time and I couldn't bear for her to be so lost, so far from who she was. I geared myself for my next visit but miraculously she was calmer. She looked at me with the eyes of a child.

'I struck lucky when I met you,' she said. Seeing that flicker of recognition felt like winning the lottery.

'I was the lucky one,' I replied again. I always said it and I always meant it. I leant over to her so she could hear. 'You are an amazing woman, my true love, and you always will be.'

On the 18th I went again. She was sitting in the main lounge in her pink coat with the badge of me aged thirty on it, but she was quite anxious when I got her back to her room.

'I'm scared.'

'What of, Bar?'

'I don't know but I think I'm going to die soon.'

What do you say to that?

'I can't live without you.'

'I'm not going anywhere, my love. I'm right here, by your side.'

For a moment or two, she looked reassured. I seized the moment and took a selfie, then we FaceTimed Ross so he could see her. 'Hello, Bar, my lovely friend,' he said.

She waved at him. 'I always want your life to be good, sweetheart,' she said. I could see Ross trying to be brave. We said goodbye and Bar lay back on the bed. She was exhausted.

'You won't leave me,' she said.

'I'm not going anywhere,' I repeated.

She smiled and closed her eyes. I watched her breathing gently then saw her open one eye, checking I was still there, then quickly close it again. It was like a little girl pretending to go to sleep. I sat and waited. Once again, her eye popped open, then squeezed shut. Treasure the moment, I told myself. Treasure. The. Moment. Only when I knew she was finally asleep did I quietly creep away, carrying the image with me like a warm ember.

26

Goodbye, Bar, I Love You

I found Bar standing by her bed looking distant and alarmed. The decline since the previous day was obvious. Her breathing was shallow and weak, but she was able to say, 'I love you.'

'Time for your pill,' said the nurse. Bar tried to kick her away, then swiped at her and, when that failed, tried to punch her. Those tiny fists, those tiny hands – 'You dirty rat!' – that I had watched for so many years gather up change from the bedside table to pay for her paper run, were flailing and missing their target. I gave her the pill. I wept on the manager's shoulder, then went to Ian's and wept on his shoulder. How could anyone have so many tears? I was trying to go every day but it was so draining.

The next day Bar was in the lounge talking to other residents, but then she would suddenly become agitated and lash out. I needed a day off after that, so I stayed home. Whenever her friends were on the telly they were asked about Barbara. Ross said he'd seen her on FaceTime but she was declining fast.

When I went in again, on 22 October, I found her standing outside her room with no wig. It startled me so much I stopped in my tracks. Only I ever saw her looking like that. She was just standing there wearing her pink coat over her nightdress. She came into the room but was agitated. She kept walking up and down the corridor. I tried to help the staff give her an injection, but she lashed out then turned on me.

'You hurt me. I'm scared of you.'

Her sleeping pattern was back to front; she'd sleep all day and then be up all night, pacing.

'She likes to have a carer hold her hand while she tries to sleep.' She would, of course. That's what I had been doing for . . . how long? I'd lost all sense of time.

'We are now officially handing over to palliative care, Scott.'

I felt numb. Hardly surprising. They couldn't put a time on it.

'Just hold on to the moments you do have.'

I was trying to feed her some ice cream.

'I want to spend the rest of my life with you.'

'You will, my love. I will always be with you.'

Hang on to the sweet moments, I told myself and tried not to weep.

One evening I arrived at 6.30pm and she was already tense and befuddled and didn't want help going to the toilet. I went against her wishes and got the nurse. She was furious and blamed me for getting them; it took thirty minutes to calm her down. I got her to take her pills, then watched with near admiration as she tried to throw one out without me seeing. Still so full of mischief.

'I love you.'

'I want to kill myself.'

'I think I'm going to die.'

All sentences. Delivered one after the other. In rapid, nonsensical, succession.

'I'm afraid I'm going to lose you.'

I would walk away exhausted, spent, empty and afraid.

On the 29th, Thursday, they called and said Bar was declining fast and was sleeping most of the time.

'The next couple of days will tell us a lot,' they said.

When I arrived, Bar was there holding her own hand, which hurt because they'd had to give her an injection. Her skin was paper-thin and everything hurt.

'You should be ashamed of yourself letting these people look after me.'

'Don't be nasty to me, Bar.'

That took her aback. 'But I love you.'

A nurse came in. 'Piss off out the room.' It was like having Peggy with us.

On Friday she was still asleep at midday, so I chatted to the team, then sat with her while she slept. She woke up a few times, kissed my hand, smiled, then went back to sleep. When she did wake up, at 3.45pm, she needed the loo. Trouble was, that meant getting help, which annoyed her. Eventually I learnt that was when it was best to slip away. By the time she was back in the room she had most likely forgotten I was there. It caused less stress than a goodbye. Goodbyes were terrible.

Bar was on quetiapine now, a strong sedative with anti-anxiety effects. Patience showed us a video of her being serenaded by her husband at their wedding. 'Isn't that lovely?' I said.

Bar screwed up her face. 'I think that's awful.' (Sorry, Patience.) Classic Bar.

On 31 October, it was announced that the UK would be going into lockdown again soon. This was the year that kept on giving. Utter misery. The only relief I had was that Bar's home gave relatives full access in end-of-life situations. My heart went out to people who were having to do this through a window. I will be forever grateful to Jewish Care for that. Many times I went and she would simply sleep through my visit. They would get her up and dressed for my arrival, but that exhausted her and she would fall asleep again in the chair outside her room. But, one precious day in November, she was awake, alert and sweet for three and a half hours. Incredible. We held hands, chatted and listened to music. It was the type of visit I would dream of leaving her on if there was a sudden turn.

Wednesday, 4 November 2020: A rare and wonderful visit.

On 5 November lockdown restarted. I got to the home at 3pm. Bar was outside her room napping again. We spent most of the time with her sleeping; me holding her hand, talking softly about the wonderful life that she had led. At one moment she stirred.

'I'm getting ready to say goodbye,' she said and gave a sweet little wave.

It melted my heart. I knew at the time what they were. Just as Zara had said, moments. Priceless moments.

Two days later the confusion was back. 'What are you doing here, Ronnie?' She must have read my face because she quickly said, 'I'm sorry but I don't know who you are.'

You never knew what you were going to get on any given day. Moment by moment.

Weak and pale. Breathing out of synch. She opened her eyes and winced in pain. They gave her liquid paracetamol. She'd had no food now for weeks, nothing but a little water now and then. God knows what was happening to her wee body. Sometimes she'd be more alert but that was usually accompanied by irritability. The pain in her stomach was crippling. I begged her to eat but she wouldn't. My Barbara was on hunger strike. She was in agony and it was torture to watch. All I could do was sit by her side and stroke her shrunken head.

On the 14th she was in a nice mood but muddled, liking and disliking the same thing in seconds. Three carers tried to get her to take her pills, but she refused.

'How about saying yes, Bar?'

'Okay, darlin'.' She took the pills from me.

'To celebrate, Dame Barbara Windsor will be rewarded with a magnificent tap-dance.'

I had no idea how to tap-dance, but it made her laugh. 'You're very good, sweetheart,' she said. So I milked it and sang along to the dance.

'You're the tops,' she said, then she nodded off. I left on a high.

On the next visit Bar looked scared and was crying with pains in her tummy. I got her to take the pills but she seemed disorientated.

'I have to go away and you have to start your new life, sweetheart.'

'Bar, you are my life.'

Other times she'd rage against the carers. Finding strength from God knows where. Her spirit never left her.

She still made me laugh as well. One day an entertainer came to sing with the residents. She did the rounds and stopped to sing a song for Bar. They sent me two videos, which I still watch today. Bar is listening but looking a bit cross. She tries to take the microphone away and tells the performer to 'shhh'. Then, with eyes to the camera, she says, 'She's killing the song, you're killing the song.' And she didn't mean in a complimentary way. But, my goodness, for a few notes of the brass section she smiled, recognising the tune.

The next day she slept for three hours with me beside her. At one point she woke up, tried to tell me something but couldn't find the right words and went back to sleep.

On 20 November they told me Bar had stabilised and was no longer at critical end-of-life stage. What?! I'd been bracing myself for the worst. Now what was I supposed to do? I went home and ate my feelings. Burger and chips and milkshake chased with a bag of Maltesers. Then I got angry with myself for eating the Maltesers. As she was no longer critical, I started going every other day to give myself a break, but we would still FaceTime every day. I was doing a bad job pretending to function. I would go to Waitrose, then home. I met Barry for a walk in the street, sat in the churchyard, socially distanced always, as I couldn't risk catching Covid. That would have been terrible.

'Why is he sitting there?'

'Who?'

She was talking to people who weren't there. She tried to tell me but she was sleepy and weak and sometimes it was hard to catch what she was saying. Then suddenly she'd change and speak in a furious accusatory tone.

'You're going to leave me here. You're going to go home, I can tell. Well, go on then, sod off.'

In her fury she threw her coffee over one of the carers. They couldn't get her back to her room.

*

December arrived and there was a further decline. It was her breathing. I found sleep almost impossible. Mum called. 'Are you coping, son?'

I found it very annoying. She was trying to ask the right questions, but my emotions were so on the edge. How could I answer that question? It was a stupid question. I think I might have snapped back. Sorry, Mum.

On the 2nd I went to see Bar in the afternoon. Julia and Patience, the carers, came in to help her up, get undressed and go to the toilet. I sat outside with the door closed, trying to block out her pain and fury as she tried to bat them off. She was in serious pain both internally and externally. I was so upset.

'She needs more help with the pain, please, she's had no food now for so long. It's unbearable. Please,' I begged again. 'I don't want my wife leaving this life in trauma.'

They agreed to increase the pain relief.

I arrived at 12.50pm the next day. She was dressed and washed and sitting on the bed. She had the glazed look that sedatives give, which was sad, but better than the terror I saw in her the day before. She slept most of the time and I was thankful she was peaceful, until it was time for her next jab. Once again I sat outside and listened to her cry in pain as they tried to get the needle into her paper-thin skin. She was so tender, there was nothing of her at this point, nothing. I consoled myself by thinking that at least once she'd had the jab, she'd be calm.

On Friday, 4 December, Zara took me outside. She told me to prepare myself. Again. She expected Bar to decline over the weekend. I had to work that day but ended up in tears on the phone with Lacey. Everyone felt helpless. We had to do this together, alone.

Zara couldn't believe the strength in Bar. She'd stopped eating but she wouldn't give up. They said the level of agitation in her was unusual. Zara gave her a morphine shot, but it took thirty minutes to take effect as Bar was resisting so much. Finally it knocked her out. In her sleep she was waving and smiling, and twice started applauding. What a woman.

I arrived at 11.15am the next day. Bar was weak but still resisting the staff as they tried to wash her. The morphine shots were now being given on a regular basis.

'Should I stay?' I asked the head nurse.

'Maybe go home and get some clothes and come back.' I was back by 7.30pm.

'You need to be strong now,' said a carer when I returned. 'And remember, her hearing will be the last thing to go. Just talk to her, she can hear you.' It was the enormity of it that made me weep, but I nodded, acknowledging her words, then I took my place in Bar's room, by her side, as I promised I would, and started to talk to her as she drifted in and out of sleep.

'You mean so much to me, Bar. I am so proud of you. I am so glad you've had the life you've had.'

Later they brought in a reclining armchair so I could try to sleep, but it was impossible because through the night the palliative care team would come in and turn her, which was a distressing process despite all the painkillers. I left the room every time, but I could still hear blood-curdling screams through the door. I can still hear them.

During the day the rattle in her chest came and went. I had heard it with Dad. It was unmistakable to anyone who had heard it before. Occasionally she'd wake and give me a little smile, then drift off, mumbling to herself. The second night the lights went off at 9pm. I got a little more sleep, but not much. The turning process every four hours was harrowing.

On Monday I tested for Covid to keep everyone else safe, though I had barely left the room. The rattle was back. 'Will you come and wait, Laurence?'

I must have thought it was imminent to have made that call to my brother-in-law. But contrary to the last, Bar got quite energetic after a shot. She tried to talk to me, but she couldn't so I went on talking to her.

'We were so lucky, Bar, so lucky to have met. We've had the greatest love two people could hope to have. I love you. I will always love you. I'm going to miss you like mad, my beautiful, talented, clever, little lady.'

Laurence arrived, was tested, and waited in the foyer all night in an upright chair. I went out to see him while they were turning Barbara. It was my third night there with no proper sleep. Towards the morning, Bar started having small convulsions. I told Laurence to go to the mews. She was battling on. It was 6am and I couldn't leave him sitting there.

The secretions on Barbara's lungs were getting louder. I got so upset.

'Scott, remember what I said, she can still hear you,' said the same carer.

'Barbara,' I said, pulling myself together. 'Sorry about the smell. Lol drove off with my clean clothes. Ross has texted, so has Paul. Everyone misses you. I miss you but, my God, the life you've had. The bloody wonderful, amazing, groundbreaking, hard-working, exciting life you've led. I'm in awe. I've always been in awe . . .'

My heart was breaking. How could this be the final scene when our first felt like just yesterday?

'Do you remember when we met?' I continued. 'I was only twenty-nine years old, you opened the door. "Hello," I said, "I'm Rita Mitchell's son, Scott."

'You looked me up and down and said, "Hello, Scott, I'm Barbara Windsor. You better come in!" Looking back, I can almost hear Kenneth saying, "Ooh matron . . ." in the background. Bar, how can that be twenty-seven years ago?'

The words were getting stuck in my throat but I was determined that mine would be the last voice she heard.

Bar was getting weaker by the minute. Her breathing was becoming shallow, then she started taking breaths in short, sharp intakes. There were noisy secretions. Lots of turning. Anti-secretion medication, morphine and . . . she stabilised. Then around 5.30pm she looked like she was slipping away. I steeled myself again, and yet on she went. My legs were like jelly. My mind was shattered and my emotions were shot. Laurence came back, as I thought the end was close, but no.

At four the next morning Lol went back to the mews. He looked as awful as I felt. I lay next to Bar's bed in my chair. Her breath was short, slightly delayed and sometimes stopping. I finally nodded off around 5am and had hideous nightmares. When I woke up I realised I'd texted people jibberish messages during the night. I was losing it.

Wednesday, 9 December 2020: Hardly any sleep again for the fourth night in a row.

Bar was going downhill every hour and I knew we were in this awful final stage. I just didn't know how long it would last. The on-off breathing was terrible to listen to in the near-dark. At one point I put the light on and was shocked to see her tiny head gasping for air. She was skin and bone. I sobbed.

Zara called me into the office with a couple of the other staff. 'It's been too many nights,' she said. 'We're worried about you and we're worried about Barbara. Often people won't go while their loved ones are in the room with them. They feel they have to fight even when they want to let go. Do you understand what I'm saying?'

'I think so.'

'There are good reasons why carers work in shifts. Each one of us has had a break in the last four days. You have not. You need a break, Scott. This is not good for you. Please consider going back home for a good night's sleep. Come back in the morning.'

'No way. Not at this stage.'

I returned to Barbara. 'If I should fall asleep, know that I will miss you every day for the rest of my life. I love you, Bar.'

There was a gentle knock on the door. An orderly brought in some supper for me. Followed by Zara. 'There is an assisted-living flat upstairs,' she said. 'It's empty. Sleep there.'

She looked at me with the kind, fierce-spirited eyes that I knew my wife would have admired and accepted. Then I sat with Barbara, as we had done so many times before, and had dinner 'together'. I chatted on about the highlights of our life, and then, when I was finished, I said my goodbyes.

'Goodbye, Bar, I love you, goodbye,' I said, as I pulled the door behind me.

Within the deep sleep I could hear a knocking in my dream. They had been trying to phone me to say there had been a rapid change, but it was going straight to voicemail. Since entering the home I'd had my phone on 'do not disturb' and I had forgotten to take it off.

I opened the door in my pants.

'Come quick.'

I fell over trying to put on my trousers. I was in such a panic. I sprinted down the hallway. I knew what it was, but still I ran and ran and ran. I can remember my heart beating so loudly I thought everyone could hear it. I knew before I'd turned left to go into her room what I would find. Her hands were clasped over her heart. I looked at her face. She was gone. I remember seeing three calm, solemn, kind carers leave the room without making a sound. I don't think I even cried. I kept kissing her forehead and saying her name.

'Barbara, Barbara, Barbara. My love. I'm sorry, I'm so sorry.'

They didn't leave me very long. I was in total anguish, clutching at the palliative care nurse. 'I said I would stay with her to the end. I said I'd be by her side . . .' I felt a pit of despair open deep in my chest.

'Scott,' she said, 'remember what I told you. She had to know that she could go and she had to do that alone, on her terms. Dying is a very private thing. She knew you were there. She knew you loved her. What more is there in this life than that?'

I walked out of the room, dazed.

'Please come and get me, Lol, she's gone.'

27

After, Life. Always, Love

At midnight the ticker tape came across Sky News telling me what I knew to be true but could not accept. On 10 December 2020, Dame Barbara Windsor had died. My phone started buzzing. I turned it off and went to sleep. When I closed my eyes all I could see was that last image of her. I remembered Laurence had come in to say goodbye, but the next bit was a blur as I said goodbye to the people who had become my life. I had called the Press Association and asked if they would hold my pre-written email until midnight so I could get home. Mum and Marsha were at the door waiting for me. I don't recall much else, except that it all felt like a bad dream.

Good Morning Britain dedicated the whole programme to Bar. Text after text, emails, WhatsApps. Every news channel talking about her. Prince Charles and Camilla tweeted. Boris Johnson, Sir Keir Starmer, they all expressed their sadness at hearing the news. Celebrities and public alike tweeted their love for her. Nothing could have prepared me for that reaction. When Prince William opened the London Palladium panto that night, he started his speech by mentioning Barbara. I couldn't really take it in. My eyes were sore. My heart hurt. I think I was in shock. I had already chosen the registrar and funeral director, so I called them and asked them to take care of my wife. Adding the image of some stranger putting her in a bag and taking her away was unbearable. It felt so callous, so brutal, so dishonourable to leave her. 'RIP Dame Barbara Windsor' was going around the top of the Post Office Tower. Also on the Blackpool Tower. My phone never stopped.

*

That first week in Sussex was a blur; I was exhausted and kept succumbing to waves of tears and sadness that seemed never-ending. Laurence was a constant rock, at my side, and helping me plan a lockdown-restricted funeral. He was incredible and I knew, even in shock, that I was lucky to have him. Only thirty people were allowed to attend the funeral. It should have been 3,000.

On 14 December I registered Bar's death and did a video for *GMB*'s 1 Million Minutes Dame Barbara Windsor Award. It was going to a palliative nurse called Nassrat, so how could I not? 'Congratulations, Nassrat. I know what a difference you make.' My God, I knew.

I was anxious and up in the night with dark thoughts about not being there at the end. It was irrational, I know, but my mind was crucifying me. She could have died at any minute towards the end. I tried to tell myself I was one of the lucky ones. At least I had spent five days by her side and, unlike so many others, I hadn't had to say goodbye on Zoom. But still, that image, the knocking on the door, why hadn't I left my phone on? Round and round went taunting thoughts.

Alzheimer's Research UK got in touch and, after having a good chat, we set up a condolence page for Barbara. It gave me a glimmer of hope that sometime down the line we would help find a cure for this terrible disease. I am as passionate as ever about that. The condolence page was doing well and had already reached £17,000 when I got a text from Lee Fenton at Jackpotjoy to say they would like to donate £83,000 – £1,000 for each year of Barbara's life. Every donation made me so proud of Bar. If only I could tell her.

Dark thoughts and images continued to haunt me. Simon Grigg, the vicar from St Paul's, the Actors' Church, who would officiate the cremation, told me that Bar's last act of love was going without me in the room. I really did try to believe and accept that, but to this day I'm still torn apart by the regret that I didn't stay with her, until the end, as I'd promised I would.

Marsha and Laurence gave me a lovely framed photo of Bar looking at me. I kissed the photo, then left the room and totally lost it. It was hard putting on a brave face for the kids at Christmas. I was not feeling it.

As the year ended an anonymous donation to her page took it up to a staggering £130,000. I woke late and turned on the telly and there was Barbara, perfectly preserved, in the 1968 film *Chitty Chitty Bang Bang*. My stomach churned. *Carry On Doctor* had been filming alongside the famous Dick Van Dyke film and she was offered a walk-on role, which she said she'd pay to be in just to work with Dick, who was one of the biggest stars of his day. By the end of the first day of shooting everyone loved Bar so much they extended her role so she was on set for another three days. The story goes that she cheered up a very miserable Dick Van Dyke. As I watched the fairground scene, I realised the finality of it all was starting to hit me. I could feel it in my stomach. There were so many emotions swirling around inside me. My AA birthday seemed more irrelevant in some ways, but in others it seemed miraculous that throughout all of Bar's illness I'd managed not to drink. I am now twenty years sober and the man who started my recovery, Jamie Foreman, is still a friend.

Each day the funeral got closer I became more terrified. I kept waking up having awful nightmares about Barbara in those last stages. The noises of her in distress and pain were haunting me. I couldn't get the image of her out of my head. It was awful so to give myself something to do I drove back to London to check on the house. There was a massive parcel of post which took two hours to read through. There were lots of letters and cards of condolence, including a handwritten one from Boris Johnson. Many of her fellow actors had written – Sir Ian McKellen, Dame Judi Dench, Dame Sheila Hancock – people who weren't necessarily close friends but whom she had known over the years. Then everyone from Sir Cameron Mackintosh to members of the public, who simply addressed letters to Barbara Windsor's husband. I don't know how they found their way to me, but I was grateful for every single one.

One night I woke up punching at the air. It felt like someone was pushing me into the mattress, like someone was there with me and it really disturbed me. I was back at home. It was very empty without her. Sure, she'd been in the care home, but this was different. This was how the house would feel with her no longer on this earth. That was the unbearable thought I couldn't escape. How could that lively, giggling spirit really not be alive any more?

But I had the funeral to keep me busy, even this small one. We had a couple of drop-outs due to illness. Paul O'Grady was gutted not to be able to attend but he'd caught an awful chest infection, followed by another who was very nervous of Covid. Replacing them was not a problem. I had a long list of people who should have been there. I just had to hope those who couldn't be would understand.

As the days before the funeral rolled on, I got more emotional. It marked the end of an amazing part of my life. I prayed to God to give me the strength to say farewell to my wife forever.

Bar arrived in the mews at 1pm. I wanted her to come back to the house one last time. I didn't want her to leave for the care home and never come back. This was her home. Our home. It was important to me.

My family were parked outside, waiting. I travelled alone in one car and the three of them followed me in a second funeral car. My neighbours had all come out to pay their respects and I was pleased her coffin looked so beautiful. There was a spray of flowers over the top, and along the sides and back three words were spelt out in flowers. What three words summed up my wife? Saucy. Dame. Babs. Saucy Dame Babs, of course. I broke down as soon as I saw the cortege. It is the oddest feeling when what is in front of your eyes can seem so surreal that it's impossible to believe. Was this really happening? I looked at my family and the neighbours, all grief-stricken. Yes, this was really happening.

We came out of the mews and turned left on to Devonshire Street and then along to Great Portland Street. I was transfixed by the word 'Babs' written so large, in such stunning white roses. We stopped at some traffic lights and I just happened to turn away and saw a man step back and put his hands to his face, shocked, sad and a little lost. It was Richard Arnold, the TV presenter. Bar loved him and clearly the feeling was mutual. Show business to the end.

Paul Bennett went down with Covid that morning, so the final guest list dropped to twenty-nine. Perhaps I was searching for signs, but I met Barbara when I was twenty-nine and that comforted me. At the crematorium the vicar Simon Grigg and the funeral director stepped in front of the hearse as we slowly inched our way to the church. A couple of people were scattered along the road. The *EastEnders* casting director, Julia Crampsie, and her husband Francis had driven across London just so they could see Barbara's coffin and pay their respects, along with others I didn't know. What would that road have looked like in normal times? I wondered. There would have been well-wishers saying goodbye as far as the eye could see. I was sure of that.

Don't get me wrong, I wasn't sad that it wasn't a big showbiz event because actually the service reflected our life as a married couple. Together through everything, just us. I sat in the front row alone, my family sat directly behind me. In the second row there were a few members of Barbara's family, her cousins Julie and Leslie and one of their daughters. The rest were our close, close friends. The people who'd been such a big part of Barbara's life. The people who'd been there for both of us towards the end and would continue to be there for me after this terrible day was over.

Anna Karen was the first one to speak. Anna was the closest thing Barbara had to a sister. They had nattered on the phone when ill health and geography had made things harder and it was a friendship Bar treasured. Even when Bar wasn't up to talking, when she was in the home, Anna would call, just to let her know she was there. At the funeral Anna talked about Bar's early life with her usual aplomb, wit and intelligence. I can't believe we've lost her too and I am sorry she's not here to read this. She meant the world to Bar. I hope the two of them are somewhere, nattering still, laughing about those crazy *Carry On* days.

Next up was Biggins, the perfect person to cover the most theatrical aspects of her life. And lastly came Ross. He gave a beautiful eulogy. A truly special tribute to a person who had clearly meant a great deal to him. As he was talking I knew it meant we were getting closer to the moment when the curtains would open. I stood on shaky legs as the service came to an end, overcome by the crazed urge to stop time, just pause, wait, for a moment. I wasn't ready. I would never be ready, and then the coffin started to move and I collapsed right where I was standing. My legs just gave way. She was gone.

I remember sobbing, repeating her name over and over. I think because it was such an intimate crowd I was really able to let go and feel her loss deeply in that moment. I didn't hold anything back. My heart literally broke. I think I loved her more than I knew and I knew I loved her. She changed my life forever. We shared something that I will never have again and I miss that, every day. I know that what we had makes me incredibly lucky. That is why it was so damn hard to say goodbye.

We walked outside to look at all the flowers that had been left. *East-Enders* had had a pub sign made of flowers for her and some of the bouquets were bigger than me. A couple of friends had turned up to pay their respects, Jamie Borthwick and Dean Gaffney. There were reports in the paper that Dean had turned up and got turned away, which absolutely wasn't the case. They just came to support me. It was awful not being able to hug them or invite them to join us, just like so many families around the country at the time. Laurence came back in the funeral car with me and, after a really quick turnaround, we were back in Sussex for fish and chips and an early night. The evening news carried footage of the coffin arriving. It was as hard to believe it then as it was when I'd seen it with my own eyes. Our life together was over. But wow, Bar, what a life.

I feel so blessed to have had what we had. Once upon a time, a 56-year-old fading actress on her uppers and a million pounds in debt picked me, an out-of-work 29-year-old actor, to help her read her lines. That lady changed the trajectory of my life and I changed the trajectory of hers. We lived on the sunny side of the street. Our relationship thrived not *despite* the age difference but *because* of it. First I had the energy to match her, then I had the energy to care for her, and I always, always loved her. I still do.

The End.

It's never The End.

I will always love you, Barbara.

Thank you for our life.

Epilogue

On 12 April 2021, lockdown restrictions were finally eased and I emerged into a world without my wife.

Since the funeral I had retreated to my old room in Sussex, ended my sessions with my therapist and allowed myself to mourn deeply, my way. I was exhausted and my incredible family let me be as sad as I needed to be and offered their unconditional support and love. Eventually I started to go out for cold, muddy, grey walks, often for miles, one foot in front of the other on my own, the weather reflecting my state of mind. As the inkling of spring returned, my energy started to lift and I walked with my family and, one day, I put on my trainers and went for a run. My fitness was awful and sometimes I would just break down and cry, but I was running and that made me think it was time to go back to the mews.

I walked tentatively through our front door, the smell of Bar's perfume Shalimar still hung in the air and her portrait loomed large in the lounge, princess drapes hung over the bed, bottles and creams covered her dressing table. It was all too much. Eventually I would move the portrait, begin the gargantuan task of sorting out Bar's belongings and remodel the house, but all that would take time. At that moment my day-to-day existence was spent walking around the park with David, Tanya or Ian.

There had been a piece in the *Sunday Mirror* debating Boris Johnson's failure to keep his promise to Dame Barbara Windsor about increasing dementia research funding. Alzheimer's Research UK and I had contributed to the article saying that, while it was disappointing that funding was still at its lowest, we understood that the pledge was made before Covid. The trouble was, all the other illnesses weren't going away. In fact, the situation was getting worse. Of course, how it read was that I was furious with the PM, so I wrote to him personally to say I had been misrepresented. I knew it would sit in a pile of mail, but I felt better for doing it.

Barbara had left wishes for her clothes to be split between the Lady Ratlings charity and Brinsworth House, a retirement home for theatre industry people. As anyone in this position knows, this is an emotionally draining task. I kept a few items back, including a jumper which still smells of Shalimar. Eventually black bags filled the hall, which is always a staggeringly soul-destroying sight, and I was glad they were going to be collected and put to good use. The shoes hit me the hardest. She had such tiny feet. Rows of doll's shoes, I had no idea who they were going to fit. Just looking at them and I could hear the signature clippety-clack of her hurrying down the road.

Monday, 19 April 2021: Another part of her gone.

On one of my walks my mobile rang. Apparently the Prime Minister wanted to talk to me.

'Scott,' said a gruff voice. 'Boris Johnson.'

He had read my letter. He told me not to worry. He did not think for one minute that I'd said those things and reiterated that Barbara's passing was a great loss. 'Please don't let this put you off campaigning,' he insisted. 'Barbara's legacy would be to help others and that was important.'

The call may only have lasted two minutes, but I will always remember it. It was the boost I needed because the London Marathon was back on and I'd already raised £30,000 for Alzheimer's Research UK from friends, so I could hardly pull out. He was right, Bar's legacy was what was important now.

On the day that would have been Barbara's eighty-fourth birthday we laid two stones in Golders Green crematorium. The one on the wall ending with the phrase 'She was a good bird'. When asked by Piers Morgan how she would like to be remembered, that is what she'd said. I hope it would have made her happy. There is a smaller personal one on the ground. Paul Bennett joined me and the family. We said a prayer and read a poem and it was another emotional day, another milestone, but important because now I had somewhere I could go to talk to her. I didn't put all of her ashes there, I actually still have some. Afterwards the five of us went to Fischer's for lunch and toasted Bar. Coming out of the restaurant I bumped straight into Zoë Wanamaker, the actress who had played Joan Littlewood in *Babs*. What were the odds of that? Call it a coincidence? I like to take it as a sign.

I ran the London Marathon in October 2021 wearing my custom-made Babs T-shirt. My legs felt so heavy but Tanya, John McIntyre and I had made a pact that, whatever happened, we would stay together. Laurence and my nephew Harry also ran, but I told them to go ahead. I was finding it tough, but I kept saying, 'Scott, I promise you we never have to do this again!' and somehow I managed to put one foot in front of the other for five hours and fifty-six minutes. Crossing the finishing line was one of the best, overwhelming, emotionally releasing moments of my life. Under six hours – a bloody miracle after the year I'd had. I collapsed on the ground. For the record, that is the end of my marathon running days, whatever Chris Evans says.

Having said that, don't let me put you off. I entreat anyone to take up the challenge. Running, and the people I ran with, got me through many dark times. I remember passing a lady when I was at my lowest ebb in the race. She caught my eye as I hobbled past. 'Babs would be proud of you, Scott,' she said, nodding at me, encouraging me on.

Such moments meant the world to me. They kept me going. They mean the world to me. They keep me going.

By the time people read this book it will be nearly two years since Barbara died and I hope it stands as both a tribute and a love letter to her. Writing it has let me rediscover the Bar I fell in love with, before illness took her away, and get to know her all over again and the many life lessons she taught me. Barbara Windsor was kind, loyal, courageous, humble and generous, and, above all things, funny.

On reflection, she wasn't a good bird, she was one of the very best.

Afterword:
What the Future Brings

One in three people born today will develop dementia and at this time there is still no cure or preventative treatment to stop it in its tracks. For every four researchers for cancer research, there is only one for dementia. Dementia is one of the biggest killers in the UK today and it is growing all the time. Barbara's willingness and courage in going public about her condition truly made a difference and that is why I became an ambassador for Alzheimer's Research UK (ARUK). To continue her legacy.

My work with the charity means so much to me and I will continue to talk about Barbara's dementia journey and keep her legacy going for as long as it still means something to the cause. I was powerless to fight what it was doing to Barbara, but I promised myself I would do all I could to join in the effort to one day find a treatment to save people like Barbara and millions of others from going through this cruel disease, or at least to ease its effects. And spare their families and loved ones too.

For those going through this now, and for anyone who will do in the future, there is no blueprint for how to care for someone with dementia. It's cunning and baffling and throws you curveballs the whole time. You will learn daily and adjust and try to do your best, although at times you won't always get it right, as I did not. Try not to berate yourself. As carers we are human and most of us have no experience, so why should we be able to get it right? All we can really do is be there and try to make our loved one feel safe in the moment. Don't dismiss them or talk to them as if they are children, even when at times it may feel like that. And remember that specialists and organisations will tell you that no two people have the same dementia journey. So not everything I have spoken about in our experience will definitely happen in yours. But I send everyone much strength and love, whatever your journey might be.

I look at Barbara's legacy as a positive thing. Not only that we use her name and image to highlight what needs to be done, but knowing that most people will see her face and, for whatever reason, break into a little smile or positive thought. Remembering who she was and the fun memories she evokes.

I am trying to look forward not with sadness, but with a true sense of feeling incredibly blessed and grateful that Barbara was such a major part of my own life. To see her smile, hear her laugh, still smell her Shalimar in my mind, and remember her sense of fun and love of life. When sadness overwhelms me, I think of Bar and hear her voice.

This was something she said to me numerous times over our many years together: 'Listen, darlin', I will go first because that's how it's meant to be, and when I do I want you to be broken-hearted and cry your eyes out and then when you are ready, I want you to pick yourself up and have the best life ever, Scott. Because that's what I always tried to do and normally I succeeded.'

Bar, I think I'm nearly ready now . . .

A Note from Hilary Evans, Chief Executive, Alzheimer's Research UK

Dame Barbara will always be remembered first and foremost as the bubbly blonde star who lit up our screens through her inimitable appearances over many decades. But towards the end of her extraordinary life, in what felt like a selfless act of defiance against her Alzheimer's diagnosis, she threw her energy into campaigning to improve dementia research, care and public understanding of the condition. Here at Alzheimer's Research UK, we couldn't have been more grateful.

Barbara was an icon – a national treasure – whose face was beamed into millions of families' living rooms each week. But when she courageously went public with her diagnosis in 2018, with her loving husband Scott by her side, she became so much more – a voice for many of those same families whose lives had been ravaged by dementia.

Overnight, we saw and felt the change here at the charity. As someone so familiar and whose effervescence made her feel like a friend to all, her openness about her diagnosis made others feel comfortable to be open, too. In the same way cancer was described as 'the big C' and wasn't talked about openly just a short time ago, the stigma surrounding dementia needed someone to drag it from the shadows and into the spotlight. And Barbara did that with both passion and conviction.

Now, Scott is continuing her incredible legacy. From running marathons and lobbying government to encouraging others to support dementia research, he's honouring her memory in the most special way. His unrelenting drive to effect change is inspiring, and we were proud to make Scott an Alzheimer's Research UK ambassador in 2021.

With Scott by our side, we will ensure dementia research continues to change the lives of everyone affected by this devastating condition.

Barbara's loss will always be felt – she meant so much to so many – but the legacy she leaves behind matters. Losing a loved one to dementia creates unimaginable heartache across families and friendships, but research brings hope that we can change the lives of people with the condition, and Barbara's memory only strengthens our determination to achieve this.

To find out more about the work of Alzheimer's Research UK, please visit our website – www.alzheimersresearchuk.org

Thank you.

Postscript

During a hot week in August 2022, one week before this book was due to go to print, I was invited to a meeting at No. 10. I was all dressed up to go to a wedding, wearing blue suede creepers, but when the Prime Minister calls you don't dilly-dally.

I was taken through the Cabinet Room, and then out bounded the Prime Minister, handing me a framed photo of himself, Barbara and me from our first meeting to discuss social care and funding for dementia research back in 2019. I'd sent him a follow-up letter in May 2022 but, well, he'd had a lot on his plate. I thanked him for being the first Prime Minister (out of fourteen) in seventy years to change the way we fund social care in this country. Thanks also to his health adviser, Will Warr, who worked so tirelessly behind the scenes to make the social care reform happen and then got the new research funding agreed. I then asked the Prime Minister how close we were to the subsequent pledge he had made to the country.

'Well, funny you should say that . . .' he said, and then told me they would be doubling the funding for dementia research to £160 million. On top of that, following on from a conference I had taken part in with Dame Kate Bingham and ARUK in April, and using the same multidisciplinary methods applied to find a Covid vaccine, the government would make available £95 million to facilitate what we had asked for: a research task force for dementia.

'With your permission, Scott,' the Prime Minister said, 'we would like to call it the Dame Barbara Windsor Dementia Mission.'

You have read this book, and you will know as well as I did at that moment how proud Barbara would be – that by sharing our story, we've helped in a small way to make a change. Ours is just one version of what living with dementia is like and there are 999,999 others out there, right now.

From the garden of No. 10 Downing Street, I looked up at the clear blue sky and could feel her smiling down. Well done, Bar. You did it.

'No, Scott. We did.'

There never was any point arguing with my wife. I held her in my mind for a moment longer.

Yes, my love. I guess we did.

Then I shook the Prime Minister's hand and bounced off in my blue suede shoes to celebrate someone else's love because, as Bar would say, 'Go, live your best life. I did.'

I am Bar. I am at peace; I am calm and the release from fear makes me grateful every day. In fact, every now and then since the hardback came out, I have experienced incredible waves of emotion radiate through me. They are joyous, warm and make my skin visibly tingle and those feelings bless me with a deep sense of happiness. It's Bar. She is there by my side, not in a haunting or eery way, but in a comforting, protective, encouraging way. It makes me feel wonderful. Writing this book was difficult no doubt but I wouldn't change a word. In fact, the only thing I am prepared to take back is the bit where I claim that whatever Chris Evans says to me, I have 100 per cent definitely retired from running marathons. Hmmm. Well, five days before my sixtieth birthday on 23 April 2023, I will be running the London Marathon for a third time (God help my knees) with a new team that we are calling 'Babs Army'. We will run for ARUK again, highlighting the government's recommitment to the Dame Barbara Windsor Dementia Mission. I personally have signed up to be a volunteer in the newly created Life Sciences Mission under the leadership of Dame Kate Bingham to expand trials and research following the highly successful Vaccines Taskforce. For the record Chris Evans did not make me do it! Bar, as ever, is my incentive. She is the one pushing me forward. I am no longer stuck in the past, instead I use the past to comfort and encourage me. Not only can I now move forward with Barbara in the name of Dementia Research,

I am also getting better at moving forward with my life. I will never find a love like ours again, but that is not the same as saying I will never find love again. Love is vital, it reveals our real strength and holds us until we are okay.

I still keep a diary and am delighted to report that most pages end with 'a good day'.

Acknowledgements

It was impossible to get the name of every person who touched our lives during this period into this book, so I would like to thank all of the following people for your love, friendship, kindness, involvement – and just being a part of my and Barbara's wonderful journey along the way. And please forgive me if I've left you out . . .

In no particular order, thank you to:

My amazing family: Mum and Dad, Laurence and Marsha, Dean and Abbie, Joey and Nico, Scott and Charlie, Lillie and Max, Harry and Amy. I love you all and always will.

Our friends: Ian and Bev Kay and family, Barry Burnett, Ross and Renee Kemp and family, David Walliams, Kathleen and family, Matt Lucas and family, Biggins and Neil, Paul O'Grady and Andre, Karan Kitter, Paul Bennett, Yvonne I'Anson, Gary Farrow and Jane Moore and family, John Reid, Tanya Franks, Derek and Anne, Mark and Deborah Gold, Sarah Piper.

Lacey Turner and Matt Kay, Jake, Alison, Buster and Amber Wood, Emma Barton and family, Adam Woodyatt, Jane Slaughter, Jamie Borthwick and family, Kellie Shirley, Natalie Cassidy and family, Pam St Clement, Carolyn Weinstein and family, Dominic Treadwell-Collins and Paul, Diederick Santer, Francis and Julia Crampsie, Mark and Jane Deitch, Teresa Williams, Richard and Joy Desmond and family, Gerald and Dame Gail Ronson, Gaby Roslin, Sir Elton John and David Furnish and family, Jo Joyner and Neil Madden and family, Debbie McGee, Laurie Brett, Jessie Wallace, Shane Richie, Jonathan Ross, Patsy Palmer, Jo Allen, Sharon Marshall, Richard Arnold, Robert Campbell, Lee Panayiotou, Stephen

Williams, Gary Cockerill and Phil Turner, Ian McIntosh, Steve Allen, Chris Evans and family, Hiten, John Yorke, Tony and Tracy Jordan and family, Jamie and Laura Taylor, Kevin Wood, Mitch and Jane Winehouse, Noel Hayden, Lee Fenton, Nick Love, Jamie and Julie Foreman, Steven Ross, all at Anita Dorfman House and Jewish Care (including Chipema, Tuzani, Elizabeth and Zara), Dr Angus Kennedy, Sam Spiro, Lord Michael Cashman, Michelle Collins, Gina Behar, Lucinda Ellery, Rita Simons, Jaq H.

Jane, Gabriella, Imola, Kristina, Lieze, Elena (home carers), Ruby Baker, Jessica Livingstone, Pete Mclaine, Steven Harris, Jeremy and Jacob Joseph, Martin Yelling, the London Marathon team (Penny, Ryan and Hugh), Henri Brandman, Jim (OBE) and Michelle Davidson, John Altman, Ashley Brodin and Jilly Johnson, Keith Griffiths, Heather Porter, the Rt Hon Boris Johnson, Sam Womack, Michael at the gallery, my friends on the checkout at Waitrose Marylebone.

All at Alzheimer's Research UK (especially Hilary and Lloyd), Alzheimer's Society, all medical specialists who cared for Barbara, Lisa Voice, Lorraine Newman, Bob Horwell, Paul Houghton, ArtsEd Year of 88, Dave Lynn, Scott St Martin, Martine McCutcheon, AA Fellowship, Hilary O'Neil, Melissa Renee.

My amazing neighbours in the mews, Peter and Lisa (flower stall), Neil Cunningham, Beechy Colclough, Ashley Conway, our many friends (and at times opponents) in the press – thank you, and no hard feelings!

To every friend and member of the public who supported my charity runs or the condolence page – no matter how large or small the donation, it meant the world to Barbara and me, and the charities. Bless you all and thank you x

For the book:
Eugenie Furniss at 42MP – My fabulous literary agent who first contacted me nearly four years ago. Thank you for being so lovely, protective, supportive, experienced and a mean negotiator. I would want you in my corner any day!

Gay Longworth – My long-suffering ghostwriter whose compassion, patience and open mind allowed me to delve deep as we worked our way through my twenty-seven years of diaries. You allowed me to talk, laugh, be brutally honest at times and on many occasions watched me cry and release my pain (and feed you endless smoked salmon and cream cheese bagels). Thank you, Gay, for all of that. You are a special lady.

Vicky Eribo and her team at Orion Books – The most incredible leader I could have wished to work with. From our first meeting a few years ago for a random chat, to securing this book and being there every step of the way with me as a calming and professional influence. Vicky, it's been a joy getting to know you and the team and I will thank you always.

RIP

Bar, Dad, Nana Lilly, Aunty Bessie and Uncle Sid, Dame Celia Burnett, Anna Karen, June Brown OBE, Dale Winton, Victor Spinetti, John Inman, Danny La Rue OBE, Brian Hall, Harold and Miriam Winehouse, Amy Winehouse, Joan Littlewood, Roger Kitter, John Challis, Paul Cottingham, Sue Carroll, Peter Willis, Dave Pawsey, Bernard Cribbins, Kevin McGee, Richard Wellington, Ian Royce – and all the other angels who have left us . . .

Orion Credits

Seven Dials would like to thank everyone at Orion who worked on the publication of *By Your Side*.

Agent
Eugenie Furniss

Executive Publisher
Vicky Eribo

Copy-editor
Lorraine Jerram

Proofreader
Martin Bryant

Editorial Management
Jo Whitford
Jane Hughes
Charlie Panayiotou
Tamara Morriss
Claire Boyle

Audio
Paul Stark
Jake Alderson
Georgina Cutler

Contracts
Anne Goddard
Ellie Bowker

Design
Nick Shah
Rachael Lancaster
Joanna Ridley
Helen Ewing

Picture Research
Natalie Dawkins

Finance
Nick Gibson
Jasdip Nandra
Sue Baker
Tom Costello

Inventory
Jo Jacobs
Dan Stevens

Marketing
Katie Moss

Production
Claire Keep
Katie Horrocks

Publicity
Virginia Woolstencroft

Sales
Jen Wilson
Victoria Laws
Esther Waters
Group Sales teams across Digital, Field Sales, International and Non-Trade

Operations
Group Sales Operations team

Rights
Rebecca Folland
Barney Duly
Ruth Blakemore
Flora McMichael
Ayesha Kinley
Marie Henckel

Picture Credits

All images from the author's personal collection, except for the following:

Plate Section One

p.5: BBC Motion / Getty (middle); Paul Clapp (bottom left)

p.8: Getty Images / Mirrorpix

Plate Section Two

p.1: Dan Goldsmith

p.3: Paul Clapp (top); Martin Spaven (bottom left and right)

p.5: Alamy / CURLEYPAP (top right)

p.7: Stuart MacFarlane/ Arsenal FC (top)

p.8: Shutterstock / Peter Macdiarmid (top left); Shutterstock / Tim Rooke (top right); Alamy / Reuters (middle and bottom)

Plate Section Three

p.1: Alamy / Lee Thomas (top left); Alamy / Lee Thomas (top right); Shutterstock / Alan Davidson (middle); Shutterstock / Jonathon Hordle (bottom)

p.2: Alamy / PA Images (top and middle right); Courtesy Bristol Hippodrome (bottom)

p.3: Studiocanal Films Ltd / Mary Evans Picture Library (top)

p.4: Alzheimer's Society (middle); Getty Images / Karwai Tang (bottom left); Alamy / Sipa US (bottom right)

p.5: Getty / WPA Pool (middle left)

p.7:   Author's personal collection / with permission from Allan Olly Scope Pictures (top left); author's personal collection / Shutterstock; Getty Images / Karwai Tang (middle left and middle right)

p.8:   Chris Harrison (top left); Alzheimer's Research UK (top right); Kyle Heller / No. 10 Downing Street (bottom left)

Quoted Material

p.47:   'Infamy, infamy, they've all got it in-for-me.' (*Carry On Cleo*. 1964. [Film]. Gerald Thomas. dir. Italy: Peter Rogers Productions)

p.56:   'How do you cope? Aren't you scared?' (*EastEnders, Episode 1388*. 1996. BBC One. 25 December, 20:30)

p.163:   'Your Majesty, it is a great honour. The King has done me.' (*Carry On Henry*. 1971. [Film]. Peter Rogers. dir. UK: Peter Rogers Productions)

p.167:   'What am I supposed to do with this?' (*EastEnders, Episode 4931*. 2014. BBC One. 25 September, 19:30)

pp.182–3: 'It's not good news I'm afraid.' (*EastEnders, Episode 5282*. 2016. BBC One. 10 May, 19:30)

p.264:   'I'm like a little old bird that's fallen out of its nest.' (*EastEnders, Episode 5286*. 2016. BBC One. 17 May, 19:25)

About the Author

Scott Mitchell was born in London and grew up in Hove, Sussex. He moved back to London at twenty-five, studying for three years as an actor. After graduating and taking on various TV and theatre roles, Scott met his future wife, actress Dame Barbara Windsor, who he shared his life with for twenty-seven years, before she passed away in 2020.

In 2014, Barbara was given the devastating news that she had been diagnosed with Alzheimer's, a day that would change both hers and Scott's lives forever. Although initially kept private, Scott and Barbara went public with the news in 2018. In 2019 Scott entered the London Marathon with a team of Barbara's friends, alongside charity campaign The Dementia Revolution, to raise vital funds for dementia research. To date it is the record-breaking charity partner for the London Marathon, raising over £4 million. Scott also ran the 2021 marathon to raise money for Alzheimer's Research UK, a charity he is now an ambassador for.